MW01092190

ALSO BY MICHAEL EIGEN

The Psychotic Core

Coming Through the Wirlwind

The Electrified Tightrope

Reshaping the Self

Psychic Deadness

The Psychoanalytic Mystic

Michael Eigen

FREE ASSOCIATION BOOKS
LONDON & NEW YORK

Published in the UK by
FREE ASSOCIATION BOOKS LTD
57 Warren Street, London WIP 5PA
and 70 Washington Square South
New York, NY 10012-1091

British Library Cataloguing-in-Publication Programme.
A CIP record for this book is available from the British Library.

ISBN 1 85343 398 5

Designed and produced for Free Association Books by
Esf Publishers, Binghamton, New York.
Printed, smythe-sewn and bound in the United States of America.

The paper and materials used in this book meet the guidelines for permanence and
durability of the Committee on Production Guidelines for Book Longevity of the Council
on Library Resources. ∞
This book has been manufactured to library specifications.

For Betty

The great lie is that we're going to live forever.
The great Truth is we're living forever now.

Michael Eigen

Psychoanalysis itself is just a stripe on the coat of the tiger. Ultimately it may meet the Tiger—the Thing Itself—O.

Wilfred R. Bion

Something unknown is doing we don't know what.

Eddington

Praise God!
Praise Him with the blowing of the shofar
Praise Him with lyre and harp
Praise Him with drum and dance
Praise Him with stringed instruments and lute
Praise Him with resounding cymbals
Praise Him with clanging cymbals
Let every soul praise God
Praise God!

from *Psalm 150*

Contents

Acknowledgments

Many invitations and opportunities to speak, teach, and write about spirituality and psychoanalysis contributed to the development of this book. Some chapters were presented at the National Psychological Association for Psychoanalysis, the New York University Postdoctoral Program in Psychotherapy and Psychoanalysis, and the National Institute for Psychotherapies. Leila Lerner, Martin Schulman, and Otto Weininger published some of these chapters in *The Psychoanalytic Review* and the *Journal of Melanie Klein and Object Relations*. Paul Marcus, Edward Corrigan and Pearl Ellen Gordon invited me to write on areas I cared about for books they edited, and these chapters are included here. I'm especially grateful to Anthony Molino for interviewing me and enabling me to use this interview as the last chapter in this book. Mark Epstein and Adam Phillips are among colleagues who have shown persistent, warm and stimulating interest in my explorations.

Gill Davies (Free Associations Books) and Florin V. Vladescu (*Esf* Publishers) have been generous with personal and professional support and practical advice. They were behind my book from the time they saw it and worked to bring it to fruition.

My heartfelt thanks to my patients and students. We open worlds together. And to my wife, Betty, and children, David and Jacob: earth, fire, water, air.

Introduction

What is a psychoanalytic mystic? Psychoanalysis and mysticism appear to be mutually exclusive. Analysis sticks pins in mystical bubbles. It traces in mysticism outlines of infantile ego states and early feelings clustering around mother-father images. It hopes to free humanity from mysticism by promoting the evolution of analytic consciousness. Many analysts believe mixing mysticism and psychoanalysis dilutes, even undermines, the latter. In this vein, Freud saw dependency on religion as one of humankind's greatest obstacles to maturation.

Still, life is not neat, and, logically consistent or not, many analysts are deeply mystical, or have a foot in mystical experience, or are friendly towards mysticism. For me, there are moments when psychoanalysis is a form of prayer. There is, too, a meditative dimension in psychoanalytic work. Psychoanalytical-mystical openness to the unknown overlap. Analytic workers, not religious in the literal sense, may be touched by intimations of something sacred in the work.

My own development has been helter-skelter. I've been speaking with God since I was a little boy, and if Wordsworth is right, living in God even earlier. I can't say that God hasn't answered. The Jewish God is quite a conversationalist. Torah says God speaks the world into being, so an awful lot of God talk is going on. I imagine my being a writer has a little to do with my God's verbal prowess.

But what if God *breathes* the world into being? *Ruach Elohim*—the breath of God, the breath of Life, the Holy Spirit. I suppose a dedicated verbalist (psychoanalysis, the *talking* cure?) could argue that breath was created so words would be possible. But suppose God breathed a long time before He felt like speaking? Perhaps God knew that once He spoke, especially after we came along, it would be difficult to have any peace. I think God was loathe to open his mouth lest the beauty and power of His words eclipse the bliss of breathing. For many, it is easier to be awed by the fireworks of words, than cradled and sprung by breath.

Before words and the creation of our world, souls probably breathed freely together. Of course, one shouldn't blame everything on words. Animals fight, eat each other. But words ignite fires, teeth and claws can't. Myriad creative-destructive fires. Wars of words, wills, territories conflagrate. What would a world without words be like?

It would be a world without a digestive system as we know it. We speak through our mouths, not noses. Speaking is weighted by a background of finding (the right word, prey, food), biting, chewing, swallowing, absorbing. Digestion-respiration follow an in-out mode. Starving-suffocation are primal dreads.

Ought we assume that God found the right Word, and this is the right World? Or are there worlds that flow with words in-out of God, akin to black hole-radiant light? Do worlds-words get mixed, so we sometimes feel in the wrong world, say the wrong thing as creative-destructive God partners? Do we say our worlds, live our words? Aren't worlds incessantly coming-going with breathing? If we sat minding our breathing all day, we'd fight a lot less. Almost as soon as we start speaking, we start fighting. The Tree of Knowledge is a Tree of Words or, at least, associates food with language. But we can't breathe and talk our lives away, although we may try, and sometimes succeed.

There are times when it is easier to find the Tree of Life through breathing, but neither breath nor word are guarantees. Both can be wonderful channels or insidious traps. Life is everywhere and anything can tap it. Even tripping on one's shoelaces can quicken the spirit, although tripping too often may stifle it. "Holy, Holy, Holy—the whole earth is filled with His glory!" Words like these express the flame that sends chills and thrills through all tendrils. The last psalms are shouts of joy, banging on drums and cymbals, blowing horns, dancing ecstatically. The shofar is a wake up call, "soul clap hands," "spirit ditty of no tone"—all tones. How much can one wake up in a lifetime?

There is an awful story in the Torah of a man stoned to death for gathering sticks on the Sabbath. The story, first of all, shows how religion, mysticism, and violence go together. Not just the violent, temper tantrum, paranoid-schizoid, infantile Jewish God (a volcano God, Freud [1939] writes). My Buddhist patients—pacifists, breathers, mindful and empty—are no strangers to controlling rages (see Chapter 10). Christian violence is well known. We dread irruptions from Moslem volcanos, worried that patriot-terrorists will use nuclear weapons. To be fair, it is difficult to distinguish violence associated with race, nationalism, and social-economic conditions from mystical violence, although these mesh in brutal ways.

There are ways to rationalize the stoning of the wood gatherer. He was closer to the moment God gave Moses the Torah: transgression magnifies as a function of illumination. But the story—without minimizing its ghastliness—also has relevance for the letter-spirit distinction.

The man was at a point when Sabbath illumination ought to have been the light lived. Why was he seeking a lesser light (a kind of death, stoning oneself, turning self to stone) instead of living the greater one?

The story cuts two ways. Mystical illumination and the facts of life need to learn how to live together. Body needs warmth, spirit illumination. Why pit one against the other? To be sure, daily chores and cares can swallow the spirit. But they *can* enrich it, and vice versa. The struggle to find the right mix at a given time, for a given person, is very much a living issue. Spirit can annihilate or inspire everyday life, as the latter can nourish or suffocate spirit.

There are mysticisms of emptiness and fullness, difference and union, transcendence and immanence. One meets the Superpersonal beyond opposites or opens to the void and formless infinite. There are mystical moments of shattering and wholeness—many kinds of shattering, many kinds of wholeness. In moments of illumination, not only one's flaws stand out, one's virtues become a hindrance (see Chapters 4, 6). Prophets attack our evil ways, but inspire us to new heights, new visions of God, new relationships to ourselves and one another.

In light of the riches of mystical experiencing, psychoanalytic focus on the "oceanic" aspect seems almost shallow. Nevertheless, Freud's writings are rich with implications for mystical experiencing. We know from his letters to Fliess (Freud, 1985) how superstitious he could be. Like Einstein, he refers to the Almighty in informal ways, and uses mystical imagery to portray creative processes. He even wrote Fliess, in passing, that psychoanalysis was akin to the ancient mystery rites. Freud wrote more books on religion than on any other subject except sexuality. In Chapter 1, I explore some of the treasures in Freud's writings on religion and mystical experience.

In Chapter 1, I also introduce the main psychoanalytic authors I use as lenses to bring out interfaces of psychoanalytic and mystical experience: Milner, Winnicott, Bion and Lacan. There are other authors I could have used, who form the background of my work, in particular, Kohut, Jung, and W. Reich. But I picked those I am most intimate with, who I read the most, and who take me places clinically and personally I need to go at this time in my life.

It is difficult to overestimate the role played by Marion Milner who, in her quiet, unassuming way, helped develop the climate for spontaneous interpenetration of psychoanalytic and mystical life. She naturally uses mystical language to portray and amplify psychoanalytic processes, and the latter to probe, cleanse, and open mystical experiencing. In her work, the pregnant void, emptiness, creative chaos, the deep unconscious, and I-yet-not-I experience are central.

At the same time, she is true to the hard facts of life, the play of illusion-disillusion, embodiment. She is a visionary spokesperson for imaginative perception (even wrote that perception is a form of imagination), ever digging into ways we communicate with ourselves and each other through mystical, bodily depths. There is no contradiction between transcendence and embodiment in her work, where surface-depth of bodily experience has its own kind of transcendence. She is a special kind of body mystic, and a hallowing of sensory-feeling life runs through her work.

Milner (1957, 1987) is virtually unique in psychoanalysis in viewing symbolic expression as a kind of ebullient overflow, expressive of the orgasmic joy of creative experiencing (Eigen, 1993, pp. xxi-xxiii, 157-176). To be sure, creative experiencing has many phases, agonizing, depressive, dead, empty, as well as thrilling and high. Milner explores ways our symbolizing capacity expresses phases of creative processes (see, too, Ehrenzweig's [1971], wonderfully suggestive explorations of this theme). Most analysts link the emergence of symbolization with loss. Marion Milner includes this but does not make plenitude a second class citizen.

While I do not write about Milner after the first chapter, her work remains a background support. For example, there is an implicit connection between the use I make of Lacan's *jouissance* (Chapters 7-9) and Milner's linking of symbolic life with an orgasmic sense of generativity. For Lacan, the symbolic capacity functions, in part, as witness, interrogator, interlocutor to our ruptured, grandiose condition (e.g., it illuminates megalomanic "solutions" to wounded fusion). Through the symbol we agonizingly reflect the fissure in the real that symbolic capacity institutes. Lacan, in grand French tradition, like Moliere, develops a dramatic critique of the ego.

As his work develops, *jouissance* and the real enter the foreground (Lacan, 1977, 1978). To undo the gap or absence that is part of symbolic mediation is madness. One accesses *jouissance* (orgasmic pleasure-bliss-ecstasy) through convolutions of a Moebius strip/boolean ring unconscious mind, in which primary repression and castration are constitutive structures. The very fact of symbolization is already a kind of castration at the heart of the real. No matter how joyous our joy, it is through a glass darkly.

No mystic would say otherwise. Nonetheless, mystical ecstasy carries very real authority which can't be dismissed as merely mad. It can obliterate structures and limits in destructive ways but, also, shine through them. It can appreciate structures at hand, without being oppressed by them, without giving them the last or only word. And if it is mad, it is a madness that makes life worthwhile.

One senses currents of *jouissance* in the twists and turns of daily life. It is part of the juiciness of life. *Jouissance* is the under-and-overside of the skin of the ego. One can more or less focus on it, magnify it. It can seize attention, overflow, carry one to beautiful/horrible places. One tries to filter it through desires.

Lacan claims to be anti-mystical. Psychoanalysis, unlike mysticism, does not claim direct contact with reality. Psychoanalysis is indirect, mediate, inferential. Yet the *jouissance* of psychoanalysis exerts special appeal. Isn't psychoanalytic *jouissance* especially tantalizing in face of (because of?) all its proposed asceticism?

Winnicott (1958, 1971, 1974, 1989) spent a good part of his professional life writing about the sense of aliveness-deadness—what conditions enliven-deaden self. I've detailed evolution of his extraordinary developmental-clinical account elsewhere (Eigen, 1986, 1996; also, Phillips, 1988). His work resonates with a sense of the sacred. He wrote of a sacred core of personality, the incommunicado self. The distinction between true-false self was real for him. He criticized deadening and degrading aspects of compliance and conformity associated with false self, and appreciated ways that chaos and madness contributed to true self aliveness. He experienced the latter as part of inspiration in sessions, writing, living. He so valued the sense of aliveness, he prayed, "Oh God! May I be alive when I die."

Winnicott did not need an other world mysticism. The real of this world was more than enough. Yet he did not want to be confined by common sense, although the latter served as ballast. He needed to let go structures, dip into formlessness, let something emerge from elsewhere, nowhere. For Winnicott, emptying-opening let something real happen. Emptiness-openness was a method for courting spontaneity.

Thus the real was not entirely or simply the three dimensional material world, no matter how important the latter. The real was associated with playing, chaos, destruction and surviving destruction, madness. Near the end of his life, Winnicott (1989) linked what is most real with a private madness one can only partly touch (pp. 119-129). Too much "sanity" kills spontaneity. A touch of madness adds taste to reality.

A muted sacramental current runs through Winnicott's work. One senses the sanctity of individual personality, reverence for the vital spark. Consubstantiation is used as an example of how self paradoxically spans dimensions. The spark of life leaps between self and other, dies out when it is localized. Aliveness wanes when confined to merely inner. Reality ceases to be real when confined to merely outer. Religion in the sense of "ties between" (neither here nor there, but here-and-there-and-between) becomes a defining ingredient of the real.

The realness of living becomes a value in its own right. In Chapter 2, I use Winnicott and the biblical Jacob to express an evolving sense of life which meets special difficulties in our day. Winnicott's depiction of a besieged "innate democratic factor" presents a special challenge and stimulus to faith in living and adds to what it means to be alive. It interweaves with aspects of Winnicott's work that enrich our sense of personal freedom.

For Bion (1965, 1970), truth may nourish and lies poison, but truth, also, is explosive. Like God, it can shatter personality if one sees it. Bion likens the sense of truth to a big bang at the origin of personality. To tame it is to lose it, but living its shock waves is impossible. He likens illumination to Messiah rupturing Establishment. We may not know what to do with the mystic-genius aspect of self, but without it life would be less inspired-inspiring.

Like Winnicott, Bion begins by exploring deadening aspects and ends by appreciating enlivening aspects of madness. He overlaps with Milner and Winnicott by linking the "void and formless infinite" with psychoanalytic openness. He characterizes the psychoanalytic attitude as being without memory, expectation, desire or understanding. As his work evolved, he placed more importance on faith than knowledge, although both felt confining. Bion refused to be boxed in by capacities he used. He kept straining at limits of the equipment he had (see Chapter 3).

Like Winnicott, to the end of his life he kept going further, shaking off crust like a cat shaking off water. Here is a quotation from the Epilogue of one of his last works:

> All my life I have been imprisoned, frustrated, dogged by common-sense, reason, memories, desires and—greatest bug-bear of all—understanding and being understood. This is my attempt to express my rebellion, to say "Good-bye" to all that. . . . I cannot claim to have succeeded. All these will, I fear, be seen to have left their traces. . . hidden within these words; even sanity, like "cheerfulness," will creep in. . . . Wishing you all a Happy Lunacy and a Relativistic Fission (1971, p. 578).

Bion uses many images and expressions from religious and mystical life to portray psychoanalytic processes. But he does more. He filters mysticism through psychoanalysis and psychoanalysis through mysticism. Psychoanalysis may be a special discipline imposed on life, but it is worse than nothing if it does not express and further life. Psychoanalysis is "a stripe on the tiger," a part of larger reality, O, that remains unknown, perhaps unknowable. Yet unknowable O is our home. We may not *know* O, we can only be O. We *are* O, parts of O. Even if we try to get outside O, there is nowhere outside to get. We *are* something we can't *know*.

Bion suggests that so-called "resistance" in psychoanalysis, is resistance to O (see Chapter 4). The impact of reality—our mutual realness— carries a certain shock. We resist the shocks we can't escape, O-jolts that shake but make us more real. We incessantly impact on each other, sending emotional ripples through our beings. One of our tasks is to help build equipment to process mutual impacts, to be able to live what we create together. To some extent, a psychoanalyst must be a connoisseur of impacts. Shocks have different tastes. Some we get used to. But there will always be enough new shocks to broaden and shift what is possible to experience.

A link between mysticism and madness emerges in the convergence of Winnicott's, Bion's and Lacan's writings on the theme of precocity, prematurity, insufficiency (see Chapter 5). Winnicott writes of unimaginable agonies that mark us before we can sustain, process or even experience them. We do not know what they are. They occur before we have frames of reference for them (if we ever do). Yet these unthinkable, unknown, perhaps unknowable agonies exert a pull. They leave intimations of breakdown at the origin of personality, agonizing breakdowns that occur when personality is beginning to form.

Our personality goes on forming and does not break as fully as at the beginning. But partial breakdowns occur and we fear worse ones. Intimations of breakdowns that occurred when personality was forming haunt us, adding to the fear of breakdown now. In therapy, we reach towards the originary breakdown, a state of affairs Winnicott calls *x* (1989, p. 128). We go through useable doses of x and get the feel of what it is like to come through difficulties that seemed insurmountable. This is less a specific cognitive-behavioral skill (although the latter may be included), than increased flexibility-plasticity of capacity to experience life. We develop a gift for spontaneous recovery from states we were certain would derail us and ruin our chance at living.

Still, madness x is inexhaustible. The sense of totally cataclysmic events happening to personality as it was starting to form never fully leaves. Neither self nor helpers can save one from early breakdowns one goes through, although quality of support in the aftermath makes a difference. The atmospheric tone surrounding breakdown can drive one further down, or lift one through (Eigen, 1992b).

Bion emphasizes insufficiency of psychic equipment in a more pervasive way. All through our lives we are challenged by impacts we can't process. We scare ourselves by imaginings which magnify dreads beyond comprehension. Yet our imaginal capacity is real and nourishes growth, as well as threatens it. Our very capacity to experience (think, feel, imagine, sense) can be too much. We do not know what to do with the range, color, intensity available. We translate bits of it into art, poetry, drama, mystical vision, intersubjective know-how. But it also produces wars and threat of greater wars—between individuals, groups, nations. We injure ourselves and each other in both crude and ingenious ways.

Our problem is not just malignant attitudes, bad as these are. But malignancy often works overtime to mask intolerance of embryonic states. So many fetal/embryonic elements of personality get rushed, blotted out, passed over, pushed aside by exigencies of living. We ignore or kill off a lot to develop a self that makes a go of it. Sometimes selection processes work decently and areas of personality we develop serve their purpose. But our attitude to what fails to develop, or what asks for development, can be critical to our overall quality of awareness or larger sense of self. If we fail to find kindly ways of relating to embryonic/fetal aspects (including aspects that sacrificed themselves so we might live), the selves we use to stake our claim to existence can run away with our lives.

When embryonic/fetal elements stir, one dreads rumblings will turn into earthquakes. It is not only a matter of built up structures threatened with collapse, significant as this is. It is, also, that one does not know what the stirrings are or what to do with them. Plates beneath our personal landscape shift before equipment to work with the change evolves. Shifts happen and we have to grow with, through, into, around them. Anxiety about collapse diverts one from deeper, perplexing quandaries: what is stirring, what can I do, if anything, to midwife or catch up to it, how can I tell if it deserves a chance at living, how can I become the kind of person to give it a chance or give myself a chance to evolve with it? Here faith may be more important than mastery, although everything we are plays a role in what we can be.

Everything we aren't/are are twins needing room. There is more than we can use or fathom in both directions. Part of the sense of mystery comes from being perpetually embryonic. Many feel that learning how to do things, becoming a scientist, takes mystery away. My own sense is that mystery motivates and nourishes science. Without a sense of mystery, science would dry up—even though science, partly, stimulates its own growth, feeds itself. Discovery deepens mystery. At present, science has never been more exciting, nor mystery deeper. If mystery ends, so will we. Mystery is the core of consciousness, while we know around and through it. Mystery-knowing permeate each other in every pore of existence.

Lacan suggests that we imagine ourselves more whole than we feel as embodied beings. This is made possible by an asymmetry between what we do and see. As babies, for example (all through life, really), we see others doing what we can't, and may imagine ourselves as complete and able as they seem to be. In important ways, image takes precedent over body, or, at least, molds, blurs, exploits body sensations-feelings. We lose touch with our body selves, or, rather, slant potential body experiencing through desires that live through images. We become "masters" of imaginal trophies—capturing desire with desire, playing off variants of wholeness-abjection. As symbolic capacity evolves (and we with it), we become more conscious of disproportions between feelings-images and mutually exploitative scenarios. We somewhat catch on to ourselves.

From Lacan's point of view, mystical feeling is an imaginary way to feel more whole. Mystical feeling feeds psychosis and perversion, undoing or distorting the framework of psychic life. To some extent, neurosis tames mystical feeling with its structures and symptoms (hysterical affect-obsessive/paranoid thinking), using fantasy conflicts as defenses. Yet the neurotic's distorted grip on reality, a reality manqué tinged with fear of reality, a kind of anti-reality, provides a bulwark against the onslaught of mystical states.

Still, beyond the equation of mysticism with madness, there is the life of the unconscious subject, giving birth to revelation-response, "pulsations from the slit," the living word, the drive towards truth, bringing silence to the brink of new possibilities, new worlds of meaning. It is not exhausted by calling it a language machine. Mechanistic explanations fall short. No matter how much we learn about it or use it or are used by it, there is a residue, a surplus, an intrigue about the unconscious subject, its determination to be free, to surprise, to excite, to shift and combine perspectives, to be somewhere else.

Whether or not Lacan would agree, there *is* a kind of mystical feeling connected with the unconscious subject, at least with some of its workings some of the time. It may or may not be associated with some version of God or *sunyata* (Lacan sprinkles references to Buddhism in his work). It may not have religious content in the old-fashioned sense. But it does carry a sense of mystery, the thrill of unknowing, shivers of awakening. It does have a sense of taking us deeper into life, opening existence.

Winnicott, Bion and Lacan overlap in emphasizing insufficiency in face of who we are and what we go through. Winnicott emphasizes unprocessable agony, a sense of agony beyond what we can experience, an agony that drives us mad. Bion emphasizes shattering, explosive force, whether evil force destroying existence, or force of terrifying truth.

Lacan emphasizes inability and fragmentation we fill with imaginary wholeness. In each case, mystical feeling interlaces with insufficiency-excess.

Mystical feeling often is aroused by a smaller psychic grouping encountering a larger, more powerful grouping outside its boundaries. The first reaction of biblical prophets encountering God may range from fear-terror to awe-dread. Freud (see Chapter 1) notes that mystical feeling is aroused by ego's apprehension of id. Political leaders appeal to nations as larger wholes individuals mystically unite with and give themselves to.

At first glimpse, it seems that Freud's association of religion with infantile dependency is right—at least has areas of validity. We fill incapacity with mysticism associated with dependency. Yet even at this level, incapacity goes beyond dependency. Bion calls attention to mystical feeling associated with shattering of dependency (see Chapters 3-6). It is precisely where controlling dependency breaks down that mystical awareness heightens. Bion's work includes Lacan's vision of mysticism covering inadequacy, but opens, also, a very real sense of mystical awareness evolving where spurious wholeness breaks down—and keeps breaking down.

Bion pays homage to the mysticism of old—the Changeless Eternal Infinite, the all potential formless Void, O itself. But he also opens to a mysticism of changing moments, a dynamic, restless O. We meet O not simply as peace, but turbulence, even catastrophe. We can not keep up with incessantly evolving O. We work with premonitions. And since we are O, part of O, we work through premonitions of ourselves.

Bion's is a kind of kaleidoscopic mysticism, fidelity to shifts in the O-kaleidoscope. Faith keeps us open to shifts in O, even if we can't handle them. If we stay open to impact as best we can, something gets through. We can and do change, even if we do not know what is happening to us. We get ideas about changes that happened to us after we realize that something made a difference and we are not the same. This is somewhat in line with the Hindu idea that the present is the past, dreaming is the present, inner void the future.

Sometimes we feel an impact without knowing what it is. We learn more about it as time goes on. At the moment we know only the jolt and sense something significant. Sometimes we learn of an impact by living its results. Events unfold in ways that lead us back to an impact we failed to notice or give its due. Somewhere Eddington may have said about the universe, "Something unknown is doing we don't know what." We are that unknowable something, as much of it as we can take.

But what if O or part of O is mad or partly mad? Winnicott, in sync with Bion, finds the stamp of madness running through our personal universe as one of its poles. We dip in and out of a madness we only partly know. It may obliterate and deaden us or help make us feel more alive and real. The impact of ungraspable madness that molds, attracts, eludes, obliterates-enlivens—colors our sense of mystery, contributes background intensity, tones mystical feeling.

Disintegration is real. There are times environmental impingement breaks us down. We disintegrate under traumatic impacts and need recovery time. Sometimes we recover in deformed ways. We harden and refuse to disintegrate, or partially harden around pockets of disintegration. We learn to face the world without going under much of the time. Nevertheless, disintegration leaves traces. Our own personality threatens us. We covertly fear ourselves and a world that provokes disintegration or can not stop it. We fear life that has horror of disintegration built into it. We know we are the kind of beings who *can* disintegrate. We step between disintegration threats like children stepping between cracks in the sidewalk, hoping to avoid fault lines of personality.

At the same time, joy is real. Coming through terror of disintegration can bring joy. So can love and beauty. There are joys of triumph, success, power—mastery joys. Cruel and mean joys. There is mad joy—heart bursting with joy. We are transported, brought to new places by joy. We bathe in streams of heavenly delights.

Often our emotions confuse us. Disintegration dread fuses with ecstatic surrender.

Increasingly violent movies portraying instant disintegration of bodies (or worlds) provide a spurious sense of mastery of dread. At the same time, they enable masses of people to taste the pleasures of disintegration by proxy, thrills of power and helplessness, tinged with a covert mystical charge. Panoramic, kaleidoscopic vistas add a dash of Infinity to the brew. It is as if we are trying to explode our sense of mystery, reduce it to rubble, to nothing, to both experience and null it at the same time.

What odd creatures we are, who try to master mystery by blowing it up. Perhaps not so strange, after all, when we're told we live in a world that had a violent beginning and will have a violent ending, not a universe beginning with word or breath. But biblical reality was violent too. We worship a God who loves and destroys, creates good and evil, is compassionate and angry, merciful and severe. We try to separate and divide these poles to gain some clarity, but often can't tell one from the other. Satan is luminous, God dark, as well as the reverse. We move between positions in which Satan is part of God, God part of Satan, desperately playing off one against the other. In so many ways, we begin to acknowledge obliteration as a way of relating to and apprehending reality.

Childhood books puzzle through emotional nuclei, shifting mixtures of might-fright, glad-bad-mad-sad, changing space-time realities, sizes, love-power paradoxes, paying homage to our capacity to go through so many states, to be mysterious to ourselves, to live in a dumbfounding cosmos. "Who am I?" asks Alice—and in writing this I wrote Alive. So much of childhood upbringing involves lies of mercy, reassuring young ones that life isn't what they think it is—but as adults they must find out it is. The chaos we climb out of as children, we nurture as adults.

Joyous, fearful, rageful, sorrowful beings. Emotions span inner-outer realities and spotlight, find, generate, weave together, break apart worlds. Mysticisms reflect the variable intensity of emotional life. There are mysticisms that go beyond emotions or take us into and through emotions, use emotions to take us beyond ourselves. There are mysticisms of emotion and no-emotion, self and no-self, filled-empty, everything-nothing, good-evil. Mysticisms combine and use ingredients of personality (e.g., self-other, body-mind-spirit, top-bottom, in-out) every which way. In an earlier book (Eigen, 1993), I explored "free floating ideal feeling," a beatific sense that could attach itself to many kinds of objects and events. We are used to opposing mystical states and everyday life. But our emotional life combines mystical feeling and practical living in better-worse ways.

Mystical feeling is not limited to what we think is good and valuable. We need, first of all, to acknowledge it is there, whatever it is, a real force or forces, working in ways we barely sense.

Science is making inroads on the physiology and neurochemistry of mystical feeling. The limbic system is a seat of mysticism and emotionality (Joseph, 1996, pp. 268-319). The Broca area may carry the voice of God (Jaynes, 1976). The autonomic system plays a role in mediating fear of God, holy wrath, sense of oneness (viz., adrenal rush in addictions, heightened states). Ideas of God and spirituality, involving symbolization, need complex cortical mediation.

Perhaps physiological and chemical know-how will someday control or regulate mystical affect. Certainly, pharmacological regulation of depression, obsessive thinking, eating disorders, and hyperactivity has demonstrated power and value, as well as raised questions about abuse. It is likely even more sophisticated advances in chemical thought-affect regulation will occur. Freud (1940) envisioned a time when neurology would replace psychoanalysis—psychoanalysis was possible or necessary only because the neurology that would make it superfluous had not yet developed.

On the other hand, Freud felt there would always be interest in consciousness for its own sake. In principle, it is difficult to envision such total control of physiology that exploration of experience becomes irrelevant. Access to physiology is through experience.

I don't think we can count on knowledge of physical processes alone to do our thinking-feeling for us. Knowledge of brain processes is not the same as joy of learning. Who we are, how we study, what we study, what we make of it—questions of value, selection, interest, tone, quality, use—such questions require something other than scientific analysis, although the latter contributes.

Our view of science is as crucial as its effects on our view of ourselves. We are, after all, people making use of science, and what kind of people we are affects quality of use. There is humanitarian, compassionate use of science, but also scientific—or pseudo-scientific—fascism. When I presented the case of Lucy (see Chapter 11) to scientific audiences, groups were split between those genuinely interested in processes that might be at work, and those who were furious that the patient was not medicated. The enraged (no exaggeration) ones were not slowed down by the fact that Lucy did not want medication, that she did not want anything (including me) to come between her and her wretched self.

Why did Lucy come for help, if she did not want "help"? What was she looking for—waiting for? She didn't know herself—yet had an inchoate sense of it. It took years of my being a background presence, lurking, bouncing back and forth, before she made the contact with life she needed. It couldn't be rushed. The most frightening depression-deprivation became a way of filtering reality for years, until the tide turned, and living became possible. Access to what Lucy really felt, or imagined she felt was crucial. No substitute for this kind of intensity was possible. The result was a profound mystical-practical affirmation of a kind only those who brave this kind of suffering cherish.

Something similar occurred with Dolores (see Chapter 5), whom I depict as a kind of "body soul" mystic. She was at the mercy of sensory-feeling bombardments for which she needed to find filters. Her managed care program demanded that she see a psychiatrist for medication, although she did not want to. She was a naked and raw sensitivity who went through agonizing upheavals with friends and myself. But the idea of using medication to make things manageable seemed foreign to her nature (although she saw it help some of her own patients). There was nothing for us to do but keep on working with the emotional fields we generated. We were filters, channels for one another, faulty, messy, leaky, usually inadequate. While we were together, we were all we had. The states we went through had infinite value for their own sake. Sometimes they were "helpful," sometimes "harmful." But they made us keenly appreciative of what kinds of beings we were. (I am not doubting the value of medication, but do not want to see individuals dictated to by those insensitive to idiosyncratic paths.)

Reading and sex are not things we know about but things we do. The pleasures and freedom that go with reading are not duplicated by knowing about the physiology of reading. While learning how to control the chemistry underlying reading has uses, the worlds, ideas, feelings that reading generates are irreplaceable. Of course, there needn't be conflict between knowledge and experience—they feed each other. They are trees in the same garden—what nourishes the garden, nourishes them. One of the best kept secrets about thinking is how ecstatic it is.

Drugs and mysticism have a long history together (in our day, LSD mystics, for example), showing a close connection between chemistry and consciousness. It is easy to imagine science and mysticism sharing interpenetrating areas. Some feel it already is happening. Others believe the idea misguided, that science and mysticism necessarily exclude each other.

I can only speak from my own experience, my life, my truth. Both psychoanalysis and mystical states have had enormous impacts on me. They've had enriching and destructive impacts. Both add meaning to my life, enrich experience, provide challenges. They interpenetrate each other. They are not separable realities, but part of one reality, what I describe as "paradoxical monism" (see Chapters 2, 10). We speak of parts of people, parts of self, and separate disciplines. There is a reality of parts, and each part opens vistas and connections with other parts. We access eternity through our grains of sand, the grain of sand, the snowflake we are. Still, my life is my life. And no one can live it for me. I am not just a bunch of separate parts but a living being, reality alive, a secret, a mystery, an intimation, just plain me. Like you.

There are a lot of people today who, like myself, dip in and out of many things. There is so much available. As I describe in Chapter 10, my interest in Buddhism began more than forty years ago. Except for intermittent and relatively brief periods, I've never been a disciplined "practitioner." But Buddhism has had enormous impact on my life, my life's "practice," my living. I sporadically dip into Hindu writings and practices and have enjoyed exposures to several Hindu and Buddhist teachers. I still benefit from these contacts. Taoism is important to me and I feel close to aspects of Sufi.

When I was a young man, I considered Catholicism, and for a time took instruction, which illness prevented me from completing. I went through quite some crises with Mother Church, but this was not to be my overt path. Truths I found through my encounter with Catholicism are very much part of me. Nothing one goes through in a deep way is wasted.

Judaism provided a powerful point of access to Divinity after my father's death. The moment of his death was a turning point. He held on several weeks, apparently unconscious for days. At last his local rabbi returned from vacation and visited and chanted, the Shma, the priestly blessing, parts of Adon Olam ("Into His hand I shall entrust my spirit. . . the Lord is with me, I shall not fear."). When the rabbi left, my mother, sister and I knew my father was gone, peacefully, as the last notes faded. The words formed in my mind, "The God of Abraham, Isaac and Jacob lives."

I studied Judaism and aspects of Kabbalah for several years afterwards. Bion spontaneously spoke to me about the Kabbalah's importance for him nearly a decade earlier (Chapter 3; and Eigen, 1993, pp. 260, 272). This aspect of my development, also, was anticipated in a paper on faith (1993, pp. 109-138), taking off from the biblical challenge to love your God, with all your heart, soul, might. This all your heart, soul, might, mind—all of you, good and evil aspects, all—there is no more passionate calling.

At this moment, I'm no longer literally observant, but a patchwork blend. A deep feeling runs through the patches, something all tributaries link up with. All the gateways, avenues of access—something pours through them all. There is a fidelity to this sacred something, the very mystery of who we are. For many, traditional religious forms can not contain or do justice to the mystery we are part of, although they try. They provide hints. Hints come from many sources. There are so many of us now immersed in and uplifted by a diversity of hints. Parochial arrogance—religious or psychoanalytic—is out of order. Mutual permeability, creative combinations, the generative unborn can't be absorbed or channeled by overly rigid postures. We are very much in process of discovering the what, how and who of experience, learning new abc's, mixtures of new-old can's-can'ts regarding the immensity of what we are given, find, and create.

We are far from free of the mirror's other sides, our ghastly, nasty selves, the monsters in our dreams as well as waking lives—ourselves, each other, our worlds, our universe. More and more, as best we can, through our selfish selves and with our selfish selves as partners, may we reach out—a little, and a little more, and keep on helping ourselves and each other, to the extent we are able, which may be more than we imagine. In Chapter 11, I try to sketch something of the way we shift and stretch, to grow with new conditions, but, also, to evolve with demands made on us by pressing inner dynamics, our own personal thorns, and the often furious suffering of others. One would think there is nothing new in suffering, but we manage to invent twists and turns that exploit this capacity, and call for creative gestures that sometimes border on the wondrous.

Chapter 1

The Psychoanalytic Mystic

Most psychoanalysts tend to be anti-mystical, at least non-mystical. Psychoanalysis is allied with science. If allied with the humanities and the arts, it is thought too ironical, too aware of multiplicity, ambiguity, complexity to be mystical. If anything, psychoanalysis is capable of deconstructing mystical experience (indeed, psychoanalysis can deconstruct itself). Psychoanalysis is too sophisticated to be mystical.

Yet some psychoanalysts tend to be mystical, or are receptive to mysticism, or make use of mystical experience as intuitive models for psychoanalytic experience. Foremost among these are Bion (1970) and Milner (1957, 1987). The greatest split in the depth psychology movement, between Freud and Jung, partly hinged on the way mystical experience was to be understood.

Most analysts relate mysticism to the ego's perception of deeper psychic structures or processes, or relatively boundless states associated with early infant-mother fusion. Freud expressed both viewpoints. In the last note (and next to last writing) published in the *Standard Edition*, Freud (1941) wrote, "Mysticism is the obscure self-perception of the realm outside the ego, of the id" (p. 300). He also relates religious feeling to a state in which nothing is excluded from the ego: ". . . originally the ego includes everything; later it separates off an external world from itself" (1930, p. 68). He gives the mother's breast as a privileged example of external reality once (forever?) included in ego-feeling.

Freud depicts early states in which "primary ego-feeling" (all is ego) goes along with "primary identification" (all is object). Or, rather, boundaries are open, so that I am part of you and you are part of me are indistinguishable (I am you ↔ You are me). In part, Freud's work is a meditation on what happens when the ego separates the external and, to an extent, the internal world from itself.

Our present ego-feeling is, therefore, only a shrunken residue of a much more inclusive—indeed, all embracing—feeling which corresponded to a more intimate bond between the ego and the world about it. If we may assume there are many people in whose mental life this primary ego-feeling has persisted to a greater or less degree, it would exist in them side by side with the narrower and more sharply demarcated ego-feeling of maturity, like a kind of counterpart to it. In that case, the ideational contents appropriate to it would be precisely those of limitlessness and of a bond with the universe—the same ideas with which my friend elucidated the "oceanic feeling" (1930, p. 68).

I am not sure Freud realized what importance would be attached to the phrase, "oceanic feeling," in future psychoanalytic discussions of mysticism. Freud's allusion, of course, was to Romain Rolland's famous letter, soon after publication of *The Future of an Illusion* (1927). The term "oceanic feeling" has been decisive in shaping psychoanalytic discussions of mysticism. I do not want to play down the importance of oceanic feeling, but I feel it has somewhat contributed to watering down possibilities of mystical experiencing and psychoanalytic discussions of the latter (Eigen, 1986, 1993).

Freud's own writings on the foundations of religious experience burgeon with complexities. On the one hand he links the ego's early all inclusiveness with a oneness with the breast or mother. Primary ego-feeling/primary (limitless) narcissism/primary identification arise in a primary maternal surround. At the same time, he speaks of primary identification with an ideal prehistoric father, prior to separation of object from ego (1921, p. 105; 1923, p. 29). This puzzling, even mysterious, coupling is subject to many interpretations.

Before venturing one of my own, I wish to acknowledge that by primary identification with the father of the individual's "own personal prehistory," Freud simply may be referring to the *Totem and Taboo* (1913) father. The father slain by the sons returns as father ideal, passed down in superego formation. Even this simple story contains many motifs, including the wish to possess the mother (sexuality), the wish to possess leadership of the group (power), love-hate (ambivalence), murder, guilt, dread, formation of/attachment to ideals. Freud depicts how ideals bind and gratify violent/sexual strivings, and act as substitute gratifications and organizers for the latter.

The *bourgeois* European father adds layering to the *Totem and Taboo* father. Freud (1930) emphasizes the need for paternal protection in face of infantile helplessness:

I cannot think of any need in childhood as strong as the need for a
father's protection. Thus the part played by oceanic feeling, which might
seek something like the restoration of limitless narcissism, is ousted from
a place in the foreground. The origin of the religious attitude can be
traced back in clear outlines as far as the feeling of infantile helplessness.
There may be something further behind that, but for the present it is
wrapped in obscurity (p. 72).

The dreaded father, the protective father, the murdered father, the
sustaining father: the father as center of psychic drama displaces oceanic
feeling in the foreground. Generations of later analysts regressed to
concern with oceanic feeling in the background, as maternal dramas
became central in analysis.

For Freud there was father after mother, and father before mother.
What can this mean? Freud's persistent association of father with ideals
suggests that the infant (from the outset, before birth) is inserted into an
ideal matrix, is a carrier of ideal realities. Part of the story of therapy is
how the individual meets the ideals he is embedded in. Ideal analysis
and instinct analysis are intertwined, since instincts-ideals are intimately
connected.

Lacan's (1977) function in psychoanalysis was to maintain a certain
primacy of the symbolic dimension in the constitution of the human
psyche. He fought against literalizing the object or drives in psychoanalytic theory. The human psyche, if it is human, is never merely literal. An
ideal dimension plays a constitutive role in human life. This is, partly,
why Winnicott (1953) says that mother symbolizes maternal functioning
as she mothers, that her symbolic functioning for the infant is as indispensable as her physical functioning.

Father before mother, ideals before drives. A chicken-egg situation.
In the Freud-Lacan line, drives and ideals are co-constitutive elements
of the human psyche. Take away either, the psyche is gone. For Lacan,
the interesting thing is the way the Freudian thing, the mustard seed of
repression, structures the way drives-signifiers work (indeed, repression
is, necessarily, a way they work). Lacan shows ways an essentially displaced psyche incessantly represents, speaks, dramatizes itself.

Lacan is admittedly anti-mystical. For him the oceanic must be an
attempt to undo repression, to undo the human psyche. It is madness,
an attempt to achieve literal limitlessness, a contradiction in terms. At
best the oceanic is part of *jouissance*, the life of the body that slides away
from and through meaning, giving to the symbolic the capacity for joy
(or terror).

The Lacanian association of the oceanic with madness adds intensity to Freud's doubt that a contentless feeling can be the basis of religion (unless one thinks religion mad). Freud argues that what is important is not the oceanic feeling as such, but how it is interpreted. Romain Rolland's sense of a limitless bond with the cosmos is one interpretation of a feeling that can assume many colors. In certain circumstances one can imagine such a feeling welling up at the moment of murder, or having sex with a stocking, or licking feces, or saluting a flag. There are many perceptual and symbolic triggers for welling up of oceanic feeling, which sometimes may go along with oneness with God or cosmos. Thus what is crucial is not oceanic feeling as such, but what it means to the individual, or how it functions psychically and culturally.

Freud (1930) candidly admits that he has been less concerned "with the deepest sources of the religious feeling than with what the common man understands by his religion . . ." (p. 74) He mainly has been concerned with how systems of belief offset frailty and dread. Freud confesses it pains him to see people behave like children, substituting wish-fulfillment for reality (God for science and common sense).

Freud says he has no personal access to oceanic feeling. It is not something he experienced himself. Perhaps he knew it in displaced form, as the joy that is part of creative work. He felt creativity made his life worthwhile. He quotes Goethe, "He who possesses science and art also has religion; but he who possesses neither of these two, let him have religion!" (ibid, p. 74) For those with only religion, oceanic feeling must signify the victory of the pleasure principle, wish over reality. For the masses it is questionable whether science and art ever will displace religion. Freud could not have imagined a time when electronic media, especially television, would conquer science, art *and* religion: victory of the commercial image, union with an ersatz, fabricated, detached and reduced mind, plugged into cosmic air waves, run by market research.

One wonders whether Freud has entirely demolished Romain Rolland's insistence that oceanic feeling is meaningful in itself, independent of established institutions, doctrines, beliefs. For Rolland oceanic feeling is an immediate experience, the live kernel that belief systems grow out of. William James (1902), too, speaks of an awakening of religious awareness beyond individual belief systems. At some point, we may have opportunity to take the dialogue between Rolland, James and Freud further. For now I wish to leave matters open, noting only that these authors speak with voices that command respect, and a dismissive attitude to any of them would be out of place.

A Few Variations

I have not defined mystical feeling because I am unable to. My hope is, if I speak around it, or from it, well enough, something of value will get communicated to the reader and myself. Discussions of mystical awareness tend to undo themselves because of the paradoxical nature of the experiencing involved.

As noted above, Freud depicted at least two states of affairs subsuming mystical experience: the ego's perception of the id, and an ego-feeling that includes external reality. The first presupposes ego's sense of otherness within the self, while the second presupposes lack of otherness outside the self. This is an especially interesting coupling in light of Freud's portrayal of ego as, essentially, less separate from id than external reality. The ego is implicated in a double illusion, feeling more separate from the internal and less separate from the external world than is so.

In the former case, the mystical feeling comes from the I experiencing a greater inner presence than anticipated, while in the latter the I enjoys a boundless fullness. The apprehension of a greater *It vis a vis* the I requires time and development, whereas a pristine all-inclusive I-ness awaits time. Both moments are naive. A contracted I is surprised by the more within the self, while an inflated I is surprised by the more outside the self. The I will learn that it and the world are bigger and smaller than it imagined.

Freud plays with dimensions of inner-outer, bigger-smaller: what is inside and outside I-feeling. That the boundaries of I-feeling shrink and expand suggests that mystical states vary, partly, as a function of what the I imagined was included or excluded within it. A sense of numinosity or mystical charge can fall more on self or other, depending on a host of variables, including disposition, mood, developmental phase, and situational factors.

Mystical moments also involve a sense of movement *between* dimensions of experience, and between self and other. A heightened sense of impact may characterize subject-to-subject meeting. In light of this, Buber (1957) wrote, "All real living is meeting" (p. 11). The self that enters an I-Thou relation is not the same as in an I-It relation. Oceanic fusion, absorption, or oneness would not do justice to the drama of self-other meeting and intersection that Buber points to. For one thing, the mystical moment may involve enormous upheaval, turbulence, over-throwing and reworking of self. A new meeting can change one's picture of what self and other can be.

Winnicott (1971) has shown that the "between" has a developmental biography. For him the sense of newness was a central element of growth. Development is revelation. Movement between self and other changes meaning. New dimensions of experiencing open as development unfolds. In "transitional experiencing" and "object usage," different relations between self and other open new worlds of experience.

In previous writings (Eigen, 1986, 1992b, 1993), I have linked Winnicott's (1971) "transitional experiencing" and "object usage" to the development of faith.

I will not cover that ground here, but wish to note that Winnicott's appeal is not simply his celebration of the ordinary. In addition to percipience and respect, a reverence for life permeates his writings. How extraordinary the ordinary and *vice versa*!

The I/not-I dance takes new turns in Winnicott's writings. For one thing, his work amplifies our conception of what an object is. An object can be packed with me-ness, otherness, a wide range of emotions and attitudes (devotion, clinging, awe, possessiveness, hate, indifference, curiosity), mommy-ness, divinity, simple itself-ness. Winnicott puts a new twist on the idea of turning the other cheek by saying we discover the realness of the object by its intact survival of our destructive fantasies. The object is important as a rich symbolic field and its ability to be itself. We could not be ourselves otherwise.

Marion Milner's (Field, 1934) early writings show what would some day make her and Winnicott friends and colleagues. From the outset, her interest was in discovering what was most real and meaningful in her own experience. She described everyday moments that stood out with special significance. Their presence transformed the day. She adopted the "dying god" image to partly organize her findings. The idea of losing self to find self was expressive of the paradoxical opening that comes with letting go usual mindsets. An uplifting sense of creativeness was linked with dipping into a deeper experiential flow. Milner's (1987) psychoanalytic writings were concerned with reaching this sense of creativeness, symbolizing it, and living it (Eigen, 1993). Throughout her writings she explored ways mysterious depths linked up with everyday surfaces. She, like Winnicott, noted symbols that expressed the connection and separation of inner-outer, self-other, like bridge, thread, overlapping circles.

Images from Buddhism, Taoism, and Christianity seamlessly seeped into her psychoanalytic writings. Not only the dying god, but emptiness, nothing, and yin-yang interweaving were used to describe aspects of creative processes. Similar language spilled into Winnicott's gropings. Unintegration, creative chaos, and nothing were, for Winnicott, important moments that enabled self to shed shells.

Freud, too, used images drawn from myth and religion to express creative processes. Note his use of the darkness-light polarity in his account of moods and struggles, and images of surrender and blindness depicting drifting with the flow of unconscious processes (Masson, 1985). Spontaneous use of mystical images to portray creative block, struggle, agony, joy, flow, and breakthrough became part of the language of clinical encounter.

Bion's (1970) work teems with use of western and eastern mystical images. He explicitly relates the psychoanalytic attitude to faith. He uses aspects of biblical narratives and terms like "O," "void" and "formlessness" to portray psychoanalytic processes. I sometimes wonder if Bion didn't have a special fondness for nihilistic mysticism. Here are a few lines from Scholem (whom Bion quotes, in a related context) describing mystical nihilism:

> The nihilistic mystic descends into the abyss in which the freedom of living things is born; he passes through all the embodiments and forms that come his way, committing himself to none; and not content with rejecting and abrogating all values and laws, he tramples them underfoot and desecrates them, in order to attain the elixir of Life. In this radical interpretation of a symbol, the life-giving element of mystical experience was combined with its potential destructiveness. It goes without saying that from the standpoint of the community and its institutions, such mysticism should have been regarded as demonic possession (1974, p. 29).

Bion combines elements of Freud's life and death drives, and Melanie Klein's paranoid-schizoid and depressive positions, in his depiction of Ps↔D operations in psychoanalytic sessions. Tearing and building, falling apart and coming together are aspects of broader psychic rhythms, if one can tolerate the shifts. Bion's writings contain the most detailed portrayals of anti-life tendencies of any psychological texts to date. He describes ways the personality tears itself apart, denudes and evacuates itself, becomes worse than nothing. His dark night seems far worse than St. John of the Cross's, and more horrifying than mere demonic malevolence. He speaks of "a force that continues after. . . it destroys existence, time and space (1965, p. 101). Annihilation goes on in sub-zero dimensions, even after destruction of personality.

I think Bion is trying to describe the worst in us. And I think he is trying to do something more. I feel he is saying we must and can survive the worst, if we are to be truly compassionate with ourselves and each other, if we are going to be partners with the capacities that constitute us. One of the great experiences in reading Bion, I think, is that over and over, we come through the worst. We survive ourselves, build up tolerance for ourselves, make room for ourselves.

The modern and post-modern mind is permanently critical, ironical, skeptical. Hopefully this saves us from gullibility (wasn't Swift's *Gulliver*, partly, a story about the vicissitudes of gullibility and irony?). Bion's work can hardly be called gullible. Yet mystical tendencies persist, and interweave with critical thinking. In Bion's work mysticism and criticism feed each other. One can not choose between faith and irony, since both are real capacities. The rule in psychoanalysis is openness to the play of voices.

In face of the worst that he can experience or envision experiencing (including total destruction of experience), Bion maintained a faith that openness to the unknowable ultimate reality (of a session, of a moment, of a lifetime) is somehow linked with growth processes. I think that Bion must have been close to destroying every possibility of goodness in life, and that he speaks from his own experience of surviving the great destruction. I think he must have discovered for himself that life erupts in the valley of the shadow of death. The sense that life survives destruction parallels Winnicott's (1969) description of the object surviving the subject's unconscious backcloth of destruction. I think Bion always had an eye on the backcloth of destruction. He always was facing the horror of himself. A faith that, in spite of all horrors, experience is worthwhile, is different from use of faith to avoid experiencing. The faith Bion fought for was linked to intensity of living and risk of openness.

Winnicott, Milner and Bion share a conviction that an originary, naked self is the true subject of experience. Internalization processes are necessary for a fully developed, human self, but something originary shines through. I think these authors would like the Zen koan, "What was your original face before you were born?" Winnicott's incommunicado self, transitional experiencing and object usage, Bion's F in O, Ps↔D rhythm, being over knowing, Milner's pregnant emptiness and I-yet not-I moment: all point to and grow out of moments of real living, in which fresh possibilities of experience uplift the self.

Ego-Self

Ego and self have many meanings in different texts and contexts. They vary along personal-impersonal-transpersonal and subject-object lines. Sometimes the ego is likened to a triangle, sharp at top, wide at bottom, imperceptibly blending into a deeper self. This is a common image in writings on eastern thought, but Freud and Milner use it as well. Jung wrote of the ego as adaptive subject of time-space reality, and the self as subject of the psyche as a whole. There are many ways to cut the pie.

Psychoanalysts tend to think of the ego as subject and self as object, although this does not quite ring right (Freud also referred to the ego as the id's object). The subject-object expression turns into a Chinese box business. What is subject in one context, may be object in another, and *vice versa*. Subject-object dialectics and paradoxes can be breathtaking, if sometimes depressing, fun.

I have heard many people say that when they focus on I-feeling and let it resonate, they sense reverberations of a deeper, fuller self, not merely as object, but as subject. I-feelings and self-feelings merge in more or less familiar or uncanny ways. One can not tie personal or impersonal to I or self in any simple way. Self may feel more intimate than I and give I meaning. *I* can feel anonymous, estranged, unreal. The complaint, "I feel unreal. I can't feel myself," is a contemporary clinical obsession.

On the one hand we speak of a feeling of wholeness, on the other we say the psyche is split through and through. I-feeling can be warm and intimate, yet I can be other to itself. It is no accident that the I, in Freud, is a blend of anonymous and personal qualities and capacities. There is perhaps a semi-free-floating sense of the personal, and a semi-free-floating sense of anonymous processes that reshape each other in search of new combinations.

One tries to find combinations that are good for one, good enough fits. It is partly a matter of body English and lucky throws of the dice. Also, blends of anonymous-personal I-self combinations good at one phase of life, may not work in another. It is a relief to admit an element of mystery and not knowing in every fiber of identity. The "I know who I am" moment can, at times, be more destructive than doubt and confusion. Who or What is the x that tries on different I-self suits, to see what fits? All combinations are compromises, some better than others for a time. We are stuck with ourselves, but not quite stuck.

Distinction-Union

The sense of connection-distinction runs through experience. We spontaneously perceive and think in terms of relations, noting similarities and differences between this and that. Children incessantly compare themselves with others: who is bigger, stronger, who has more or less of whatever one sees or imagines there is more or less of? So many fights seem to hinge on a sense that there should be sameness where difference reigns, and vice versa.

A parent tells two brothers, "I'm treating you both the same." But the brothers see or imagine differences that irritate them. On another occasion these siblings may be mad because they are not treated differently enough. At the same time, each may be absolutely certain that the other gets the better deal. In the latter case, one's lacks and the other's pluses are magnified. Cain and Abel capture the feelings of the child, whatever God may say or do. Deal another hand, and Cain and Abel become allies, united in common cause against parental winds that go against them.

People who are close together may exaggerate small differences, and those far apart may exaggerate minimal similarities. How the sense of sameness-difference functions varies with many motivational, situational and attitudinal factors. At times we feel united with all existence, moved by a sense of commonality. Another moment, differences lead to war. Some individuals seem more attuned to differences, others to similarities. The mixtures keep shifting. We play up-play down sameness-difference in ceaseless, complex ways.

The sense of union may attach more to sameness or difference at different times. Union doesn't only or mainly mean same. One may be repelled by sameness, and attracted to difference. For many mystics, the difference between self and God is what makes union possible. A patient, Claudia, once said, "I was amazed at feeling close to John. He is so different from the sort of man I'm usually attracted to, so different from me. A breath of fresh air. I felt a deep union with him. I was free to feel union with him, because I would not be trapped by it."

The need for union looks for targets, but does not always find constructive conditions. Claudia's need for union always led to trouble. She hung her need for union on some perceived or imagined area of sameness between herself and her partner, only to feel suffocated and recoil. In the end, she had to run from those she united with (or they from her). With her new man, there was more space to begin with, so that she could exercise unitive needs more freely.

There is an ecstasy of difference, as well as ecstasy of union, and all sorts of mixtures. Often when we try something a little different, we feel better. Winnicott's (1969) use of object account expresses an ecstasy of difference. His work emphasizes freshness, beginnings, movement, aliveness. In a somewhat reverse case, I remember a man so tied up with his girlfriend, that when she wounded him, he literally saw stars and heard bells ring. One night, after a particularly cutting injury, he walked outside and the sky looked like Van Gogh's "Starry Night." He felt so free, such radiance. The experience was so decisive that he could not return to a relationship in which union was defined by injury. His hunger for new kinds of difference-union combinations eventually led to a workable marriage.

Paradoxical Monism

What sort of beings are we that we can have such radically different experiences of life, and adopt such radically different viewpoints towards our experience? At times I am alive in the world of the psalmist. My heart cries out to You, O Lord. You are closer to me than I am. Chasms separate us. Nothing is between us. You smash me, lift me up. I cry my heart out to you, with you, in you. You are with me in the shadow of the death that you are. You are my life. In your light do I see light. Such darkness, such radiance. Such closeness, such abysses. We struggle with words like in, out, between, through, beyond. Winnicott speaks of an incommunicado self, but also interdependence. In experience, bread and wine may delight the spirit, but also may symbolize spirit, or body, or spiritual body, or even *be* divine. For hundreds (thousands?) of years experience of God has been expressed in inside-outside terms: God is in us, yet outside us, immanent, yet transcendent, near-far. This dovetails with sense of self as detached and immersed.

Such terms are useful but we also go beyond them. God is everywhere, all is holy, poets and mystics exclaim. "I-yet-not-I-but-*moshiach*-in-me," says St. Paul. In moments of grace St. Paul no longer knows where he is or what is body and what is not. The spirit-flesh division that torments him becomes irrelevant. His exclamation, "God is love!" signals the awakening and opening that transforms him, a placeless place where one is free and ever born anew.

At other moments we leave the personal or superpersonal, and plunge into anonymity. "I am not my body, I am not my mind, I am not my I," the Hindu may say. Anonymous processes produce the same I in everyone. With the scientist or Buddhist we become aware of groupings that feed the I-field, all the multiple identities and identifications that enable the psychoanalyst to wonder, "Which I-You mixture is doing what now?" The Freud-Klein line has developed variations on the theme of the I in you and you in me.

With another turn of the kaleidoscope, we may speak of I or you as forms of energy, interdependent parts of causality streams proliferating in all directions, fading in time. A Buddhist may say, "Form is Void and Void is form. There is no relativity or Void outside each other." But because our knowledge is not absolute, we stay open to fresh awakenings.

Viewing myself as transformations of energy or Form ↔ Void has been quite helpful, not only in freeing me from myself, but enabling me to be myself more freely. My Jewish soul pops back up and my relationship to my God begins anew. The cry from the heart, the joy, the intensity of being, fierce sweetness, longing, intimacy: my God and I are back together, so many dramas lie ahead. I do not find a problem in moving between more anonymous, and personal moments, and their various amalgams. To say New York City exists does not mean Chicago doesn't, although many New Yorkers can not imagine real living goes on elsewhere.

In Hebrew one can turn various nouns or verbs into names of God. One calls God the place, the blessing, the song, the compassion(ate one), as well as the infinite One. There is a plural as well as singular name of God, apparently referring to the many-in-one, and one-in-many, the God of time, and the timeless One. I love the part of Judaism that speaks of the living God, a God of life. St. Paul confessed it dreadful to fall into the hands of the living God, but it is more dreadful not to.

I am writing this passage the day after Yom Kippur, after stripping away everything that can be stripped away, until there is nothing but naked contact with one's God. One's life flashes before one's eyes, all one's deformations, deficits, shortcomings. Dread, awe, sorrow, joy commingle. One makes contact with something more than the sum of selves, including one's psychoanalytic self. We are invited to return, turn again to the Source, a movement through death to one's birthplace.

The psalms are filled with references to this process. Repeatedly we are crushed like grapes, only to drink from the stream of divine delights. We go to bed weeping, but in the morning there is a cry of joy. Destructive tendencies and events threaten us from within and without, but we come through, chastened, seasoned, more able. Some of us do not make it. We reach out to brothers and sisters as the earth swallows them. Our turn will come. We hope we can touch fingers extended to us when the time comes, and that we keep reaching out to the unknown in others, whatever the odds.

I was not surprised to feel tears well up as the shofar sounded its long, last note to signal the end of the At-onement Day. But I was surprised to find myself wanting to hold on to it, wanting it never to fade, feeling I would miss it so in the year to come. I could not bear the idea of not hearing it for one whole year. What would I do for one whole year without that sound, the soul's tuning fork? In a few moments the congregation was shaking hands, exchanging glances. We would be shofars for one another. We would not let each other sleep away our lives. We would call each other to ourselves, over and over, throughout the year, often unpleasantly, but also, at times, with stunning sweetness. We were living in the God of life.

We are encouraged to seek God's presence, and do so incessantly. Seek and you will find, says one aphorism. I think more important than finding, is opening. Seek and you will open. *Seeking is opening*. When I read religious texts I stay open to experiences they induce in me. I need these experiences. They reset, deepen, redirect, renew me. They provide nutriments for further growth of experiencing.

I read psychoanalytic texts the same way. I need texts that add to my life, that open experiencing, that speak to my condition. I am not in psychoanalysis merely as a business or intellectual exercise. It is a life and death matter. It is my life I am spending in it, my time. Either I get the most I can from it, or it is worthless. I also want others to get the most they can, or why bother? I would be deeply gratified to think my writing (or some of it) evokes experiencing some people can use.

I can go back and forth between psychoanalytic and religious writings, moment to moment, each feeding, correcting, amplifying, opening the other. I say this because I think there are many of us who do, but are afraid to own this double tendency. Either we are put down for being psychoanalytic, or put down for being mystical. I had a similar difficulty as an undergraduate. My English teachers criticized me for being too psychological, and my psychology teachers criticized me for being too literary. It is awful to think one must stay on one or the other side of a permeable membrane, and try to stop the flow.

Cross fertilization between disciplines is a path of creativity in our time. Who knows what efforts this will give rise to, what odd beasts slouch toward Bethlehem waiting to be born? Let those who want to keep some version of psychoanalysis pure do so. But there are others of us who must go where the spirit blows and see what happens. Some of our products are better than others, but we are very much in the business of discovering how to live our way into processes that keep opening us up.

I have a stream of associations to Bion's O, his ambiguous notation for unknowable reality. Something unknown is doing we don't know what, is the way a physicist, I believe Eddington, somewhere put it. Milner speaks of Bion's O as zero, but O is also *Omega*, everythingness and nothingness. At times Bion uses O to signal the unknown emotional reality of a session, or of a series of transformations, or of group events, or of the cosmos. O may represent the impact of the Other, the shock of impact that sets off waves of feelings, sensations, presentiments. As we ride these waves we may utter a rapturous "Oh, Oh!", or an "Oh-Oh!" of trepidation. O is for the orgasmic element that permeates, charges and sustains experiencing. O is for One, one God, one cosmos, whose streamings we are. O is a circle, the rounds and rhythms of life, eternal returns and reversals, crisscrossing currents, a geometrical representation of the constructive-containing mind that pulsations explode, the Opening of the O.

O is a mark or utterance, a signal or notation for something it can not contain, perhaps not even represent. We try with language to point to the unrepresentable. We can not succeed with language (after all, language is the Tower of Babel), but we can not do without it. We have many partial successes, codes, sign systems that evoke experiences that can not be represented. How can we say that language evokes what it can't represent? The Kaballah speaks of *Ein Soph*, the unrepresentable infinite of infinites, then develops representational systems portraying channels of infinite flow. We never tire of speaking about what can't be talked about. We are filled with mystical and psychoanalytic gossip, our own little news briefs, our "Have you heard?. . . ."

If we are all made up of somewhat different combinations of the same or similar processes and share a common anonymity, the processes that we are have variability built into them. Without tensions and inhomogeneities, there would be no shared processes. It is a leap from the formation of the solar system, to the formation of language. Yet we like to think the solar system *is* a sort of language, and link God's word with birth of worlds and life. But earlier than word is breath, and while word is associated with the Tree of Knowledge, breath is associated with the Tree of Life.

Lacan used Boolean rings and the Moebius strip as images for the life of meaning and intertwining of language and psyche. If it is true one can't step into the same river twice, it is also true one can't step out of the river, whether the river is life, meaning, time, consciousness. It is a truism that consciousness can be conscious of being conscious of being conscious, yet can't catch itself. Time and language point beyond themselves. Movement is built into processes, and the Judaic God is a God of movement, a God of processes, partly explosive, partly conservative.

We are those processes, the temper tantrum big bang God, slow to anger, compassionate, treasuring the beauty of each soul, destroying multitudes. Just ordinary people, you and I, but what we go through in a single day is enough to ignite existence into flames, and burn, like Aharon's sons, into a crisp of glory. The blessing of fatigue and sleep saves us at day's end.

Fire and air (breath) seem more linked with the Jewish God than water, although the latter is important. What images we use to express the unimaginable make a difference to our psychic economy. They reflect and direct nuances of intensity and interplay between tensions and tendencies. What funnel systems we choose (or choose us) determine the directions of our lives.

I remember once being in emotional agony on a bus in my 20's. I doubled over into my pain and focused on it with blind intensity. As I sat there in this wretched state, I was amazed when the pain turned to redness, then blackness (a kind of blanking out), then light, as if a vagina in my soul opened, and there was radiant light. The pain did not vanish, but my attention was held by the light. I felt amazed, uplifted, stunned into awareness of wider existence. Of course I did not want the light to go away, and was a bit fearful that it would, but above all was reverence, respect: it could last as long as it liked, and come and go as it pleased. It was an unforgettable moment. Life can never be quite the same after such experiences.

I would not say I was one with that light. It was precisely its difference from me and my state that was so uplifting. There was a sharpness, a quickening, a thrilling rush, an awakening and heightening that blew me through myself. I was not engulfed or encompassed, so much as brought up short, opened. Breathtaking radiance and oceanic oneness are perhaps different aspects of mystical experience, the former more mental or transcendental ego, the latter more body ego, although such distinctions keep shifting. It is apt that Freud described libido in both electrical and liquid terms.

Often the impact of the Other is more than we can bear. Part of the job of primary process is to begin processing potentially overwhelming impacts into affective images and symbols usable for growth. The psyche repeatedly breaks down. It can not keep up with or metabolize what is happening to it. It may numb or get rid of itself and its products, or partly put itself out of play. Chronic rigidities are ways of freezing psychic flow and gaining partial mastery over some subsection of events. Today production is so far ahead of metabolization, that we substitute the flow of products for life.

In therapy we use mutual impacts of self ↔ other (therapist ↔ patient) to help constitute psyches more capable of working with the impacts that therapy generates. If therapist and patient can't respond creatively and usefully to impacts they have on each other, it is unlikely they will do much better with portions of life outside therapy. In therapy we give ourselves time to catch up with each other, to catch up with ourselves. We give ourselves time to give life a chance.

There is no reason to place artificial limits on where or how far therapy should go. Throughout my career I have heard that therapy is not a religion, and must stop short of the religious dimension. Perhaps this is true for many practitioners but it has never been so for me. Therapy is a holy business for me and was so from my first session, as patient and as therapist. I have not always lived up to its calling (as therapist, or patient), but I have thrilled to its call. The light I discovered through an opening in my agony in my 20's, comes back to me daily in the face of my patients. There is nothing we can't come through together, no hell, no death we can't face, if only we give each other time.

I think it important to recognize how much we get from our patients. Our patients are holding environments for us, as well as we for them. We organize ourselves through their presence. We immerse ourselves in them on a daily basis, and this immersion restores and enriches (not only drains) us. They give us the chance to use our minds and feelings creatively and usefully. We come up against our (and their) walls, and find ways to keep flowing.

Many patients have mystical experiences. Some have the power to transform lives. Others are misused and become destructive. Therapy can help people use their mystical capacity more fruitfully. Any experience can be reduced to its defensive aspect. One ought not prematurely close down the flow of experience and meaning by too strict an ideology or well meaning bias.

I want to close with a quote from a letter sent by a former patient, Sal. Sal came to me because he felt his earlier therapists closed down (and closed him down) when he opened the possibility of horrendous, limitless deadness. He felt helped by past therapies, but always felt somehow evasive. With me he got into the deadness that terrified him, but could not get out of it. There did not seem to be resources in his life to help him. He fell into a bottomless, malignant regression. I felt awful when he left me. I felt I failed him.

His letter surprised me:

> I left the therapy really to get therapy from life. I can see that more clearly now. It seems to be working. Something's going on anyway and I'm not really sure what it is.
>
> As I read stuff here and there on magic, occultism, esoteric stuff, I bump into things that describe experiences to be expected, but *after* I've had them. It's reassuring because of my training and with my bullshit I psychologize stuff or you know, attack my own belief in my experience.
>
> Where the world blew up on me before and left me in this ruined place, I'm now *beginning* to find myself in a different universe altogether. It's like a second explosion is occurring to clean up the mess of the first one. And I have the tiniest glimpse of this new place.
>
> That horrible dead thing, that empty experience, is still there but it is

becoming more of a tangible landscape. It's like it occurs on the level of the psychological but that's only a reverberation of something spiritual. And I don't experience "spiritual" as abstractly as I used to.

One of the most important things you ever said to me was that I was part of the universe. That was a seed that's bearing fruit. I *never* felt that way before, not really. The involvement in magic is a door. I said I would break through because I *must*. Maybe now I don't have to *break* through but the door can be opened. The *best* in analysis approaches practical magic. I don't know quite what I want to write about, but it's probably *something*.

I said Sal's letter surprised me. But deep down, deeper than my sense of failure, I hoped something would happen. Anyone can do well with benign regressions. Malignant ones are the ultimate challenge, the edge. If I were deeply honest with myself, I would say I had faith something good would come of my work with Sal. But I dared not let myself know that, lest I be wrong.

Sal found a mysticism very different from mine. But our worlds touched, and we are both better for it. Will his god and mine make friends, are they friends already, or eternal enemies? Let the gods decide. I think there is a bond between Sal and me that no god can break, because God made it. It is a bond that deepens our awareness of what freedom is. Therapy may involve skill, but is also a form of prayer.

Chapter 2

The Fire That Never Goes Out

Freud never ceased being impressed by the plasticity of psychic life and the reversibility of states. When he gives a reason for not abandoning hope in the treatment of psychosis, he points to the vast changes we go through on a daily basis, as we pass from ordinary consciousness to the madness of dreams and back again. What most moves us today in Freud are his descriptions of one thing changing into another. His complementary emphasis on fixity and structure acts like brakes for incessant movement described as liquid and electrical.

Winnicott takes up Freud's emphasis on movement and comes down on the side of movement over structure. He is one of a handful of psychoanalysts who wants his terms to be alive and fresh and suggestive of movement. He insists on this: "The word intermediate is certainly useful but the word transition implies movement and I must not lose sight of it otherwise we shall find some sort of static phenomenon being given an association with my name" (cited in Rodman, 1987, p. 42).

Winnicott's terms relate to freedom: transitional experiencing, use of object, use of madness, unintegration, the incommunicado core (Eigen, 1991). They depict different aspects of feeling fresh and free, new and alive, linked with a sense of creativeness. For Winnicott (like Freud), the sense of creativeness makes life worth living (Eigen, 1983). Out of this sense arises the prayer Winnicott was to use at the beginning of his autobiography: "Lord, may I be alive when I die."

Above, I wrote that Winnicott affirms movement over structure, yet how can these be separated? Perhaps this is possible only conceptually or as a matter of faith. For Winnicott, there is a kind of formless moment that is the home base of the self. Bollas (1989) points to this moment when he writes: "In our true self we are essentially alone . . . the absolute core of one's being is a wordless, imageless solitude" (p. 21).

Bollas had Winnicott's "incommunicado core" in mind, but he could add patternless to wordless and imageless and point to Winnicott's "unintegration." Here is where Winnicott differs from gestalt psychology: "You with your affection for gestalt psychology seem to me to be taking the pattern-making as a primary state, whereas for the psychoanalyst the pattern-making is a secondary phenomenon related to primary unintegration" (cited in Rodman, 1987, p. 31).

For Winnicott, it is important for the personality to be able to rest in unintegration, to float or drift between organizations, to dip into formlessness or chaos or nothingness. At this Sabbath point of personality, one takes time off from self. It is important to have time between choices, time simply to be. What a relief not to have to be this or that, not to have to force oneself into a particular shape ("shape up").

In letters and informal clinical discussions, Winnicott is not afraid to say that, often, the better part of wisdom is to play for time. The psychoanalytic holding environment puts the patient's personality on hold, gives the person time to thaw out. The psychoanalytic situation creates a context capable of absorbing and outflanking an individual's self-destructive patterns. At least this is an aim, a hope, and often a possibility.

Often, therapy suffers temporary breakdowns when the therapy partners are overly taken in by one or another swing from one tendency to another. For example, brittle self-tightening temporarily may prompt an illusion of greater stability and security, only to make a swing to promiscuous bleeding of personality all the more frightening. In the long run, therapy survives these swings, and a person learns that it is possible to survive the self.

What a relief not to have to side with one aspect of self against another, to let each current or tendency make its contribution. William Blake described heaven as war in which all aspects of personality had their maximum say, and all were increased by each other. What a blissful, wishful outcome to the necessary agonies of conflict.

Winnicott's unintegration provides time outside or below conflict. Here, one no longer tenaciously grips slivers of self. Out of this formlessness one or another organization or tendency may emerge, and one can ride these currents. Perhaps this is a kind of Taoist vision, where alternative aspects of self come and go, contributing to the evolution of the whole. There is always the inexhaustible background of formlessness and more forming. In true self-activity, there is a double directional flow between void and aliveness.

Is Winnicott's vision a reversion to ancient philosophical wisdom, a recycling of complementariness of opposites, of transcending or subtending the flow of opposites? We know that Freud and Jung invoked Heraclitus in this regard. Is psychoanalysis a modern revision of an ancient vision? Yes, of course, it is, in new keys.

There are psychoanalysts whose thinking is a reworking of ancient visions. Ehrenzweig's (1971) "undifferentiated preconscious ego matrix" and Matte-Blanco's (1975) "symmetrical unconscious" are striking and beautiful reworkings of Freud's primary process thinking, in which everything may be everything else. Various workers describe variants of zero points of personality, "no-places" where distinctions collapse or meld and personality can reset and regrow. Balint's (1968) "interpenetrating harmonious mix-up," Milner's (1957) "overlapping circles" and "pregnant emptiness," Bion's (1970) "O" and "formless void" are examples.

Winnicott's writings are without religious imagery; yet, he could not avoid the word "sacred" in pointing to the incommunicado core of self that shines through unintegration. For him, this was a living reality, a rock-bottom affirmation. At the same time, he was aware of its fictional character: "I thought to myself 'really it is only in split-off intellect that one can be 100% honest; as soon as living processes come in, then there is self-deception and deception and compromise and ambivalence'" (cited in Rodman, 1987, p. 192).

What a wonderful mixup we are left with. The true self for Winnicott is anything but pure; nevertheless, something pure runs through it. It is no ideal self, but it is not without an ideal core. In real life the true self is dirty indeed; yet, isn't there room for trueness?

A Detour Through Jacob

There have been times in my life when memories of the Biblical David and Jacob have sustained me. So indebted am I to these Biblical models for my survival and development that I named my two sons after them. Recently, I read Harold Bloom's comments in *The Book of J* (Rosenberg and Bloom, 1990) and wondered how I might dare write about my heroes after the way he covered the territory. However, I feel compelled to at this moment, for bringing together Winnicott's concept of the true self with David and Jacob is illuminating. In the present chapter, it is enough to limit myself to some remarks about Jacob and the true self.

In my life, Jacob has been a carrier of true-self feeling. But what is this true self? In Jacob's case, it is a self that goes from one messy situation to another, from trickery to heartbreak. He begins life in conflict with his brother, coming out of the womb gripping his brother's heel. From the outset, the narrative sets the tone of struggle.

We know Jacob will catch up to and surpass his brother. But how? He takes advantage of situations, moments of destiny. His brother, Esau, the ruddy hunter, comes in tired from the field and wants food. Jacob sells him stew for his birthright. Even as this happens one thinks it must be a joke: Surely, neither Jacob nor Esau will take this seriously. But we read on in a state of suspended disbelief. It is all too serious and cannot be undone, an oddly telling moment that scarcely makes sense.

All the details somehow fit together, although we do not quite know what to make of them. Esau is the physical man and his father's favorite. Jacob is a man of the tents, his mother's favorite. Esau seems to be the plainer, less complicated man who likes the outdoor life and takes the women at hand. Jacob "stews" more, plays the waiting game, and is more patient and closer to the Unfathomable. He possesses the more inexhaustible and resonant consciousness.

Jacob has acquired deeper powers from his mother, Rebecca, who gets him to trick Isaac, his father, into giving him Esau's blessing. Rebecca herself prepares the meal that inspires Isaac's tongue, gives Esau's smelly clothes to Jacob, and puts animal hair on him so he will feel like Esau to Isaac's touch. Again, a preposterous situation that seals the direction of lives.

We can laugh it off as a charming tale for children (which it is). But our heads reel if we try to penetrate it. The story twists and turns; reversals are endless. The rabbis try to unravel it by myths of both polarization and integration. First, the myth of polarization: Esau is evil, Jacob good. Jacob was conceived first, born last, so is really older. The oldest son is entitled to twice the inheritance of other siblings, but also has more religious duties, like officiating at sacrifices. Jacob valued the latter more than Esau. What did he do in the tents? He studied and prayed. He developed his sensibility, his tie with God. Jacob was more tuned in than Esau. He had a deeper sense of God, the more intense connection to God.

How Esau cried! Why did rabbis call him evil? They pointed to his impatience, some lack of inner power. Jacob would *never* have sold a birthright, nor married women who vexed his parents (his women would have better character). Esau wanted to murder Jacob (who wouldn't?). Esau was a murderer, the rabbis tell us (associate Esau with Cain and Ishmael, the wild man). The lines are drawn. The blessing and the one meant for it find each other.

The myth of integration sees Esau as part of Jacob, a part he had to master, transcend, and use (a myth of sublimation or assimilation of the shadow side). Esau was Jacob's evil inclination or impulse life. One gloss has it that the angel Jacob wrestled with was really Esau or Esau's guardian angel, Jacob's lower self and guardian of that self.

Some rabbis teach that we need to wed Esau with Jacob (integration); others say we have to choose (polarization). All opt for a primacy of Jacob, whether as context or choice. In the Biblical narrative, neither Esau nor Jacob is all good or bad. Esau has heart; he weeps at his loss of the blessing. After their long separation, he weeps and embraces Jacob. He wants to please his parents but makes mistakes. Certainly, he does not have Jacob's intuition but perhaps he is better off without it.

On the other hand, Jacob is no angel. He cheats, cons, and steals, but some cheating is for love of God. We are told explicitly of his mystical tendencies: the Jacob's ladder dream and wrestling with God (or angel, or devil, or death, or Esau, or all of these), a decisive image for Western consciousness. We are let in on this intimacy, so that we participate in Jacob's sense of the holy, his worshipful self, his awe and love of Yhoyva. I think we see that Esau also loves God in his way, but we do not share the intimacy of this love as we do with Jacob.

Rebecca's imprint is reflected in Jacob's intimacy with the holy, but Jacob is his own man too, not just another mother's boy, not simply one or the other. Something original in him is mediated by mother. Another Esau would not change the course of Western consciousness, but Jacob's life bore witness to a change that contributed to a new sense of what personal being might be.

One feels Esau got a raw deal from the rabbis; however, I believe they were on to *something*. In current analytic terms, Jacob could contain the blessing and pass it on, something Esau could not do. Jacob was surely an imperfect container, although more able than Esau for this purpose. If nothing else, his greater complexity, resonance, and psychic invagination made him more fit. He was capable of undergoing more, experiencing the multidimensionality of life more. He was the greater vehicle for containing a multitude of crosscurrents.

This is not to say that being a vehicle for *the* blessing was such a blessing. Jacob paid a price for the privilege that Esau was spared. Esau seems to have had the happier and easier life overall. He reacted and got on with his life. His extroverted life moved along its own path without getting sidetracked by excessive ambition. We are not even told that he fell in love.

Jacob's life ripened through suffering, hard work, and love. When he met Rachel, he kissed her and wept, then was tricked into marrying her homely sister. He worked 14 years in payment for the beauty he loved and another 6 years to secure his own flocks. We associate patience, persistence, and perseverance with Jacob, as well as a certain haplessness. Circumstances forced him into fatherhood with four women, although his heart was with only one of them. He remained loyal to all, although Rachel was his beloved. Competitiveness, frustration, and bitterness are part of people living together, so the story tells us.

If Jacob was a trickster, so was he tricked by life and faith and God, horribly so. Rachel died, and the son most dear to him, Joseph, was sold into slavery and thought dead. If Jacob pulled the rug from under Esau, the ground of his life was wrenched by God working through angry egos. Those whom Jacob loved most were taken from him. His payment for closeness with God (and mother) was dear. We are not told of any comparable catastrophes in Esau's life. In Jacob's old age, he is reunited with Joseph, an irony that virtually mocks the theme of reconciliation. Perhaps there is some fulfillment in exhaustion.

Every last drop squeezed out of Jacob's life was paradoxical. *Jacob was paradox.* Being schooled in suffering was to be schooled in paradox and vice versa. Paradox in Jacob's life was not intellectual but lived: wholehearted, living paradox embracing divisions and deceit. Esau was a straight thinker compared with Jacob. His life seems relatively linear. Jacob's was more involuted, filled with depths of love and grief, touched by an undercurrent of intunement with time itself.

Perhaps here we are close to the heart of the matter: Time is a main character in Jacob's story. *The story of Jacob is the story of time.* We feel the rise and decline of a life with all its main lines. In a few deft strokes we sense all a man can go through. Life enriches and ravages. A loving self comes through but not unscarred. Jacob's wish to be Number One is caricatured by Joseph's number oneness, which leads to Joseph being ripped away. Jacob is punished for being Jacob. Time boomerangs and recoils but does not stop. Time goes on, and Jacob cannot be reduced to any one version of himself.

As if to show that Jacob is more than the sum of his traits, he is given a new name, Israel, after wrestling with the angel. Rabbis say this refers to his transcendent nature, his higher self. He will need all the help he can get, for the worst moments in his life are yet to come. There is no end to the depths of suffering, and discovering one's transcendent or higher self does not change this. In Jacob's case, becoming Israel initiated new horrors.

The story of Jacob-Israel is the opening of time. Circumstances and contingencies play on and reflect his character but have a life of their own. Deceptions unify the twists and turns of events and run through his story from beginning to end (beginning with his deception of Isaac, ending with Joseph's deception of him). In the end, deceptions are undone but we know they will have a long life in history. Yet, each turn opens possibilities of experiencing, each turn makes a difference. A picture of life as a whole matures.

One of the great things about Jacob is that we do not have to choose which self is his real self: We feel trueness and realness running through his varied aspects. He is weak and wise, strong and naive, prayerful and self-reliant, influenced by others, yet treads his way. Above all, he is vulnerable. He can turn away from life. Another blow is always possible, as is also the shock of joy. The linear aspect is there too. Life goes on; daily functioning continues. One shoulders blank time as well as pregnant time and dies rich in years, steeped in experience.

We do not have to choose what is more or less real about Jacob because *he* does not choose. This or that situation comes and goes, and this or that aspect of personality has its moment. Jacob is not this or that but unfolds in time. He is a basically good person but is prey to all that flesh is heir to. He is fully human. He is a good model because of his Biblical monism. He does not try to stamp out or stifle aspects of self, or think it odd to move between different worlds of experience (they are part of One Reality, One World). He does not idealize one area at the expense of others. He is a living being, a living soul. His vicissitudes are those of *a feeling self* in the midst of experiencing the rocky flow of events.

His life has branches, tributaries, but a lifeline runs through derailments and reroutings. One feels the real self, the true person like a heart beating through all. I was once told that a cactus branches out wherever it is wounded: If there were no traumas, it would grow forever straight. I do not know if this is true of a cactus, but it has a ring of truth for us. In time Jacob's strength wanes, and he begins to fade. Nevertheless, even on his death bed he passes on the gift of paradox in his blessings to his children. He knows who they are and what he may say of them.

True Self/False Self and Paradoxical Monism

Jacob suffers the pains of human existence. His main blows involve loss of those he loves most. His suffering is not yet that of tormented consciousness as such (there are portents of this), but wounds that are part of whole-hearted living.

King Lear is tormented consciousness. Like Othello, he is tortured by signs of not being loved, tormented by his own internal Iago that is one with his consciousness. His model may be King Saul, but Saul was punished for not being cruel enough, whereas Lear is his own punishment.

Lear is no longer the suffering journey of a whole-hearted soul, but the agony of a demented brain under sway of disguised passions, puffed up by self-deceit. Cordelia is what is left of the whole-hearted self that runs through Jacob's life, but Lear cannot get to it (she is little more than a fairy tale princess). The modern age has begun.

Winnicott's emphasis on true self seems almost Biblical in face of the fragmentation that followed upon Lear's explosion. At the height of Elizabethan England, one reads in Shakespeare forebodings of the collapse of monarchy. Soon enough, newly released and highly charged particles of mind, feeling, and body would be creating new forms of government, lifestyles, livelihood. Scientific, industrial, and technological revolutions would unleash new democracies on the world. Fascism and communism tried to bind things into forced cohesion. Winnicott links true self to democracy, although he feels democratic living (even in so-called democratic societies) may be achieved by relatively few people.

Winnicott (1950) speaks of an "innate democratic factor" created by "ordinary good homes" as support for democratic machinery of social systems. Any group contains a variety of antisocial, immature, and healthy elements. For Winnicott, "a whole (healthy) person . . . has the total conflict within, which enables him to get a view, albeit a personal one, of total external situations" (p. 249).

When speaking of democracy, Winnicott gravitates to the language of "wholeness." He has a definite vision in mind. He experiences or imagines a capacity to hold opposites or acknowledge contradictory tendencies. He contrasts this to the tendency to oversimplify and brutalize one split-off aspect of self or society with another:

> Hidden antisocials are not "whole persons" any more than are manifest antisocials, since each needs to find and control the conflicting force in the external world outside the self. By contrast, the healthy person, who is capable of becoming depressed, is able to find the whole conflict within the self as well as being able to see the whole conflict outside the self, in external (shared) reality. When healthy persons come together, they each contribute a whole world, because each brings a whole person (p. 244).

One cannot coerce wholeness. It is a path that has to be created/ discovered through ordinary good living. On this journey one finds ways of making useful contributions with the paradoxical materials that characterize self and society. Ideally, our contributions grow out of true-self activity, but things are not so simple.

Surely the feeling of wholeness can be dangerous. Fascism makes people feel whole. The sense of wholeness makes people kill each other: My wholeness is right, yours wrong. That is why Winnicott includes the capacity to be depressed in his definition. One must somehow find space in oneself for the Other's viewpoint, so that wholeness is no easy oneness. One also can be uplifted and relieved by discovering the realness of the Other's view ("Thank God I'm not the only one in a universe of zero").

Perhaps wholeness is a direction, a tendency, a striving, a changing vision, or something sensed. How odd it seems for Winnicott to insist on the importance of "unintegration" and then to stress "wholeness." In most psychological literature, wholeness is associated with integration. Winnicott stresses the open-ended aspect of wholeness, sensitivity to the "known unknown," the Otherness within the self.

Jacob's wrestling with the angel all night before meeting Esau after 20 years away from his homeland is an example of such openness. I have heard it said that without this struggle Jacob surely would have missed the mark. Perhaps he would have been too scared, or too provocative, or defensive. He would have failed to find the right mood. In the morning, he found his way to Esau's heart because in the night he wrestled with his own.

This moment of destiny was no final moment. Esau's and Jacob's paths crossed and each went his own way. Their descendants wrestle to this day. Psychoanalysis is one modern offshoot of this struggle. It is too easy to equate Esau with id and Jacob with ego, mind over matter. Psychoanalysis wounds Jacob with Esau: the ego is first and foremost a body ego. Freud delighted in humiliating the Western ego, no longer master in its own house. In this sense, psychoanalysis is Esau's guardian angel.

But Freud never ceased speaking of mastery and gaining some pocket of control over the wild man within. Perhaps we can learn something about channeling a bit of Esau's energy, like we channel electricity. We need to protect Esau's raw vitality if we are to use it. Freud swings back and forth between letting Esau carry Jacob and letting Jacob channel Esau. As I noted earlier, Freud's swings back and forth are more alive than taking sides with one or the other.

What may not always be noticed is that Freud's depiction of id, ego, and superego means that we are not one with any or all of them. We are more than the sum of our stories. This sensed "more" is what, partly, makes our stories so poignant. We measure ourselves not only by what we are, but what we might have been. What have we done with what we have been given? What can we do?

Jung (1958) points to the "more" by writing of a "transcendent function" that makes use of one-sided profiles but is not limited to them. Green (1975) writes of a "tertiary process" to indicate a position or function that takes into account primary and secondary processes. Winnicott uses terms like "transitional experiencing" and "potential space" to suggest movement *between:* between inner and outer, self and other, mind and body, id, ego, and superego. He is more concerned with processes that give rise to symbols than imaginative elaboration of symbols. He no longer finds it adequate to pit traditional categories against each other and fight holy or unholy wars. Winnicott's work is a call for radical psychic democracy. We do not always have to take sides in order to grow. We can look for ourselves between positions.

Freud, the conquistador, often used military, hierarchical imagery. Psychic life involves warfare, higher versus lower capacities or forces: conversion of lower into higher, collapsing of higher into lower. At wonderful moments up and down work together, fuse, then fall apart and the struggle continues. Is there anyone so utopian or Appolonian as to be able totally to deny the reality of this picture? Thousands of years of literature and art are filled with depictions of this versus that. Ideologies of higher versus lower permeate the history of our culture and characterize outer and inner realities of every sort (see Eigen, 1986, Chapter 6).

Winnicott cannot grant us immunity from struggle, but he enriches the place we struggle from. Life cannot be less than struggle, but it is also more. He taps a sense of being allied with the feeling of creative aliveness. His (1970) emphasis is not on repression (a political-economic-military image) but on "existing" as "a basic place to operate from" (p. 39).

His image of democracy is more cooperative than competitive. It is not a capitalistic system driven by economic greed and envy. Nor is there a psychic voting booth tallying the votes of each aspect of personality so that the majority wins. Winnicott's psychic democracy is outside the system, a free time and space. He is a spokesman for the saving value of experiencing as such. What miracles aliveness and experiencing are! How freeing to immerse oneself in being and shake loose from ideologies.

Yet, Winnicott's being is not brute or dumb being. Winnicott's sense of being is filled with paradox: the self is stamped with paradox. We move from one paradoxical moment to another. All Winnicott's developmental concepts have paradoxical elements (the infant's finding-creating the object, the "between" of transitional experiencing, the destruction that creates in object usage).

Psychic Deadness

If Winnicott's work is a paean to the sense of creative aliveness, his main clinical concern is psychic deadness. One associates his theme with existential writings on loss of meaning, alienation, and estrangement, and with further twists to late nineteenth century writings on entropy (loss of energy, annihilation, zero point of variability). T. S. Eliot's "The Hollow Men" and "The Waste Land" are paradigmatic, and it is no accident that Winnicott refers to Eliot's later work, in which meaning and aliveness are recovered through memory (a sense of intimacy with what is hidden) and the now of time (including loss and finding the capacity to experience).

Winnicott does not flinch from the horrific voids his patients face. In a posthumously published paper, "Fear of Breakdown" (1974), he delineates "primitive agonies" overwhelming psychic life. The psyche lacks equipment to bear what it produces. The capacity to experience and process states breaks down. To some degree, one gives up contacting self out of fear of the unmanageable. One builds a second self expert at circumventing incapacity. Early terror drops into a void filled with busy work and symptoms.

For Winnicott, the "malaise of civilization" is not only linked with sexual or political or economic repression, but with a false self that tries to handle the unmanageable by pretense and subterfuge. Sexual life is a privileged area linked to defensiveness, rerouting of energy, and hypocrisy, but the problem is more pervasive. The simple fact is that an infant cannot care for itself and survive. It needs help. The fault lines of personality are chronically etched breakdowns molded around breakdowns of help needed to support maturation.

The false self has, at least, two horns: toughness and compliance. One toughens to handle breakdowns if one wants to survive and triumph. One learns to bull one's way through or past experiences that might drag one down. This may entail flying over experience or wearing blinders or crushing life under foot as one marches or runs along. Toughness does not mean deadness: Toughness makes one feel alive. One tries to get what one wants or do what one can. There is hope in toughness, but there can also be secret despair.

The positive side of toughness is the I *can*, the I *will*, of healthy self-reliance. The underside is a forced element if one has learned that help is useless. One discovers that help breaks down at crucial moments and one must get over these ruptures on one's own. Pleasure in growing abilities is erected over an abyss of failure. With every I *can* there are many more I *cannots*. *So* many bits of help cover scars of helplessness.

Healthy toughness easily conjoins with a hidden and deadly self-hardening process, insofar as one must keep pockets of hopelessness under control or out of reach.

In time, toughness cannot be counted on to maintain a sense of aliveness. Personality becomes a caricature of itself and a sense of unreality seeps in. One may try to tough it out by further hardening processes and barely manage to get through life without a major psychic heart attack. Iced over pools of hopelessness become ghosts of unreality, and one may never be at home with the haunted house of personality.

A frequent side effect of bulldozing over oneself is the injury one does others. If one rides roughshod over the sad, angry, fearful child in oneself, one is likely to ignore or bully the child in others. One may grow intolerant of weakness and relative shapelessness and seek to impose one's own idea of order and control. If such a person successfully masks intolerance and rigidity with seductive control and sufficient charm, he or she may manage to rise high enough to tighten arteries of an entire civilization until the inevitable reversals occur.

The twin of toughness is compliance, the great villain in Winnicott's writings. The child complies with parental pressures to falsify him- or herself in order to get along with others. This seemingly innocuous fact of daily existence becomes the basis of Winnicott's lifelong meditation on what makes life feel unreal. The false self begins in infancy as the infant molds itself along support-and-breakdown lines of its caretaking milieu. If things go decently, one learns to give the environment what it wants or needs in exchange for provision. One distorts oneself to make life smooth and possible (Winnicott's false self overlaps with Freud's adaptive ego).

Winnicott points out that it is precisely one of humanity's advantages, its plasticity or adaptiveness, that contributes to a sense of falseness. One tolerates a certain amount of falseness as part of human interchange. False self can protect true self feeling, which may persist in a hidden way. In more severe cases, false self acts as a cocoon in which true self sleeps or waits for better circumstances. If one is less fearful, false self can act as a vehicle for true-self activity, a link can be made between the incommunicado self and adaptive action (so much depends on the fit between false self and true self).

To a variable extent, the true self always remains shell-shocked. It takes more than a lifetime to thaw out and begin recovery from the shocks that go with developmental processes. Nevertheless, true self activity is possible and happens, and one feels uplifted and redeemed by these moments that knit a life together.

False self also knits personality together, but hopefully not at the deepest levels. Compliance in infancy is passed on to adulthood as compliance with one's own personality, especially false-self elements, lies one lives. What remains of true self may live through false self, or be mesmerized by false self and comply with false-self scripts. True self becomes a false-self addict and the result may be what Winnicott describes as the great sin against the self: alteration of the core of true-self by false-self elements seeping in through all protective membranes. Here, false self fails as a sealer and poisons what it meant to protect. This is the condition for what Balint (1968) describes as "malignant regression" and takes us to a cutting edge of therapy. At this point, all that is left of toughness-compliance may be explosiveness and/or fading away.

The true self/false self double helix and double sense of reality/ unreality are part of Winnicott's version of tormented consciousness. He focuses on the sense of being unreal to oneself. This is perhaps externalized in Hamlet, who battles with the pretender, the false self that has become king of one's personality. Winnicott accepts the spin into fragmentation, the fact of decentered agony. The wholeness he writes about is not a defense against falling apart, not a dominance of one over another (whether person over person, class over class, ego over id, reality over illusion, integration over unintegration).

Winnicott's wholeness refers to the "innate democratic factor" and faith that personality works well enough if proper space is provided. Wholeness is not writ in stone. It is more a growing ability to process and taste experiencing than any victory of integration. one of Winnicott's (1986) patients hints at this growth process when he says, "There seems now the possibility of a blend, which is different from seeking a midway path. The blend includes both extremes at the same time" (p. 33). Winnicott's proposed title for his unpublished autobiography fits his patient's remark: *Not Less Than Everything*.

Clare Winnicott touches my theme by quoting T. S. Eliot's poem "East Coker" to begin a collection of her husband's (1986) papers:

Home is where one starts from. As we grow older
The world becomes stranger, the pattern more complicated
Of dead and living. Not the intense moment
Isolated, with no before or after,
But a lifetime burning in every moment.

As we grow older, home becomes the wholeness of "a lifetime burning in every moment." In Winnicott's terms, it is a lifetime embracing true self/false self, not limited to either. It includes deadness and alive-

ness, unrealness and realness. One of the wonderful things in Winnicott's cases is the room he provides for experiencing unreality, nonbe-
ing, deadness, so that an aliveness one can say "yes" to has a chance of
emerging.

The Biblical call to whole-heartedness appears in a new key. It can no
longer be the whole-heartedness of exclusion. Blake's heaven is within
us now: The legitimate claims of all the devils within us, the valid rights
of all inner and outer interests—we dare not ignore any whisper, shout,
or shriek. What will we do with the multitudes within and without? What
will become of us? Will the new, universal democratic striving destroy us
or transform us? What are we becoming?

We are part of one great paradoxical monism, a wholeness that
thrives on fragmentary processes, bits and pieces throbbing with significance. O Lord, teach us to listen, teach us how to be. Let us survive our
own opening, as we O and O and O.

Opening

With therapy comes opening. Rather than merely speaking about
undifferentiation-differentiation (terms Winnicott does not use), one
speaks of closing-opening (not quite the same thing). The circle opens
or begins to open. One begins to branch out from the living center, just
as one had closed oneself into the dead center. The true self can wait a
long time for rescue, for a chance, for an opening to begin to pour itself
through.

Clinically speaking, when one is walled off one is not simply merged
but also isolated, not only fused but entirely separate—not just the "oneness" of merger, but also the "oneness" of being self enclosed. The two
go together, a two-in-one or a one-in-two, but in life losing ways. In such
cases, supermerger goes along with superseparateness (superisolation),
both being dissociative aspects of a larger system. The omnipresent
distinction-union structure suffers warp, so that something goes wrong with
the back-and-forth movement (Eigen, 1986; 1991; see Chapters 4, 7,
and 8).

It is the back-and-forth movement that is most important. The
patient needs to achieve the ability of allowing him- or herself to move
back-and-forth, between one-and-the-other. We are so afraid of this
movement; we feel it is not right to let it happen or be part of it or do it.

That the patient retreats does not mean he or she has retreated to
undifferentiation. One tries to find what point of safety he or she can.
The closed circle may well be super-assertion of uniqueness in a super-
self-protective mode, so afraid of violation that there is total closing off

and shutting down. Or massive shut down may be an attempt to so control the Other that the Other is brought totally (as a delusion or hallucination) within one's boundaries (and vice versa). Perhaps one tries a crazed gripping of what remains of true-self feeling, unable to let go, as if killed while biting an apple (breast *and* knowledge) and now is forever frozen in the biting, stuck in a clutching position. One always can find both distinction/union elements in various keys or warps. What matters most is not the state or moment one is stuck in, but the loss of movement, the pulsation at the boundary, the crossing. The patient grows in the ability to cross over.

The center of the drama is *a feeling self*—whether in the midst of joy, suffering, emptiness, unreality, or bleakness. The dead self is such an important part of psychoanalysis now. The child self (like a real child) needs to be helped to let its own natural swings encompass the back-and-forth movement between deadness and aliveness in so many ways. It really is bewildering and frightening, the upsurge of life and its vanishing. People too eagerly push for a decision so as to organize themselves in one direction or another. Winnicott's work says there is value in indecision, in letting either side of what might have been a decision play with each other, and growing goes well enough without always taking sides.

Chapter 3

Infinite Surfaces, Explosiveness, Faith

No psychoanalyst I know has confessed more self-hate in print than Bion. Reading his autobiography (1982, 1985) is an exercise in tolerance of self-laceration. Yet vivid pictures of his life emerge: his devastating yet rich early childhood in India, the horrors of an 8 year old's school life in England, the gradual emerging of a tough, super-sensitive man with insect endurance, an athlete, a war hero, a doctor, a psychiatrist, a psychoanalyst.

One of the most painful passages in Bion's autobiography depicts his walled off immobility when his young daughter tried to move across a yard towards him. He sat in autistic-schizoid silence, unable to reach out to her. I think Bion was permanently horrified by himself (his inability to respond), horrified by what people did to each other, what *he* did. He felt he lost his daughter and was grateful when his second wife made family come alive, and saved him from himself. He felt he died in the First World War. His first wife's death as a result of childbirth during the Second World War heightened his embittered sense that there was no end to dying. His writings are concerned with interweavings of destruction of personality and affective intensity, with deadness and aliveness of self.

One of Bion's most terse and telling depictions of destructiveness was of "a force that continues after. . . it destroys existence, time and space" (1965, p. 101). How can a force continue after it destroys existence, time and space? Isn't that a contradiction in terms? Yet it is just such impossibility that give his formulations their special punch. The idea of destruction going on in sub-zero dimensions, feeding on deadness, endless worlds of deadness: it brings us up short and deepens our realization of what we are up against. Destructiveness challenges us and we dare not ignore it.

More Preliminary Remarks

Most psychoanalysts would be surprised to find no use of the term "drive" in Bion's major works. One would think he has Freud's life and death drives in mind, especially the latter as developed by Melanie Klein. Yet he calls himself an object relations theorist, a field theorist, and the term "drive" is glaring in omission.

Bion focuses on transformations of affect. Instead of drive language, affect language. For example, he traces the play of love (L), hate (H), knowledge (K), and faith (F). The value of any these elements depends on its function in a given context. Any can be more creative or destructive, contribute to or impede personality growth at a particular moment. The analyst needs to stay open to fresh perception of relations, close to the impact of moment.

Bion uses many images drawn from diverse fields as intuitive models for impacts he experiences in psychoanalytic sessions, as tools for making observations, and as tracers to illuminate interplay of variables, functions and attitudes. Many analysts would be bewildered, even alarmed, at the array of religious, philosophical, historical, and mathematical images Bion uses to describe or evoke psychoanalytic experiences.

The garden of Eden, the flood, the tower of Babel, the Sphinx and Tiresias in Oedipus are used as lenses to bring out psychoanalytic dramas involving curiosity, the passion to know, punishment, anxiety and guilt, and the omniscience that prevents learning from experience. Bion is also drawn to mystics, like Jesus and Rabbi Luria, who show that not only curiosity and the desire to know get one in trouble, but birth processes of new experiencing involve cataclysmic processes. Faith, as well as knowledge, opens doors of perception that unleash disturbances. Faith that is merely comforting is probably as deleterious to growth, as knowledge that is cut off and schizoid (although comfort and cuts have uses too).

Ideas and images from Plato, Kant, Poincaré, Fregge, Milton, Freud, Klein, Scholem, physics, astronomy, medicine: Bion battled to feel free to select what he needed from the writers and influences that mattered to him. He dug deep into the well of his experience. If psychoanalysis does not grow from the depths of being and reflect who one is, what good can it do? How can psychoanalysis be a catalyst for growth, if the analyst evades his personal destiny? Bion always seems to be wondering what psychoanalysis is, and what can it do. He takes running leaps, opens, comes back with another bit of the elephant. He encourages us to do the same with our version of whatever it is we are doing. For Bion psychoanalysis is no fixed thing to be subsumed by formulas, but an unknown to be created and discovered.

His famous formula for the radical openness of the psychoanalytic attitude (an act of faith) expresses his passion for fresh starting points. He (1970) describes the psychoanalytic attitude as being without memory, desire, understanding, expectations. Over and over the analyst stays open to the impact of the patient. Of course, understanding, memory, expectations grow from this impact. But it is to the impact the analyst returns, an affective core of experience, which gives birth to images, which give birth to symbols, which give birth to ideas.

Bion's brand of openness leads him to depict, in varying ways, states involving maximum-minimum emotion. We might place double arrows between heightened emotionality and emotional vacuum or void (e.g., maximum emotion ↔ minimum emotion) to suggest interchangeability, reversibility, oscillation, opposition. An extreme would be catatonic excitement-stupor. But silence and explosiveness play a role in many phenomena. Bion was fascinated with various ways emotion-emotionlessness could be structured, and he leaves us a rich treasure of observations.

My suspicion is that Bion did not, finally, alienate those closest to him (he remained endearing), because he could be *felt* experiencing the desolation that haunted him. Even in gone, black hole states, *someone* was there, clinging to life. The vacuum or void was a measure of intensity in reverse. At times, the formless infinite void became thoroughly alive and enlivening. Nevertheless, I believe Bion knew the zero states whereof he spoke, and weathered them. Life never lost its relish in a final way.

How can maximum emptiness-fullness exist together? The law of contradiction does not hold in any simple way for emotional space, where one *can* be in two places at once, perhaps must be. How can a dead man be alive, and an alive man be dead? Bion bears witness that such simultaneity is possible, necessary. After immersion in the Bionic universe, one wonders whether it wouldn't be less than human not to taste something of the everythingness-nothingness that forms the background of experiencing.

Another example of the well nigh indistinguishability of seemingly opposite currents, is Bion's discussion of the commingling of health and sickness in certain psychotic individuals. A person may feel his "well being and vitality spring from the same characteristics that give trouble. The sense that loss of the bad parts of his personality is inseparable from loss of that part in which all his mental health resides, contributes to the acuity of the patient's fears" (1965, p. 144). One suspects Bion, partly, has his own eccentricities in mind when he speaks of aliveness and disturbance flowing from the same source. Such sentences in Bion's work are barriers against analytic smugness.

As is typical, Bion maximizes the tenacity, provocativeness, and acuity of his formulation by listing a group of traits that might be taken as indices of illness or health, depending on how they function, or one's view of them. They are: ambition, intolerance of frustration, envy, aggression, and uncompromising belief in a fulfilling ideal object (1965, p. 144). Most of these belong to what Melanie Klein describes as the paranoid-schizoid position (more infantile, primitive, pathological). Bion emphasizes that they are or can be part of the patient's endowment of health and virility, with origins "in a *normal* physical state" (ibid).

Kleinian writers note contributions paranoid-schizoid capacities make to normal functioning (e.g., the importance of splitting, projection, denial, idealization), but the overall thrust is on "making" the depressive position, where one is capable of perceiving/introjecting a whole object, feeling remorse over one's destructiveness, and undertaking reparative activities. Bion's emphasis is on the back-and-forth, the incessant contributions of both poles, the life (as well as death) giving aspects of the most elemental resources. He is a spokesman for what is valuable in what seems most ill (and the ill in what seems healthy by conventional standards).

In my sessions with Bion in New York (1977), he startled me by talking about the Kabbalah (Eigen, 1993, pp. 272-274). He seemed to feel the latter was relevant for my problems, but also for his, and for the sort of psychic processes that interested him. As I struggle now to convey something of the essential quality of his work, I think of a teaching of Lurianic mysticism. God contracted to make room for the world. This resulted in divine sparks being buried in dead and evil places. It is up to us to recover these sparks and unite God with himself. Bion has done his job. He has gone into realms of evil and deadness, and redeemed what he could. He joins Freud and Luria, too, in helping us live with what is unredeemable, although we do not know exactly what that might be. Wherever we turn (including sub-zero worlds of infinite horror and deadness), there is much we *can* do, together with the ever present can't.

Multiplicity and Explosiveness

The next sections of this chapter springs from two images Bion uses, one from geometry and one from physics: (1) a geometric solid with an infinite number of surfaces; and (2) explosiveness (as in the big bang vision of the universe's origin). The former pertains to the many ways any moment of a session can be viewed (by analyst or patient), and to the sort of space an individual is able to constitute. The latter points to turbulence that is part of change, beginnings and destruction. It is tempting to say that the former has to do more with cognition and the latter with emotion, but there is so much overlap and reversibility that a clear-cut distinction would be misleading. For example, there is explosive thought and deadening interpretation. Nevertheless, we will follow, as space permits, some of Bion's uses of these images. In so doing, we get a sense of the flavor and thrust of his vision through selected details.

Infinite Surfaces

Suppose two people agree that what they say to each other is selected from other things they do not say, and that what they notice about what they say is selected from other things they do not notice. Neither insists his view is the only view, yet both try to communicate some bit of experience. It is possible that these individuals will make room for the impact of each other's communications, partly because neither claims his contribution is exhaustive, nor excludes the other's. Neither negates communicative efforts on the basis of what is unable to be communicated. These lucky individuals are able to work with the restrictive nature of communication. They go on speaking, while tolerating recognition that what they say (or paint, or write, or compose, or build, or legislate) is possible only on the basis of what is left out or not sayable.

However, there are individuals who remain silent in face of the unsayable. They are unable to communicate what they might, because they are held captive by what evades limits of communication. They can not take their eyes off what they are not saying, in order to say what they can. At other moments, such individuals may say too much too quickly and jump around in dizzying fashion, trying to say everything at once (again, nothing can be left out). To such a person, nothing the analyst says seems useable, as there is always something that is not said, and what is not said may seem more important than what is said.

In the fable I am developing, the *everything-at-once* or *all now* individual is unable to take for granted the infinite in every moment. He can not abide representational restrictions, not even restrictions meant to represent the infinite in every moment. Bion offers images to convey infinite possibilities of timing and meaning in a session. This situation "could be represented by a visual image of a figure in which many planes meet or lines pass through a common point," or "a visual image of a geometric solid with an infinite number of surfaces" (1970, p. 8). The *everything-at-once/all now* individual can not suffer spatial representation of infinite possibilities, even in pretend (analogical) fashion. To represent the infinite in terms of a visual image is idolatry, and psychoanalysis, like ordinary daily life, is blasphemy.

The medical model of psychoanalysis commits the opposite error, since it treats the psyche like a physical body. The physician uses his senses to study instruments and see and touch bodies. But thoughts and feelings are not localizeable: "anxiety has no shape or color, smell or sound" (1970, p. 7). The analyst works with the felt impact of the patient, and affective-ideological transformations of this impact. The felt subject-to-subject link (or lack of it) is crucial.

The analyst, who goes beyond the medical model, neither treats the psyche like a physical thing, nor evades use of spatial models. With the psychotic, he intuits the infinite unsayable. But he allows ineffable intimations to contribute to personality growth. A vision of infinite surfaces of a moment or session can be awesome, but the fact this can be represented and talked about can make for shared appreciation. Part of therapeutic work involves finding expressive language (images, narratives, metaphors, statements, outbursts, drawings, songs, movements etc.) for aspects of the impact we have on each other, and aspects of the impact life has on us.

Bion is especially interested in individuals who can not endure growth of experience. They can not take the impact of events, nor can they communicate disability in a way that might help. If the presence of the analyst is a challenge to grow, the very being of the analyst must be obliterated. Obliteration may be out of envious hate, but also results from being too damaged to support the impact of the other. Part of the task of therapy is to help build capacity to work with the interchanges therapy generates. This places considerable pressure on analyst and patient alike.

Individuals who can not tolerate evolution of the capacity to support growth of experience, may evade this painful challenge by discounting anything the analyst says on the grounds that the analyst is saying it. For example, an individual with eyes glued on the formless infinite (and who unconsciously demands everything at once now), may be hyperaware that whatever we do reflects selection processes. If the analyst says something about the patient, he must also be saying something about himself. Whatever the analyst says may be used against him. The patient may not be wrong in arguing that the analysis is more about the analyst than the patient.

Similarly, an analyst can not cover all possible meanings of any moment. A patient may move the analyst to try more inclusive interpretations, until the analyst is driven to impotent silence in face of incapacity or impossibility. The analyst may react against this pressure by adopting a subtle moralistic stance or by some other urge to action (implosion leads to explosion of the analysis). Thus the analyst is brought to the point where he, too, is unable to tolerate experiencing, particularly when experiencing is of destruction or collapse or undoing of experiencing.

The analyst must become an expert or artist or adept at living through collapse of analysis. He studies processes that undo themselves. Little by little he learns something of what working with destructive processes entail. His growth in capacity to live through and work with destruction signals the patient that such a capacity is possible. If the analyst can survive therapy, perhaps the patient can as well.

Instead of negating growth because it is too hard or uncertain (why bother—one's going to die and know nothing anyway!), the analyst models the realization that only uncertain growth is possible. When he tries to communicate with colleagues, he must struggle to find models for his experience that are not too general or concrete, not too inclusive or exclusive. A parallel struggle goes on to find intuitive models or images to communicate with patients. Myths of destruction and creation encode processes that go on in sessions. Which image is valuable when? What lens, at what distance, provides most mileage at a given time?

Bion never tired of painting problems inherent in communication of mental states. How do we communicate what goes on inside? What is inside? What does it take to discover a feeling? How do we know what we feel, or feel what we feel, or let another know? Can we know without an other? We discover our feelings as we speak them, but aren't they changing as we discover them? We can not keep up with affective transformations, but we also *are* them. How do we communicate with ourselves and others? Often we discover the other has heard something quite different from what we said, or thought we meant to say. Dare the analyst ever take for granted his and the patient's understanding of one another? Bion knew from experience how difficult it is to feel understood, to understand oneself, to understand another. One wonders, from reading Bion, if it is more unusual for people to understand each other than is ordinarily imagined. The sum of violence issuing from misunderstanding testifies to the importance of the difficulties he highlights.

The infinite surfaces of time and meaning of every session always give analyst and patient a way out. They may never have to pass through the eye of the same needle. They can always find ways of being somewhere else, of pointing elsewhere, of failing to meet. Even when they want to meet, it is always possible to miss each other. Nevertheless, multiplicity and uncertainty do not completely obliterate impact.

Meeting flows from impact. Authentic therapeutic struggle gravitates around points of impact analyst and patient have on each other. The sense of impact is the raw datum analyst and patient have to work with.

Part of the adventure of therapy is learning to discover and communicate bits of impact that make a difference—not only impacts of events and people, but impacts of thoughts, feelings, sensations, our own impacts on ourselves. Can we take a little more, let a little more intensity build and work its way through affective expressions, so that we begin to notice what calls us into life or prevents us from living?

Explosiveness

Bion (1970, pp. 12-15) uses a reverse big bang image to describe individuals who can not let experience build. He imagines an explosion so violent that constitution and use of viable mental space is obliterated. Psychic life is blown up. The individual or the analogical space that involves symbolic life is blown away. Coordinate or mapping systems are useless. The individual can not find a workable orienting frame of reference. What might pass for thoughts or feelings turn out to be bits of flotsam and jetsam floating away from each other with accelerating velocity, scraps of an explosion aeons away.

This is a reverse big bang because it destroys rather than creates potential for living. A well meaning analyst may think the patient is making meaningful communications, only to seethe in frustrated bewilderment when the work keeps collapsing. It may take some time for the analyst to realize that the patient is no longer there, that the latter's emissions are light years away from what is left of the patient by the time they reach the analyst. An analyst who enters such a patient's force field is in danger of having his own mental processes blown away as well. Meaning is jammed because the kind of emotional/symbolic space meaning depends on has been obliterated. What reaches the analyst might more profitably be taken as signals of a self-obliterating process that began long ago, is ongoing, and sweeps up whatever comes near.

Thus Bion allows for the possibility that a good deal of what the patient says or does is incoherent and meaningless, indices of catastrophe in progress. The individual who sees the analyst may be very far from the point of the original explosion. A second, or third, or fourth personality may have grown in place of the original. These, too, are parts of catastrophic processes. An analyst who has some inkling of the catastrophic processes he faces, tries to avoid inflicting the surplus torment of talking to the wrong patient. Finding which patient to talk to when is a major part of the therapist's struggle.

A psychoanalysis, like a person's life, "can be seen as a transformation in which an intense catastrophic emotional explosion O has occurred (elements of personality, link, and second personality having been instantaneously expelled to vast distances from their point of origin and from each other)" (Bion, 1970, p. 14). The analysis is like "one moment in time stretched out so that it becomes a line or surface spread out over a period of years—an extremely thin membrane of a moment" (ibid, p. 14). The analyst uses temporal-spatial images to portray his sense of the patient's loss of space-time. He uses images like explosive obliteration in hopes of bringing the patient's non-existence into focus, a lens to allow the one who isn't there to achieve a measure of visibility.

Bion (1970, pp. 13-14) traces the fate of a scream as an example of transformations explosive processes can undergo. He puts together a psychotic patient's references to not being able to get ice-cream over two years. The patient begins by saying he could buy no ice-cream, and after two years says there was no ice-cream. Such remarks triggered in Bion a vision of the patient's linking capacity. In the beginning there was the link with a good object (ice-cream), which underwent destruction or spoiling. When destructiveness showed up, the individual's scream became a link between two personalities. Screaming over loss or destruction of goodness replaces the good feeling link.

Screaming provides a link (or calls for linking) as goodness vanishes. Screaming may demand restoration of goodness, but can also blindly feed further destruction. The good object turns into an "I scream" link, which builds its own momentum. As the scream builds, the individual may become less accessible, more caught in panicky fury. The other may not be able to respond suitably, and even if there is response, the latter may not be able to fan the good link into life, or sustain the bad link for long. Insofar as "I-scream" fails as link, it transforms into "no-I scream." The scream dies out or implodes, or is lost in stupor.

Destruction snowballs. The good link transforms to the scream link, which transforms to no scream or nothing at all: mute stupor, deathly silence, or meaningless, chaotic noise. One could imagine a happy infant becoming a screaming infant becoming a stuporous infant. Yet Bion goes farther. The explosion of linking processes he depicts involves, also, a succession of explosions. The dying out of the scream (fatigue, hopelessness, negativistic refusal, stupor, numbness) ignites explosion of mental space as such.

The congealed scream may at first be a refusal to scream. Why scream if it does no good, if it fails as link? At first, the individual may be alive enough to ragefully stifle reactivity. But negativism spirals, eats itself up. The no scream (silent refusal) starts as desperate linking attempt, silence meant to draw the other in (silent people hope to be unseen, but may also hope others will come to them). But stifled reactivity can lead to dying out (loss) of reactivity. The numbing process swallows the individual. The linking capacity explodes into nothingness, an agony of anesthesia forever reaching a vanishing point.

The link moved from nourishing connection, to screaming connection, to no screaming connection (a mutated mute connection, void connection). The no link is a connection of sorts for a time. But the no link (no scream) itself explodes, and loses much of its capacity to attract or repulse. The individual may finally be lost in spacelessness, no individual at all. Explosion and black hole become the same.

A scream can be an explosion that grows from pain and then obliterates pain. One might take screaming as a sign of the explosiveness inherent in our nature. But, it is important to note, the destructive explosive process Bion points to, sweeps the scream along with it. A scream is usually on the side of life. It expresses pain or distress or terror or fury. It is failure of the scream to meet with corrective measures that further's the subject's spin out of existence. Even the no scream (angry or frightened silence) may harbor the hope or demand or wish for a saving presence or a righting of affairs.

Bion does not develop a causal account of the explosive destructiveness he envisions. He sights it and traces its moves. It appears to aim at linking processes. Wherever one finds it, it is destroying links, or mushrooming through nothingness after links have been destroyed. It destroys the good, sweet link (ice cream), it destroys the scream link, it destroys the no scream link. It drives the subject further and further out of existence. The destructive force seeks and destroys any place the individual tries to make contact with himself and others. The linking capacity undergoes successive detonations, its generative ability ever nulled.

The analyst may imagine fragments of a link as "dispersed instantaneously over infinite space" (1970, p. 14). But psychotic destruction in the patient may be so immense that the idea of infinite space is not viable, since any space may be too restrictive. The challenge for the analyst is how to link up with a patient in whom the space where links are possible has been destroyed. How does one grow or re-grow a world and psyche in which linking processes can evolve and in which life is possible?

One can imagine that Bion knew well the destruction of existence he depicts. As mentioned earlier, he felt he died in the First World War. Years later he could be imprisoned in immobility (compressed into a sepulchral self) in face of his child's spontaneous needs. He knew in his own being what it is like to lose goodness, to become a scream stretched over years, to become a scream that dies out (a useless scream), an impacted silence collapsing into nothingness.

His writings are like SOS messages sealed in a bottle thrown into the sea. We open them and at first it is like reading in the dark. When our eyes adjust, we glimpse worlds of deadening processes in ourselves we dared not imagine. Bion used to remark that by reading him, at least, one gets to know what having a patient like Bion is like. I suspect there are many psychoanalytic writers who write from the depths of their beings, hoping to create a therapist who can cure them, or communicate through deaths with another living flame.

Generative Explosiveness

Bion also uses the image of explosiveness to describe generative, as well as destructive, processes. There are positive, as well as negative, aspects to explosive processes. The birth of a new idea or feeling or intuition may have explosive properties. Growth can be explosive. Beginnings have explosive aspects.

Bion's emphasis on explosiveness in development can, partly, be understood in terms of the resistance of any established status quo state to change. The saying, "The good is enemy of the better," touches on a certain inertia in human nature. Bion is especially sensitive to barriers, walls, blockages both on individual and social levels. He (1970, pp. 62-82) uses terms like Establishment vs. Genius or Messiah to depict conflict between conservative and radical elements in life. The new idea or intuitive vision is experienced as both life giving yet also destructive from the vantage point of the established order. Ideally, the old and new achieve a useful symbiotic relationship, each contributing to the other, facilitating growth of knowledge and being (of individuals, society). However, one must not expect things to go too smoothly, since boundary tensions can be incendiary.

In addition to the explosiveness of the new in relation to the old (and, conversely, the violence of the old vis-à-vis the new), Bion points to something inherently explosive about psychic birth processes in themselves. The big bang that begins the biography of the universe is not simply an explosion of the old. The beginning is itself explosive, an explosiveness intrinsic to beginning. As a model for psychic processes, one would expect new beginnings to be explosive, not merely because they disturb the old, but because they *are* explosions: explosions into life, life explosions.

In Dante's *Paradiso,* the soul keeps opening. More and more heaven is possible, no end to opening. It is no longer a matter of resistance of the old. There is only more and more opening, more and more divinity. It is only a matter of what the soul can tolerate. Apparently for Bion there is something intrinsically explosive about the journey towards infinite opening. Opening is explosive.

In our conversations, Bion brought up the importance of the Kabbalah in thinking about psychic reality. He used it not only to locate psychic life, but as a vehicle for experiencing more intensely. Kabbalah (Steinsaltz, 1988) has its own versions of big bang processes, explosive beginnings. The *Ein Soph* or Infinite Infinite is beyond conceptualization. As it descends towards knowledge and understanding a kind of explosion takes place. At times divine movement is depicted as a lightning flash, or white light (all colors contained). It explodes downward (into knowledge, understanding, feeling, action) and upward (through and beyond intuition) simultaneously. The birth of consciousness is likened to a blast of light. For Bion consciousness is an explosion.

Bion uses the experience of truth as one example of explosive consciousness. If lies poison, truth explodes. Facing truths about one's life explodes the lie one lives. Psychoanalysis can be dangerous because it can overturn lives. The analyst is necessarily (partly) a subversive support, insofar as he midwives the resetting and reshaping of lives.

Many people fear going into analysis because they sense the truth of their lives will upset what they've built up. They fear they will have to act upon truths they keep closeted. Their adaptations include comforts, pleasures, and habits that are reassuring. They would like analysis to diminish pain or dysfunction without too much cost. Perhaps, in some ways, analysis is "easier" for those who feel their lives and persons are disasters, who do not have too much to lose. They are already so badly injured that analysis can not cause them too much harm. They have reached such a level of desperation, that truth seems saving, cleansing, nourishing, rather than disastrous.

Bion is keenly aware of the destructive and generative impact of emotional truth. On the one hand, he feels truth is necessary for psychic growth, as food is for the body (1970, Chapter 1). On the other hand, he is aware that people may be ill equipped to take the impact of truth. He suggests there may be evolutionary, as well as individual, factors involved. A mental apparatus which evolved to handle problems of survival, may need further evolution to work with problems of integrity, emotional truth, and *how* we survive (*quality* of *being*, and not simply material being).

The human psyche's concern with issues of emotional integrity is an evolutionary explosion, a new dimension. Humans discover it is possible to live a lie, to be poisoned by the lies they live. Bion is one of those who suggests this "sense" of emotional lying-truthing has an aesthetic element that needs nursing. How do we "know" we are on a track that is right or good for us? What is this intimation of being "off" or "on" as we go along, this *feeling* of linking with ourselves, or being far from the mark? Under what conditions do these intimations work generatively, destructively? And aren't terms like generative-destructive awesomely crude?

Bion is attracted to difficulties inherent in psychoanalysis. He has a way of exploding hypocrisy with laconic black humor. For example, the question, "Can a liar be psychoanalysed?" Bion suggests if a liar can't be psychoanalyzed, no one can, since a liar (the psychoanalyst) also does the analyzing. Is anyone exempt from lying? Bion (1970, p. 2) trenchantly remarks that only a liar could disregard lying's pervasive nature. Analyst and patient struggle with the same basic problems. Our common task is how to become better partners with the capacities that constitute us, a never ending journey. Our job is not to stop lying (an impossibility), but evolve further in our relationship with this tantalizing capacity.

Part of wisdom involves dosage, a sense of context. Truth kills, as well as frees. In an earlier work (Eigen, 1992b, Chapters 4 and 5), I described an analyst, Ben, who used truth to ax others (and himself). He was a truth addict, gorging on truth orgasms. He had a scent for what was false in life and went for the jugular. In doing so, he was in danger of destroying his closest relationships, and losing everything dear to him. His sense of truth-falsehood needed deepening, broadening, contextualizing. He did not see the destructive way he used truth, the megalomanic bludgeoning, the lie.

Among other things, Ben needed to metabolize or process his destructive use of truth. He needed to develop a more resonant context for himself and others, a larger psychic field. He needed to grow a psyche capable of tolerating more of himself and others, one that could let the impact of the other grow, one that could let his own being grow. His precocious (intolerant) use of truth short-circuited growth of experiencing and its Moebius strip "truth-lie" mix. My writings on Ben document his (our) struggle to grow more of a psyche capable of tolerating more growth.

Bion's discussions of consciousness as an explosion, the ubiquity of lying, the need for truth as psychic nutrient, truth's destructive and generative impacts: all such discussions shift the center of therapeutic gravity towards what it takes to let experiencing evolve. It is not a matter of the Oedipus complex, maternal envy, sibling rivalry: all these (and more) are useful at particular moments. They represent particular organizations of relational tensions, pressures of diverse affective intensities. What is at stake is whether an individual (or group) can take its own capacity for experiencing. To what extent is emotional life, and mental life in general, too much for us? How much of ourselves can we take and allow to develop? Can we do so in life giving ways? How do we relate to our destructive tendencies? How best we make room for ourselves? Are we creatures destined always to have relatively low tolerance for ourselves, or can tolerance for ourselves and each other truly grow? Psychoanalysis is always an open question as to how far or in what ways analyst and patient can constitute themselves with reference to the conditions and capacities that make their lives possible.

Faith in O

The radical openness of the psychoanalysis Bion (1970) envisions is given dramatic expression in his description of the analyst's attitude as an *act of faith* (F) (pp. 41-54). One feels Bion's description of faith is itself an act of faith, and that there has been a growth of the O in faith as Bion's writings evolved. In earlier works there was more of an emphasis on evolution of K (knowledge, insight, understanding), and attacks on K links. He traced psychotic hatred of emotional reality and destruction of knowledge of emotional life. By his last major, formal work (1970), Bion was explicit in grounding psychoanalysis on something deeper than the drive to know. It is not simply knowledge that psychotic intolerance destroys. The faith that supports living is at stake. In his writings on faith, Bion comes close to envisioning what must be a contradiction in terms: a psychoanalysis without words.

Of course, psychoanalysts and their patients go on speaking. Bion wrote and spoke to the end of his days. But he affirmed something more important than words. For Bion, nonverbal emotional reality has a certain privilege or primacy that give words value. If words do not grow out of and mediate or signal movement of the emotional substrate, they are useless, even dangerous (since high altitude verbalization can lose contact with or falsify the affective core). The greater part of psychoanalytic movement is wordless.

Psychotic processes not only attack the analyst's capacity to know and put things together and make sense out of a life (or segments of a life). Psychotic processes undermine the faith that makes meaning meaningful. In psychosis the faith that makes emotional aliveness possible (and desirable) is undermined. The faith that makes an alive analysis possible is threatened. What comes under attack is the analyst's faith in the analytic process. The analyst is not only in danger of losing his mind, but his faith that mind and life are worthwhile. What suffers damage or destruction is his conviction that being in the analysis is worthwhile, that *being* is worthwhile.

As mentioned earlier, Bion envisions (a real experience, I believe) a destructive stripping of everything worthwhile, a denudation of personality and life past the null point into sub-zero dimensions: "a force that continues after. . . it destroys existence, time and space" (1965, p. 101). What can possibly meet or face or address such a force or state or deadening process? To the death without end, Bion proposes its counterpart: a faith in infinite O'ing. Can this faith outflank, outlast, undercut, absorb and partly metabolize, or somehow go beyond ever increasing deadness? Can faith survive analysis? Can faith survive (and contribute to) life?

Bion, partly, describes faith as a stripping away of mind. He advocates a disciplined eschewing of such mental capacities as expectation, understanding, desire, memory, and sense impressions. He relates this generative zero state or radical openness to Freud's free floating attention, an artificial blinding (suspension of usual use of mind), so that intuition of psychic reality builds. He writes, "If the mind is preoccupied with elements perceptible to sense it will be that much less able to perceive elements that cannot be sensed. . . . It is important that the analyst should avoid mental activity, memory and desire, which is harmful to his mental fitness as some forms of physical activity are to physical fitness" (1970, pp. 41-42).

It is as if Bion tries to find an Archimedean point of being that destruction can't destroy. He achieves a state (or vision of a state) in which there is nothing for the destructive force to feed on. One must ask, if one contracts until nothing is left but naked intuition, can't the destructive force feed on the latter? Bion seems to feel that (at the point of ultimate contraction) it may always be possible to open a little more, to keep on opening, so that faith provides more room (because it is "spaceless," infinite) than destruction can exhaust. Faith keeps opening as destruction keeps destroying: one infinity opening vis-à-vis the other. Such a statement, of course, is an act of faith.

The attitude of faith provides a "resistanceless" medium in which it is possible to observe destructiveness at work. Bion is concerned with how it is possible to make a correct clinical observation, especially observations of destructive processes: "I am concerned with developing a mode of thought which is such that a correct clinical observation can be made, for if *that* is achieved there is always hope of evolution of the appropriate theory" (1970, p. 44).

The starting point is always the impact of being on being, psyche to psyche, and transformations experience of impact undergo. What state of being best registers these impacts and their transformations? To what extent can we let experience of the other's impact "obtrude" and build? For Bion theory is secondary and follows observation of waves of impact.

Theoretical work, indeed, can be part of the ripple effect of one being impacting on another, ceaseless attempts to provide orienting frames of reference for mutual sensitivity.

Of course, the term "resistanceless" is a fiction, since nothing is resistanceless. The pain, disorientation, and insecurity the analyst feels in trying to achieve the openness Bion calls faith, show how difficult the analytic attitude is to find and sustain. It is not simply a matter of blowing dust off a mirror. It is human for patient and analyst to share difficulties in their work, since they are both defensive creatures struggling with disabilities. Analytic time is a mixture of hardship and joy for both parties, as they fight for and against each other and work with processes that support, defeat and challenge them.

Bion blasts the idea of the analyst as *knower*, since it is openness to *unknowing* (perhaps the unknowable) that grounds the analytic attitude. One tries to keep opening to shifting impacts and transformations of impacts. Can one ever know what is impacting on what? The analyst's experience of the patient is not the same as the patient's of the analyst. Furthermore, the analyst (or patient) may have difficulty achieving consensus with himself as to what he is feeling, or what his feelings mean. Nevertheless, one speaks from the point of impact, or from experience of evolution of impact. To connect with and voice intimations, hunches, and convictions from the pressing plethora of alternatives is itself a kind of faith. No two voices can be identical.

The voice that comes through Bion's climactic writings expresses and conveys the faith he speaks of. It is a strong and passionate affirmation of the human spirit via the analytic attitude, almost a musical evocation of the faith he fights to live from. His writing is an act of faith: it tries to convey the faith domain it grows from, alive in twists and turns of the living moment. Let me quote a passage that is an especially clarion call:

> Investigation of the problems involved depends on F. This means that the understanding of the patient and the identification with him that have been regarded as sufficient hitherto must be replaced by something quite different. The transformation in K must be replaced by transformation in O, and K must be replaced by F (1970, pp. 45-46).

One can not know O. One *is* O. The center of gravity shifts from knowing to being. We can talk about O and work with this or that bit of knowledge (always open to revision) about O. But we also *are* O and evolve in O as O evolves. "The problem in discussing O is that the discussion can only be about evolved characteristics of O (K) whereas F is related to O itself" (1970, p. 45).

The analyst's true home, when being an analyst, is living transformations in O, evolving in O, being in O through F. Since Bion (1970) associates O with infinity, "The analyst has to become *infinite* by the suspension of memory, desire, understanding" (p. 46).

Tall order! Not the usual description of the analyst and the analytic function! The analytic attitude is F in O, and can never be rationalized. Insofar as it is rationalized, it is not the analytic attitude, not F in O, not radical openness to impact, not living transformations in O. We are explosive nutrients for one another. Only by living O through F do we stand a chance of connecting with and hearing each other, as we speak through and from our O's, our shared O.

O

I have postponed, to the last, discussion of what Bion might mean by O. My inclination is to use the notation as the moment suggests, and let usage acquire tonality with time. In Milner's (1987, pp. 258-274) chapter on mysticism, Bion's O is zero, a null state, emptiness, void, nothingness, a quasi-oriental O. She associates analytic openness with pregnant emptiness, creative darkness, the power of non-existence, the goodness of absolute vacuity, the matrix of the sense of self, the divine ground of one's being, the experience of breathing. It is as if we surface momentarily at different points of an infinite pool. If we live only at the surface point, we cut each other (we are very pointy). But it is also possible to dip into background interlacings, where our roots interlock.

For Milner O is inherently orgasmic, albeit a muted (and extended) orgasm in analytic work. Bion tends to emphasize negative aspects of experiencing O in his explicit "descriptions" (analogical evocations). For him impact of O tends to be dreadful: "The emotional state of transformations in O is akin to dread. . ." (1970, p. 46). This is not so much a matter of psychodynamic resistance, as a matter of equipment insufficiency and unfamiliarity. Not even an analyst is used to *being* an analyst. Few of us are used to exercizing the capacity Bion calls F in O. Bion is actually calling for an evolution of our O, our capacity to be an analyst, our capacity to live F in O. To let go usual modes of being and knowing is frightening.

One wonders if too much analytic training goes into making believe the beast isn't there. What happens if one discovers the psyche is alive? An analyst discovering the living psyche is akin to a praying person overturned by prayer, shocked by more than he bargained for. If one of the faces of O is emotional truth, one is always in danger. One can, perhaps, control falsehood easier than truth (it is possible to own or claim a lie as one's own, but truth belongs to everyone—although any ideology of control is insufficient).

Bion (1970, p. 47) presses the point home by suggesting a kinship between increase in the power of F (as the analyst practices it), and experiences of severely regressed patients. At a certain phase of opening one may feel the pull of sleep akin to stupor. As contact with O sharpens, experience heightens and intensifies, so that emergent perceptual and sensory configurations may be painful. Not only must the analyst evolve with these shifts. Intimations of the latter are possible only by letting go ordinary grip on reality. Artificial blindness is, also, a kind of artificial madness.

Bion touches upon a sort of necessary analytic madness when he points out that the analytic attitude suspends both pleasure and reality principles. The deprivation of desire, memory, understanding and sensation that opens F in O

> corresponds to displacement of the pleasure-pain principle from its dominant position. This would not matter were it not for a simultaneous apparent deposition of the reality principle. . . . The disciplined increase of F by suppression of K, or subordination of transformations in K to transformations in O, is therefore felt to be a serious attack on the ego until F has become established (1970, p. 48).

O can be the ultimate reality of a session, emotional truth of a session, growth of experience of an analysis, the ultimate reality of the personality. It can be creatively explosive, traumatically wounding, crushing, uplifting. To a certain extent, one can select what O to focus on when. One spends a lifetime discovering one's O, tuning in, connecting with, becoming at-one with whatever one imagines it to be, whatever it makes itself known as. If one is lucky, one learns more about working with one's O as one goes along.

But I still have not said what O is. Kant's thing-in-itself, Plato's Form, Eckhart's godhead, Milton's formless infinite, Kaballah's Ein Soph, the Christian Incarnation, the weekend break in analysis, the weekly session in psychotherapy, the point of meeting or of not meeting, the impact two people have on each other and how they process their impact, the awesome shock of being alive, revelation of who one is or isn't, gifts and horrors of history, the shell that entombs one and the fire that burns the shell: O keeps changing meaning, finding new forms of expression, evolving, transforming. O as a notation explodes itself.

Our ideas of what science is must be transformed by what science is asked to deal with. A science (psychoanalysis) of the ultimate reality of the personality, O, has nothing to hold on to. It is a search for ways of making correct observations of what is unknown and ultimately unknowable, "a science of at-one-ment," since one *is* the O one studies (1970, pp. 88-89). It is more important to *actually* evolve, than talk about evolution. But it is also possible that what we say provides analogies for processes beyond words. The evolution of the relationship between the wordy and wordless is ongoing, and we are very much engaged in mediating quality connections, gaps, leaps.

What Has Bion Done?

Let us stand on both sides of the looking glass: on the one side, faith, and, on the other, a force that goes on working after it destroys existence, time and space. Two immense denudations, strip downs. One eats up everything, infinite Pac Man, feeding on true self, false self, no self. The other keeps Opening. O'ing and O'ing. I suspect, finally, there is a primacy of Opening over Oblivion. But Bion retains a certain democracy, equality of voices, a perennial binocularity (or multiocularity).

Blake writes of heaven as a war in which all voices have their maximum say to benefit of all: no compromises, total fullness of expression of all realities of Reality. O seems to have endless plasticity, transforming into what the avenue of approach of moment can use. Yet Bion's O is not prior to the moment of creation, the living now. O is evolving now and we with it, as it is us and we are it. Our oneness with it is part of the psychoanalytic method, one with the evolving O of moment.

One has to admire the achievement of one who felt denuded of life, and uses denudation as a means of finding life. I think of Zen masters who speak of becoming like a dead man as a way of opening. It is, also, possible for life to open life, a more orgasmic path than Bion explicitly describes. The senses, of course, are nutrients, not only nuissances or barriers to enlightenment. Bion does not deny this. However, one of his special achievements is to pull away the skin of sensory goodness, insofar as the latter masks destructive processes that are crucial for us to learn about.

His analysis has wide application in a day where materialistic pleasures are substituted for emotional realities, where addiction to sensory goods (often manipulated by media images and market research) obscure destructive forces. Can we even tell what is destructive and what isn't? Bion suggests that F in O is a way of cleansing our equipment to the point where what is happening to us can begin to register. We discover our naked sensitivity to life's impact at the point where everything has been thrown overboard.

Chapter 4

Musings on O

It is impossible to know reality for the same reason that makes it impossible to sing potatoes; they may be grown, or pulled, or eaten, but not sung. Reality has to be "been": there should be a transitive verb "to be" expressly for use with the term "reality" (W. R. Bion, *Transformations*, p. 148).

Bion makes a lot of the distinction between knowing (K) and being (O). For instance, there is a difference between knowing about psychoanalysis and being psychoanalyzed. The psychoanalytic experience is not the same as knowledge about it. Patient and analyst are faced with the problem of passing from the wish to "know thyself, accept thyself, be thyself" to becoming the reality such words suggest. There is a gap between knowing about x and being x.

O represents the realness of anything (Bion, 1965, p. 147). Psychoanalysis supposedly helps individuals become more real. One way it does so is by becoming more real itself. It is one thing to get credentials and build a practice and another to become what one professes, actually to be an analyst. To be and be and be an analyst. We become more real and keep discovering what reality can be. How real-unreal one is appears to be fathomless. It is odd to speak of degrees of reality. Yet we mean something when we say with conviction that someone is not real or perhaps too real.

O is inaccessible, unknowable, yet nothing is more accessible, since O is everywhere and everything. One can not know O, but what else can one know? The issue is set in the story of Adam and Eve and the apple, in which the Tree of Knowledge and Tree of Life are separated. Fierce angels guard the Tree of Life. But what can we be and know outside life?

Nothing is more threatening or nourishing than the realness of anything, any O. Resistance is resistance to O, suggests Bion (1965): "Resistance operates because it is feared that the reality of the object is imminent." "Resistance is only manifest when the threat is contact with what is believed to be real" (p. 147) To id, ego, and superego resistance, add O-resistance. One wants and fears nothing more than what is real— something or someone real.

Does this mean it is easier to be unreal than real? Does one need to find ways of regulating how much and what sorts of reality one can stand? The problem of building tolerance for reality is basic for Bion. Lying, illusion, falsehood help regulate the dosage of O that is bearable. We may get so embroiled in deceptions that O fades, until we are rudely awakened by the gap between pretensions and the flow of events. Deceptions protect against and manipulate the real, but nothing is more devilish than so good a fit between pretensions and reality that one never wakens.

To state that the fundamental reality is unknown, although we can be nowhere else, provides protection against necessary and inevitable deceptions. If we really know we are an unknown bit of unknown reality, we leave something open for further experiencing, knowing and lying. This sounds sophomoric, but the consequences are very real. So many individuals on the public stage and in our office leave little room for unknowing. So much destructiveness follows in the wake of feeling right about what one knows. It is harder (not impossible) to pull a trigger while exercising curiosity, doubt and wonder.

"The fundamental reality is 'infinity,' the unknown, the situation for which there is no language—not even that borrowed from the artist or the religious—which gets anywhere near to describing it" (Bion, 1992, p. 372). In one passage, Bion (1965, p. 151) tries out the notation, "ultimate object" to express the O of O, but he is dissatisfied with expressions. To call the ultimate object a group is an oversimplification, to call it infinity is too mathematical, to call it the infinite is too mystical, to call it the Godhead is too religious (ibid, p. 150) But can one stand there all day saying, "Ugh!" or sit going "Gulp! Wow! Zap!?"

Bion did not abandon use of mathematical, mystical or religious expressions. For example, he described the ultimate object as a group "containing in itself the potentiality of all distinctions as yet undeveloped" (ibid, p. 150). One binds the groupishness of the group by a name and distinctions emerge which call for further representation. Thus God may be a name for the infinite unknowable, which is a name for whatever God is a name for, which is unnameable. Omniscience, omnipotence, justice, mercy factor out of the primal affectively charged mass or emotional density (a sort of numinous, ur-group suffering development) and become objects of thought about the ultimate object. Groupings of experiences and thoughts about experiences percolate out of primal ur-group pressures, which keep rippling.

The idea of God as a group overlaps with the idea that identity is a relation (Heidegger, 1957, pp. 25-42) or networks of open relational sets (Matte-Blanco, 1975). Christianity's emphasis on the tri-un God expresses this intuition, as does the Kaballistic Sephirot or the Hindu panoply of creative-destructive gods. Some primal ur-group called mystical experience ripples through time and space, like variable light energy producing colors.

Bion notes the surprising degree of agreement by mystics expressing their meeting with ultimate reality. Similar paradoxical descriptions emerge in many times and places. Mystics agree that their expressions are inadequate. One might take their agreement as a general model for the insufficiency of words in the realm of feelings, but that would not do. There are, also, many instances in which surprising conjunctions of words create new possibilities of feeling. We change O as we change with it. The current popularity of "constructionism" acknowledges the importance of our contribution, although it does not circumscribe the reality that "constructs" itself through us or with us and as us. Creation includes, but is not limited to, construction.

If religion is an illusion (Freud, 1927), Bion (1992) called it a *basic* illusion (p. 374), a term that recalls his "basic assumptions" in groups (1961). "Any particular religion changes with the prevalent fashion, but the fundamental thing, religion itself, does not" (1992, p. 374). The generic group called Religion manifests in subgroupings like Judaism, Christianity and Buddhism, but also in sects and experiences not yet formalized or formulated. Bion repeatedly writes that he can not do justice to whatever religion—the fundamental thing—may be. He is not up to describing the O of religion. Yet he feels there is an O that words like religion bear on and that relationships with O are evolving and very alive.

Bion (1992) notes that religion—the fundamental thing—is a powerful force, although we do not know exactly what this powerful force is. In fact he calls it a *very* powerful force (p. 374) and recalls the Death Pit at Ur and the deaths of 900 followers of Jim Jones in Guyana in 1978. To think we know what this force is is to prematurely trivialize it. It will not stop exerting itself on account of our trivializations.

Religion is no mere construction. Whatever it is partly constructs/destructs us. We are far from knowing what to do with the multi-edged resource religion is. Bion tears at conventional notions of religion by noting how destructive the O of religion can be. We can not count on the niceness of O. Bion (1992, pp. 370-371) makes a little list of religious stories to show how God does not fit boxes. Jesus, resourceless on the cross, feels more betrayed by God than Judas. Job knows no arguments for what confronts him. Should we imagine that what we call God and the devil are indistinguishable, split conceptions of elusive, omnipresent x?

To wish to become all good or all evil is to wish to be absolutely unreal (absolutely split). O represents ultimate reality, good and evil (Bion, 1965, pp. 148-149). It is possible to live O by splitting O. But since O is O and ever shall remain so (O keeps O'ing), the split recoils from itself and boomerangs on the splitter and split one. One *can* use splitting processes by realizing the latter tries to bite off bits of O for partial digestion. One can turn splitting to profit by making it part of creative work that goes on and on. That is, one takes some of the edge off splitting by using it provisionally: one splits without losing touch with O. In Job, a kind of splitting became part of a larger movement. No matter what happened, Job kept his eye on the bouncing ball. Job didn't give a damn about the devil. He placed the whole thing in God's lap and wouldn't budge until God Himself made an appearance. Was it worth going through what Job did to see a bit of God? Is there any other way to become O? (Eigen, 1995, pp. 173-193).

Bion's portrayals of O tend to be in the key of terror. He speaks of "the terrifying unknown" (1992, pp. 369, 371). Religious and poetic expressions, evocative as they are, tend to obscure the raw terror of encounter with O. The most authentic art dresses what forever must be naked. The Bible has many references to the terrifying power of O. Prophets fall down in dread when God contacts them. Aharon's sons burn to a crisp trying to get too close to God by their own means. The ground swallows Korach, who claimed to rival Moses in knowledge of a God no one controls. Moses binds Israel with laws that act as filters for divinity, to lessen destructiveness. God's raw power irrupts, nonetheless, and many die before it temporarily subsides or is modulated, a drama that repeats itself throughout history. You can add your favorite stories or speak from your experience.

Bion ups the ante by wondering if the O of psychoanalysis can be experienced through the latter's ability to destroy. The destructive power of whatever psychoanalysis is appears in many guises throughout Bion's work. In an especially nasty passage, Bion (1992, p. 378) points out that the truth of psychoanalysis does not necessarily depend on whether or not it does good (i.e., "cures" anyone). Psychoanalysis may be "verified" by how much destruction it can cause. In physics a theory is good if it leads to a bomb that destroys Hiroshima. Psychoanalysis may yield interventions that blow up individuals or groups. For example, psycho-analytic theory might enable "increased memory and desire to a point where they rendered sanity impossible" (1992, p. 378).

The destabilizing moment takes many forms. A patient was able to share good news with me. After years of work, things were coming together. He was more in contact with himself, his marriage was more alive and sexual, his family was thriving, his professional practice over-flowing, his writing freer and truer. Then he shared a disturbance that occurred in a small group of colleagues. He seemed to split the group. Some members noticed his change and valued it. Others were uneasy. One man announced with patronizing concern that he was worried, apparently fearing destructive acting out, even a breakdown.

My patient was thrown off balance for a time. Should he be worried about himself? Was something bad happening? He felt better. His life was better. Things were on an upswing. Was this cause for alarm? It gradually dawned on him that he might be doing better than the man who worried about him. Success stimulates envy and resentment. He no longer needed the pity and worry this man displayed, at least not now. He probably caused a disturbance in this man, although not for the reasons the latter voiced. Their relationship required revisualization and renegotiation, since my patient was no longer in a position below. Slow changes over years broke into public visibility and solidly so. The disinte-gration worried about referred to the breakup and change this man's picture of my patient would have to undergo, which included redistribu-tion of psychic power in the group.

Can growth occur without waves of disturbance? Even growth of good feelings is troublesome. My patient was amazed he caused such diverse reactions. He was not used to making waves.

Love makes waves. Which is more disturbing, love or hate? What kind of love, what kind of hate? Bion (1992) notes that the term, "the love of God" (p. 373), introduces a challenge to stretch beyond ordinary sensa-tion, perception, emotion, action. It can not be reduced to what usually passes for love. It may find expression in sensuous life, as in the "Song of Solomon," but it is not circumscribed by sensuous reality. Bion associ-ates love of God with absolute love, requiring growth of capacity beyond creaturely love. Love of God may threaten other love attachments, although the former can bring the latter to fulfilment. Whether destruc-tive or generative, love of God invites and pressures us to find and give more of ourselves more totally to what lifts us through and beyond ourselves. We need "a language of infra-sensuous and ultra-sensuous, something that lies outside the spectrum of sensuous experience and articulate language" (ibid, p. 372).

Where does love of God come from? It certainly has played a crazy role in human life, feeding much destruction. Yet the call to love God with all your heart, soul and might pressures psyche to evolve. Can one ever love with all one's heart, mind, soul, might? Is there all of anything? Intractable problems engage our most powerful efforts (Bion, 1965, p. 152). We may not "solve" a problem, but change ourselves trying to. For moments we glimpse and feel love of God with all our beings, and if we place such moments rightly, life is not the same.

The story of Abraham's near sacrifice of Isaac brings together, in ghastly fashion, two powerful loves, love of God and children. That there is no way to rationalize the horror of this story, suggests we are dealing with terrifying forces. How can God tell Abraham to sacrifice Isaac? For the moment, let us take it as a parable expressing the significance of loving God. There is no doubt that Abraham would have done what God asked, like a madman. Yet Abraham's lie to Isaac, that God would provide the lamb, turned out to be the truth. Abraham was a crazy old man, crazy for God. Could he love God more than Isaac, more than Sarah? Rabbis tell us Sarah died of a broken heart when Abraham took Isaac to the mount. It was not the first time Abraham sacrificed Sarah, but this was more than she could bear. It's a crazy story, Sarah dying because the child she thought she'd never have was taken from her. Yet it portrays life in extreme pain, at the edge, at the breaking point.

What does crazy God ask? Isn't he asking, "How much do you love me? Do you love me more than Isaac, whom you love more than life?" Abraham hears and does, foreshadowing the Hebrews' response at Sinai. If the lover asks, the beloved does not ask why. But Abraham is capable of asking why. He has reasoned with God when God has seemed unjust and cruel. He has tried to change God's mind. We have learned from Abraham that we can speak with God—that we *must* speak with God. But Abraham does not try to change God's mind when it counts most, when his son's life is on the line. Abraham, the idol breaker, the traveler, the bargainer, the hospitable one, succumbs to his mad God.

As children, we were taught to admire Abraham's faith. The story is part of the morning service, read seven times a week, each week, each year. Our teachers did not seem to be sensitive to its gristliness. They imprinted it on our souls, a psychospiritual circumcision. They probably took sadistic pleasure in our latent horror. Abraham is our father. God saves us from our crazy father. But who saves us from our crazy God?

We grow up and discover that God is dead. It is a waste of time to be masochistic. But as years go on, many of us become fathers, and learn about sacrifice. My God, so that's what it's about. There *is* sacrifice. So that's why so much space in the Bible is devoted to details of sacrifice.

Life is *sacrificial*, sacramental, fusions of atonement and celebration. The link between sacrifice and celebration is inexhaustible. God breathes again, as new dimensions of living keep opening.

Teachers conveyed a pride that Abraham would have sacrificed Isaac but didn't. Moses encoded this in law. Not only no human sacrifice, but no penitential wounding of body. You are proud to be part of a tradition that prohibits sacrificial murder and wounding oneself. Yet the Bible is littered with bodies devoured and discarded by God and men.

Proud of Abraham. Proud of God. Proud of Isaac. They found ways of letting each other live. *L'Chaim*—to life! Each moment we are challenged. Can we take each other's aliveness, can we let each other live?

One peers into the Abramic kaleidoscope, after another turn, and sees that it is not just about saving child from father, but saving both from parental narcissism. A missing ingredient in the parenting of *every* "borderline" and "narcissistic" and most "psychotic" patients, has something to do with respect. Most patients I have worked with met with insufficient respect as individuals from birth on. Many were subject to love without respectful boundaries. They were treated as parental possessions, play things, plugs to fill holes in parental psyches, rather than as persons in their own right. They were loved to death, or to madness, in some way crippled by love. In these cases, parental love was intensely egocentric, so that the child was flooded by parental needs. The child was bound on the parental altar, under threat of destruction by what was life-giving, simultaneously supported and drowned by love.

Biblical warnings against idol worship apply to parental ego worshipping child, expecting to be worshiped in return. Ego becomes a mad, twisted god, parasiting on the selves of others. Paradoxically, excess of love unmitigated by respect, becomes indistinguishable from lovelessness. Children often feel dropped into an affectless void, as parental attention swings between too much and too little. The parent who idolizes the child and expects idolization is, also, indifferent, insensitive, and self-absorbed, so that the child goes from feeling pumped up with admiration into wastelands of neglect, too visible one moment, invisible the next.

The child's psyche is seared and imprinted by the parents' mad ego and deeper deficiencies and deformations. To kill Isaac is the greatest wound to parental narcissism imaginable. The story strikes with black precision at the parental jugular vein. Abraham would rather rip his heart out than kill Isaac. Our crazy God fingers our most raw and vulnerable point, our heart-to-heart umbilical tie with our children, our favorite child. God plays favorites, but God help you if you're favored! God rips at the very ties He establishes, yet the ripping sometimes has a strengthening, as well as annihilating, effect.

At some point or another, Abraham sacrifices all major ties as part of God's journey: his parents, uncle (Lot), sons, wives. He becomes a stranger who is kind to strangers. Yet his is not a story of abandonment. Ties persist, if altered. Isaac's wife will come from his father's family and Isaac and Ishmael will bury Abraham. No one is forgotten. As the tale moves from change to change, one is transfixed by a mute, unbroken thread, as if the Bible has its fingers on the pulse of Abraham's living soul.

Still, the Bible tells its stories by marking discontinuities, a narration of disruptions. Disruptions within disruptions. Infanticide-matricide-patricide are ancient themes. That most criminal murders occur among familiars today echos ancient motifs. Disruptions of intimate ties often are violent and give rise to violence. Violence is part of growth processes but may also attempt to forestall, avoid, or end growth. A king may kill sons in order to escape destruction, but literature tells us rivalrous destruction is inescapable. Freud (1913) amplifies this theme and proposes that destruction of fathers by sons is a nuclear force in the evolution of civilization.

Perhaps the greatest biblical disruption is the attempt not to be violent in a violent world. Abraham, God and Isaac swerve from violence in the nick of time, but threat of destruction remains in the background, ready to irrupt. Peace—*shalom*—is included in so many prayers because it is so difficult to achieve, more wish than reality. Not to destroy requires immense effort, as depicted in Freud's (1914) essay on Michelangelo's Moses. To abstain from murder as a solution to problems fosters psychospiritual evolution. By not murdering, a psychical field opens in which one can picture oneself murdering and/or not murdering, and going beyond these alternatives.

In fact it may not be possible to live without murdering and being murdered (in some sense). Anyone who thinks he is harmless is dangerous (everyone *is* dangerous). Yet it is important not to be content with being a murderer, even if one can't help it. This is one of those intractable problems that keep one growing. Coming to grips with the eternal Cain-Abel soul drama makes one resonate differently than refusal to acknowledge such facts.

Cain goes on killing Abel 'till the end of days: all states are eternal. But Cain builds cities marked for creative work, while Abel becomes part of the soil he ever tends. The two souls partly crisscross in Esau and Jacob, who manage not to kill each other. Esau (an incarnation of Cain's soul) sports Abel's naivete and gullibility. Jacob (an evolution of Abel's soul) has gone some way towards assimilating Cain's guile, since he takes what he (or his mother) wants from Esau without a physical blow.

The pairs Ishmael and Isaac, and Jacob and Esau, survived each other, although they could not live together. Still, they established, with great fragility, the principle of crossing souls for psychic evolution. This is not an achievement that always holds up. There is danger of regressing to Cain and Abel (e.g., Hitler slaughtering Jews; on a lesser scale, Arabs and Jews slaughtering each other), where splitting counts more than crisscrossing. Dread that cross-fertilization makes differences vanish (clinging to racial purity, fundamentalism) overwhelms faith in evolutionary possibilities. Clinging to splitting wipes out O.

Jacob is a model of psychic invagination (Eigen, 1992a). He makes room for many others inside him, but goes on with his own life. The bible writes of the pain he causes and suffers, no pain simply caused. Responsibility always is shared. Identity undergoes transformations in O, and God changes Jacob's name to Israel, to express this. Shared existence requires not only continuous adjustments to one another as conditions change, but reciprocal transformations in O, as we learn how subject to upheaval we are to each other's impacts.

We, also, are subject to impacts from within ourselves and get to O by attending inwards. We get insights, visions, ideas, feelings, intuitions that have potential for altering our approach to living. This happens in many ways in everyday life. For example, a student cried over how badly she was treated by her supervisor at work. She feared confronting him would make things worse, yet she felt she must find a way to let him know how awful it was for her. She could not bring herself to tell him. How amazed she was when her supervisor called and apologized. He *saw* what he was doing and realized he totally missed *her* and hoped to rectify things before the year was wasted or worse. The distress he caused affected him and led to the realization that he impeded rather than helped another life. Not all people in a position of power (eg., parents, teachers, psychotherapists, as well as politicians) are changed by the pain they cause, although many are.

We do not know exactly what went on inside this supervisor, but something did. By allowing himself to be sensitive to his own internal changes, he was able to approach shared reality differently. It is a process partly made explicit on *Yom Kippur*, when we ask each other's forgiveness for harm we've caused throughout the year. Perhaps this supervisor needed to maximize his supervisee's distress before he could sense the approaching disaster, the disaster in progress. People often need to inflict suffering and make it mount before believing it is real. An inner shift in this supervisor enabled a bit of growing, a bit of *Yom Kippur* in daily life. He used disaster anxiety as a signal to make life better, rather than complete the plunge.

In such instances, it is not clear whether we get to O or O gets to us. Perhaps guilt builds until perception changes and leads to reparative action. It is also possible that we see ourselves in God's light and tremble, not merely guilty, but genuinely shaken by the difference between our habitual selves and other possibilities.

Bion (1965) writes of a process in which the patient's "godhead" consents to incarnate in the person of the analysand (p. 148), rather than the reverse (patient becoming god). A bit of godly knowledge or revelation becomes real in a person, who begins to live it. In the example above, it is possible that the supervisor was shaken by the fact that he was supposed to be a supervisor and not a tyrant or baby or blind propagator of a narrow position. Driven by his godhead in process of incarnation, he let his supervisee know that he knew she did not have a supervisor this year and he would now try to be one. The supervisor in him broke through his resistances and made itself known in a way that made him want to be the supervisor he could be. He now ached to be a real supervisor, not whatever it was that was ruining their year. To really be a supervisor challenges ungodly personality elements that have unsupervisory things in mind.

To be anything good is an invitation to greatness. To be a good citizen, political leader or follower, surgeon, teacher or student, therapist or patient, requires perseverance and refusal to settle for the worst one can be. Once tasting the good, better, and best, one knows the difference. One endures and enjoys lesser moments much of one's life, and it is important to make peace with who one is most of the time. But if one omits incarnating one's special bit of godhead, something fallen or collapsed results where the best should be. One needs to incarnate godhead in order to rehabilitate oneself. If one voids this struggle, one swings haplessly between inflation (becoming god) and degradation (refusal or inability to incarnate, relate to, or root oneself in one's share of God).

Bion (1994, p. 138) speaks of the call of Brasilia to its citizens, a new city calling for new life. Will its citizens collapse into destructive inertia (business as usual), or make of the new space the great city it *could* be? One thinks of Jonah sent to Ninevah. Will the city rise to what it can be, die on the vine, or habituate to the lowest common denominator so that prophesy can not stir it. For the city's O or godhead to incarnate in its citizens, individuals would have to undergo the painful transformations that make a city great *and* good.

"Ought I remain a god or become a human being?" is the issue of the schizoid soul. Becoming a human being is a lifelong task, even if one can never be anything else. God hardened Pharaoh's heart to show His greatness. So many dead Hebrews. So many dead Egyptians. What a violent process. What kind of God is this? Where is God's heart? Doesn't God hear His prophets?

One works all one's life to have a heart, to be a person, to get it right or better, only to meet a heartless God who keeps demanding more heart. The miracle is there *is* more heart. It is possible to die from self-hardening processes. One's heart grows harder, tighter, uglier until it loses value as a pump. But hardening-opening has a rhythm. Deeper no, fuller yes. Eternal Yea and Nay are parts of psychical circulation. We may not bake well and God comes along and hardens us beyond imagining, but—Oh my God!—what openings! Not everyone discovers the heart that can't stop opening, but once discovered there seems to be nothing that can't be faced.

Bion calls us to recognize the ubiquitous reality, guises and uses of emotional explosiveness and mental turbulence. Emotional life is real. We are real. To what extent can we learn to work with difficulties sensitivity to emotional experience brings? To what extent do we hide or collapse in order to make ourselves bearable? To what extent can we find and actualize the greatness each soul is? Do greatness-goodness nourish each other or must they war? Is their reconciliation our impossible task?

We see an evolution in biblical brothers from Cain and Abel through Moses and Aaron. Abel does not survive Cain. Ishmael and Isaac go separate ways. Esau and Jacob have a complex relationship and barely survive each other, finally going separate ways: trickery, reversal and individuation, instead of murder. Jacob's children unite to kill outsiders (the story of Dinah and Shechem) and barely avert killing one of their own (Joseph). They cooperate for good and evil. On his deathbed, Jacob remembers Shimon's slaughter of Dinah's lover and his blessings bear few illusions about the sons he loves.

Moses and Aharon cooperate to do God's bidding. They follow God's, rather than their own or parental wishes. Their wills become intermittently indistinguishable from God's, yet each has characteristic weaknesses. Moses flies into rages and Aharon gives in too readily. Rabbis view Aharon as a peacemaker. We should imitate him trying to reconcile people to one another. Yet making the golden calf to keep the peace prevented him from reaching the promised land. On the other hand, Moses's striking the rock at Meribah, instead of speaking to it (as God bid), prevented him from entering the promised land.

Striking a rock instead of speaking to it does not seem a terrible crime. But little things summarize big tendencies. Not that getting water from a rock is such a little thing. Getting water from a rock by speaking rather than hitting marks a moment of evolution missed. Moses missed an opportunity to grow. For the moment he set a bad example: beating is easier than speaking. We are still learning to speak rather than hit to get water from each other. Psychoanalysis is part of the evolution to open hearts with words, a tendency that needs to spread throughout the social body.

The Bible has a deep rigor but is not tidy. Those who follow God are in for trouble, but those who don't are in trouble too. It is not often clear which trouble to prefer. Moses draws up rules for getting closer to God, but God often seems to break His own rules. Sometimes the closeness achieved by breaking rules is more acutely satisfying than the closeness achieved by following them. A moment's closeness to God is its own reward.

Winnicott's Agony: the X of O

Winnicott (1992, p. 128) wonders if it would be useful to use a symbol, X, to indicate a state of affairs involving some basic derailing or reshaping (or mis-shaping) of self when the personality is being formed and organized. Something untenable happens to a person that precipitates premature reorganization of a personality that is in process of becoming organized. The individual is forced to deal with wave after wave of re-organization before there is enough organization available for such work.

Flood and shock are terms which try to express what happens to the incipient self-in-evolution. Noah's ark expresses some ability to ride out the storm and begin anew. But what survives is only a remnant, a sample of all that was lost. A bit of semi-goodness survives, but it does not take long for the evil inclination to flood it once more. So much bad-good stuff gets decomposed by the sea. Perhaps some of it is metabolized and distributed as nutrient throughout the psychic circulatory system.

Winnicott asks what happens when an ark that can survive the flood has not yet been built. The personality is in danger of permanently being overwhelmed. Some individuals describe themselves as going through life as if submerged or in process of drowning. One may grab what one can and hold on for dear life, even if this means rigidly organizing oneself around part of the caretaker's personality, often the very caretaker who precipitated the storm or failed as an ark. Grabbing on to some bit of the other for dear life may make it impossible to grow in a spontaneously fuller way.

Winnicott (1992) suggests that what "remains absolutely personal to the individual is X" (p. 128), the alarming sense of the personality getting derailed or deformed and not being able to right itself. He depicts a scene in which the environment fails to support the developing individual, who tries to mend this failure by premature, skewed, defensive over-identification with aspects of the failing environment. This is like grabbing the opening of the trap door one is falling through. One pastes oneself to some bit of object to stem oblivion, but the object is composed of the same components that are part of the problem.

One may stay stuck in agony because the capacity to undergo, pass through, or process agony has not evolved. There are tales in which one creature sticks to another in endless fashion, until something or someone comes along to right things. In Winnicott's scenario, attempts to right the situation can exacerbate the problem, if they fail to locate and make room for the X that is off.

One makes the most of one's special skew, amalgams of ego-object elements pasted together, composites of native elements and streams of identifications. But an inner eye remains magnetized by the thorn in one's side, apple in one's throat, the X that is off. Warp or poison or skew—whatever the image—the sense of something being wrong must be given its due.

There are individuals for whom only the X that is off is real and everything else is phony. But there are individuals who value many things in life, yet need to keep reaching for the X that is off. In order to reach X, a person may need to provoke or undergo experiences which might seem or be crazy. Winnicott (1992) writes of "localized madnesses" that have to be lived as part of the therapy relationship: "Constantly the analyst is bewildered by finding that the patient is able to be more and more mad for a few minutes or for an hour in the treatment setting, and sometimes the madness spreads out over the edges of the session" (p. 128).

The response to bewilderment ought not be doctrinaire. The analyst might be tempted to set things right by getting the patient to "see" his madness as mad. The appeal to rationality often is surreptitiously moralistic and tempts the patient to add yet another layer of sanity (or pseudo-sanity) to insulate the mad core. The patient has spent a lifetime insulating madness with sanity, exacerbating dread of self. It is less important for the therapist to throw cold water on the patient's delusions, than to allow "the madness to become a manageable experience from which the patient can make spontaneous recovery."

Openness to experiencing enables growth of openness to experiencing. It is thrilling when a fearful patient discovers faith enough to risk spontaneously going through mad moments, to risk recovery of spontaneity. When one begins getting beneath words like sanity-madness to realities they mask, one grieves wasting so much time knowing what they meant.

Wading more deeply into the O of X has rewards and dangers, but for some persons, missing this venture is even worse than failing to wake up for one's life. There are people who live better staying away from X. The O of X does not seem to haunt them, chase them, not enough to warrant prolonged attention. There are others who appear to be better off missing X, since finding it can mean waking up in a nightmare. But there are also those who need to wake in that nightmare, and keep on waking in it, until the landscape becomes familiar, and one begins to feel the impact of other O's.

Chapter 5

Mystical Precocity and Psychic Short-Circuits

Precocity and Prematurity

Winnicott's False Self and Lacan's Imaginary Ego

Winnicott (1958, 1965, 1971) was concerned with precocious development of mind as substitute for emotional maturation. He wrote psychoanalytic poetry portraying split off mental organizations enabling the individual to survive, at the price of mounting deadness and unreality. He developed networks of terms (e.g., "caretaker self," "reactive self," "False Self," "splitting of the *psychesoma*") expressing facets of alienation in service of survival.

Winnicott's emphasis is an instance of a more generic, anthropological, structural concern, and links up with Lacan and Bion. Lacan (1977) placed decisive importance on the premature birth of the infant. That the infant is born long before it can care for itself, functions as a symbol of discordance that runs through experience. Lacan especially emphasizes the gap between what the baby sees/imagines, and inability to coordinate motor responses to keep up with vision. The eyes are far ahead of what the baby is able to do.

Prematurity is linked with a kind of visual precocity, an eye-mind nucleus of ego precocity. Lacan describes how the infant substitutes a visual image of self-completion for somatic streaming, awkwardness and incompletion. An imaginary I takes itself to be more whole than anything is, and reads its own and other's desire in terms of megalomanic scenarios: ego worship in place of truthful struggle. For Lacan, the imaginary, narcissistic I is necessarily paranoid and aggressive. It is forever molding self and other in terms of ideal images that funnel larger subjective-intersubjective flows. The I is inherently violent, since it is dedicated to trapping self and other by its versions of experience (or versions of experience it identifies with).

Winnicott's (Rodman, 1987, p. 31) reaction against gestalt psychology gains in richness when coupled with Lacan's picture of the I as overextending visual perception of wholes, units, outlines (a sort of *visual capture*). Winnicott's false self can partly be described as a dissociated eye-mind pretending (or falsely believing) it and others are more whole, integrated, complete than reality allows. He writes of the positive value of unintegration, chaos, doing nothing, so that welling up of fresh experiencing is possible. When Lacan (1978) describes spontaneous outpourings of the unconscious subject as "pulsations of the slit" (p. 32), he connects on a verbal level with Winnicott's (1971) "ticking over of the unintegrated personality" (p. 55). Lacan's imaginary I or Winnicott's false self do not have the last or only word.

For Lacan the violent I conditions object relations, and is not simply the result of the latter. Bad object relations may exacerbate and give direction to I's violence, but no amount of good object relations can "solve" or end I's aggressivity. The I always will have a tendency to precociously close or alter or funnel experiencing according to its scripts. It will always read itself in terms of the Other's desire and vice versa. It is in the nature of the I to do violence to life. It does not easily *let be*.

Winnicott's emphasis on parental provision of a milieu that facilitates true self evolution seems, at first glance, to speak against the inevitability of a precocious I that ruins things. But he also notes that no amount of good parenting can do away with sadism, although parenting may play a role in how constructively-destructively the latter is used. Indeed, for Winnicott, instinctual sadism plays a role in the true self's affirmative movement. The false self, like the imaginary I, does not end, but is incorporated in the tensions of a growing personality.

Psychic Breakdown

Winnicott (1974) immeasurably deepens his own and Lacan's work when he portrays the repeated breakdowns the psyche endures in face of its inability to process its own experiencing. The infant subject or self undergoes psychotic agonies that the immature psyche can not process. To a greater or lesser extent, one may give up on ever being able to deal well enough with equipment that produces states it can not handle. One lives, as best one can, through defensive organizations that ward off dread of being overwhelmed by agonies one lacked ability to work with. It is as if the psyche is injured by its own states and by its own immaturity. As one matures, a second, or more adult or competent personality grows over the debris of the first, and one learns to hide evidence of immaturity, disability, and helplessness vis-à-vis disorganizing emotional tides. Thus we always develop too soon and too late: too late to endure our early agonies, too soon to process them.

I think Winnicott here stresses a deeper immaturity than Lacan. He feels himself into a more pervasive experience of failure than the gap between seeing and doing, important as the latter is. For Winnicott there is a primal disproportion between agony and incapacity to sustain and process agony or overwhelming states (recall that for Freud the primal trauma was flooding: equipment can not sustain, handle, or keep up with states it is called on to undergo). Dread of environmental failure is the outer shell of a deeper dread of failure of one's own equipment. The environment tries to make up for what the individual can not do (and vice versa), but never with more than partial success. We rely on each other all life long for help with agonies we can not handle. The human race in its entirety is hard pressed to handle the collective agonies it is ever heir to.

The state of affairs Winnicott depicts is less structured than Lacan's. It is not simply a matter of tensions between different ways of processing experience, but a breakdown of processing ability (whether primary or secondary processing). To be sure, Lacan's portrayals are filled with irreducible paradoxes, reversals, and allusions to what eludes linguistic webs (the overturning of scenarios by the banana peel impact of the real, or the mercurial play of *jouissance*, the never ending ouch and yum of things). Lacan's and Winnicott's analyses do not exclude each other. On the contrary, they fill each other out. But it is important to note that the abyss Winnicott points to is not the cut or bar in language, not a gap between or within systems, or the wound of the real, or the opacity of primary repression: but *a cataclysmic failure of the psyche to live through its inability to sustain dire agonies*. We are not concerned here only with misdirection or redirection of experiencing (metonymy and metaphor), but loss of capacity to experience, because the capacity to process (sustain) such a capacity was lacking.

Deficit, Malevolence and The Embryonic Self

Bion complements Winnicott and Lacan. His work, partly, can be viewed as a meditation on the psyche's inability to tolerate experiencing (precocity is substituted for experiencing). Bion delineates at least three modes of intolerance of experience, which I am here summarizing under the names of malevolence, deficit, and embryonic self.

Malevolence

Malevolence has a long biography in Bion's oeuvre, stretching from his early to late psychoanalytic writings. It would be too much to give a full account of this evolution here, but some mention of facets of his work will be helpful. He depicts ways that hate attacks links between thoughts, between feelings, between thoughts and feelings, between self and other, between mind and body. Something in personality can not stand linking processes.

In early essays Bion (1967) depicted the attacker as a precocious superego taking the place of ego development. A warped, malevolent, hypertrophied superego preempted and usurped ego functions. For example, a moralistic life-condemning tendency left no room for thinking. Hate filled the gap where thinking might have been.

Bion meant more than paralysis of secondary process thinking. Indeed, secondary process thinking is often commandeered by a moralistic, life-hating superego to justify destruction. As his worked evolved, Bion depicted ways that destructive tendencies aborted or warped processing of affects at their inception. Malevolence can damage the psychic apparatus, so that metabolization of traumatic impacts is not possible. That is, primary process thinking can be damaged, as well as higher level cognition.

The breakdown and reworking of traumatic impacts into material suitable for dreaming can be stifled, or poisoned, or deformed. A crippled primary process can not begin the transmutation of *raw trauma globs* into usable feeling/imagining/thinking flows. Raw, unprocessed-un-processable trauma globs, together with chards of aborted, deformed thoughts-affects (scraps of failed psychic movement), agglutinate and further block possibility of movement. One may depict this state as stagnant, as a graveyard, or garbage heap: a dead or inert or wasted psyche. Yet malevolence gives this graveyard an eerie gleam. The psyche is at once dead and radioactive: its deadness takes on a poisonous life of its own, contaminating and destroying whatever comes near.

It is not just thoughts, feelings, and sensations that are deformed. The space where *sensing-feeling-thinking* might have been, is altered. Instead of openness, a black hole. Instead of intensity, annihilating explosiveness. Not only space, but time is degraded. The personality condenses into a demand for everything now, so that anything that takes time is impossible. The little the analyst has to offer is rejected, because it is not all at once.

Intolerance of time and space makes it impossible for life (or analysis) to build on itself. Bion developed a grid depicting evolution of psychic processes. As a metaphor for massive destructiveness, Bion imagined the grid working in reverse. Instead of feeding trauma into primary process, where traumatic impact may be worked into images, which give rise to symbols, which give rise to thought, a stunning reversal occurs: any achievement gets deconstructed back into originary trauma elements, which remain unprocessable. Raw, everlasting catastrophe takes the place where a psyche might have been. The psyche (what there is of it) becomes a *catastrophe machine*, grinding any bits of possible experiencing into horrific nothingness.

The primary task in personality growth is permanently undone. Bion (1965) writes, "The earliest problems demanding solution are related to a link between two personalities" (p. 66). Far from being able to "solve" linking problems, the personality set in destructive mode can not even sustain them. It gets rid of them, attacks them, implodes-explodes them. Finally, it ends problems by getting rid of itself. In one of his most dramatic portrayals of destruction, Bion writes of "a force that continues after. . . it destroys existence, time and space" (p. 101). Annihilation goes on in sub-zero dimensions, even after destruction of personality. Bion does not offer a causal account of how such a destructive movement gets started, but once underway nothing escapes it. Malevolent precocity does not give the psyche time or space to develop.

Deficit and the Embryonic Self

Malevolence often masks and is triggered by a sense of deficit. Malevolence may even damage the psychic apparatus, so that it creates or adds to defective functioning. Nevertheless, *inability* has a biography in its own right, and can not be understood merely as a cause or effect of malevolence.

Psychoanalysis usually understands deficit to refer to some lack or ill in environmental provision, a deficiency in personal or social nutrients necessary for growth. Bion does not exclude this, but his concern is broader. He calls on us to face the fact that our ability to process experience is not up to the experience we must process. This is not only so in infancy, but all life long.

Difficulties inherent in tolerating and processing experience can not be written off as malevolent attacks against aliveness or failure of environmental provision, although these are important. We come against limits, walls, holes in processing ability every step of the way. Part of failure of provision reflects a general difficulty human beings have in working well with their own and others' experience.

Bion attributes part of our deficient processing ability to the embryonic nature of self, psyche, mind. If our mental apparatus evolved in service of survival (adaptation), it may be ill equipped to handle issues of integrity or emotional truth, important later in our history. Our capacity to work with tensions between integrity and adaptation may be embryonic. The tension between conflicting claims may give rise to new ways of being a person. The very idea of what it means to be a person may be embryonic, in process of development, getting ready to be born.

We must make room for the idea that we are eternally embryonic. Perhaps our ability to do *any* experience justice is embryonic, the more so our ability to make the most of conflicting experiences and approaches to experience. The idea that we are embryonic takes the edge off deficit. If we are embryonic, there is hope we may grow. The embryonic self carries the possibility of becoming, an ever open *not yet*. Yet it is important to note that Bion does not have a utopian idea of growth. No amount of growing and learning will supplant or eradicate the permanent embryonic dimension of living.

Neither the malevolent self nor the embryonic self exhausts the area of deficit. A hallmark of defective hardware, equipment, or mental apparatus is an incapacity to let experiencing build. As noted above, this runs deeper than failure of secondary process. For Bion, the capacity to let experience build begins with the transformation of an impact into dream work, myth, symbolization, affective images and primal narratives. The deficiency in our equipment begins whenever processing of experiencing begins, a primary process deficiency. We can not keep up with experiential impacts. Production of experience outstrips assimilation. Our equipment produces states it can not handle. It is doubtful we can ever catch up with ourselves, or do ourselves justice, whatever level of processing we tap.

We are too much (or too little) for ourselves. Bion amplifies ways we can not support ourselves and each other. We get rid of, evacuate, shunt, or turn off our experiential capacity, our sensitivity. This may involve destructive and embryonic processes, but in principle goes beyond them. The inability to support ourselves is built into the way we are together. If we do not make room for inability to support ourselves and relationships, if we do not make room for deficit, we place too great a burden on what we *can* do. We may try to do *too* much, overextend ourselves, substitute omnipotence for openness, ravage ourselves with mastery rather than discover what partnership can mean.

Summary So Far

We have linked precocity of ego development with the infant's premature birth. Aspects of ego functioning outstrip the slower, more gradual development of psychomotor coordination. Image outstrips ability. We wish we could do things we can't. As infants, and all through life, we imagine ourselves able to do what we see others doing. There is a gap between what we see, imagine, wish, and true achievement. There is an *eye-mind* we can never keep up with.

The time lag between and within our selves also has deeper roots. The impact of trauma, and emotional experience in general, is often too much for our equipment to process. We are not up to the agonies that beset us. Our equipment produces states it is not able to handle.

It is easy to imagine an infant unable to process turbulence it undergoes. But I think it helpful to confess a processing incapacity all life long. Our religions and psychotherapies offer frames of reference for processing unbearable agonies, and perhaps, also, unbearable joys. At times, art or literature brings the agony-ecstasy of life together in a pinnacle of momentary triumph. Good poems are time pellets, offering places to live emotional transformations over lifetimes. There *are* moments of processing, pulsations that make life meaningful, as well as mysterious. But I think these aesthetic and religious products gain part of their power from all the moments of breakdown that went into them.

We have developed a rhetoric equating falseness with defensiveness, a rhetoric of the double, or counterpart, or substitute self occupying the place where a true self might have been. We picture the substitute self as a second self, more complete, less subject to breakdown, tougher skinned than the first. Underneath is pure sensitivity, without muscle, bone, or skin. At the same time we associate the originary, true self with wholeness, or with spontaneity and impulse. The substitute self is a kind of runner up, what we make do with in real life in order to deal with hardship. Yet substitute pleasures make up for a lot, and sometimes are all we have.

We become diffuse by filtering our personalities through too many versions of self, and rigid if we take too few too literally. Part of processing includes symbolizing facets of self and relationships to self. We develop expressive forms for breakdown or ruptures in processing, and how we relate (or fail to relate) to incapacity. We symbolize, also, orgasmic-ecstatic moments, as well as the hard work of problem solving, turning things over, chewing on things. We show each other mixtures of metabolized-unmetabolized bits of wrestling with materials we are drawn to, objects that light up self in this or that way.

Our communications impact on each other's sensitivity, setting off more processing work, some of which bears fruit. Whether we defend, modify, amplify or deepen our positions, we need the work of the other to bring out our own. We feed on each other's work, allied processors, friends or enemies, at work together.

The Mystical Capacity and Sense of Rightness

It is important to spend time thinking about the different states one goes through in a day. In one day, even a few hours, one may feel one with God, explode in fury, quiver in fright, weep, work hard at something. One may be a skillful hunter ready to take on the world, or roll up in a ball in bed.

Freud marveled at the plasticity of the psyche, its changes of state. He felt this capacity held out hope for treatment of psychosis. If we go back and forth from dreaming in sleeplife, to common sense in wakelife, why prejudge what is possible, what transformations of self await us? Meditating on our capacity to change states may enable us to be a bit freer from entrapment by any one state, and to get as much as possible from the states we go through. Dwelling with changing states deepens our inner-outer texture (our inside rings grow, our outside bark multiplies ripples).

There is a mysticism of changing states. The very *experience* of changing states can be highly charged, numinous. The amazing diversity and extremes of experiencing can give rise to a sense of awe and mystery. How can all we experience be possible? What sorts of beings are we? What can we do with the restless palate that gives life its colors? Surely we can do more than point and nod, as the great display slides by.

Often the mystic of changing states is manic. His panoramic vision flies over vast psychospiritual landscapes, scanning for prey. Now and then he swoops down and turns a few captured moments into prayers or poems or plays or papers. Or he may gaze unblinking into the vast shifting navel of vision and throw stones. Such a mystic keeps shifting positions in order to maintain exuberance. Every movement opens new vistas, new thrills. The passing years leave no rings inside, no ripples outside. He is as blank at the end, as the beginning, although his life may be in ruins.

The manic mystic short-circuits the states he spies. It is enough to see them, to taste them a bit before spitting them out as aesthetic, religious, or psychological products. The manic mystic is able to avoid being changed by the states that thrill him. This is different from the mellowing of the seasoned mystic, who is deeply affected by what he goes through, and undergoes corrective transformations.

The seasoned mystic gets something out of the changes he goes through, and does not merely luxuriate in hyper awareness of change. He does not simply ride the waves, nor masochistically go under, although he may do each at different times. He is brought up short, revisualizes himself, rediscovers life where the real becomes symbolic, and the symbolic becomes real.

There is a mystical agony when one sees everything wrong with oneself magnified to infinite power. One patient dreamt of this as a bug inside the pearl (Eigen, 1992b, pp. 148-151, 234-235). The shock of bottomless malevolence, madness, and deficit brings one to one's knees. One hungers for truth about oneself, even if it is impossible to bear. The beatific vision is complemented by vision of one's ugliness. One needs input of both for balance. Both are real, both imaginary.

The ugly vision rubs our nose in what is worst about us. It is important to know the worst. The mystic who grows from the ugly vision takes the latter's impact. Wave after wave of horrific destructiveness pour through him. There are many types and gradations of response to vision of destructiveness. One may cry from the heart, pierced by agony, "Lord help me, I can't help myself." One may open one's eyes until they go blind. Qualifying thoughts may come, "But I'm not all bad." One may try to wash away bad vision with good vision. One may lose consciousness and start over.

The vision of destructiveness (like destructiveness itself) can never be fully integrated, transformed, metabolized, processed, converted into something useful. Our ability to injure ourselves and others never ends. It is cruel to rationalize all destructiveness as secretly useful, as hidden good. I think we must make room for the possibility of destructiveness as such. Making room is not indulgence. Making room for the possibility of really being destructive without precociously rationalizing it, makes room for spontaneous growth of protective measures. If one confesses one's viral (virulent) self, one's touch may soften.

This is not a matter of saying, "I'm sorry, I'll be good," nor a matter of making resolutions. One knows such attempts spiral out. Being touched by vision of destructiveness (one's own, others', life's, the broader currents one is part of), cuts one to the core, makes one less hardhearted. One becomes less harsh and strident and spongy. Facing one's destructiveness is no immunization, but it gives one a different smile and glance, a different "feel."

In a recent session, a patient (Dolores) with years of immersion in mystical experiencing, began speaking about losing "the analytic stance" in sessions. She was taking courses in psychoanalysis, and feeling badly

about not keeping "the analytic stance" with her patients. Other therapists in her peer group were taking courses too, and sounding more
analytic. Dolores was a very sensitive, gifted person. I found myself
repeating the words, "*the analytic stance*."

Dolores was wounded to the quick. She furiously withdrew, cried,
then attacked me. She felt I was making fun of her, putting her down for
not being analytic. As far as I could tell, I was trying out her phrase for
size. The analytic stance? I had visions of analytic pretentiousness I
encountered over the years. Here was Dolores, so psychically prescient,
adept, intricate. Many analysts seemed crude and butcherous by compar-
ison. Was she measuring her ability by some Procrustean phrase?

After enough time passed to absorb some of the emotion in the room,
I remarked, "If anything, I was making fun of the phrase, not you. What
the hell *is the* analytic stance?"

It was a momentous event. In an instant, puff! Puff went her picture
of me ridiculing her, her conviction that her rage at me was totally
justified. An instant visionary flash exploded all the times she raged at
the other, feeling justified by her sense of injury, never doubting her
perception. At such moments her vision of the other's destructiveness
threatened to doom her in an abyss of worthlessness, which she raged
against. Her sense of rightness was absolute.

"The analytic stance," I mumbled. "Puff," I trailed off with a wave of
my hand.

She laughed and laughed, free from certainty. We smiled at each
other, and felt spread of feeling circulating back and forth, a good
permeability, free of sensitivity rape and paranoid rage. A prison she
hadn't known she was in momentarily disappeared. Self and other could
not feel quite the same again.

Mystical Moments

For Dolores, life was essentially mystical. So much of her experience
was highly charged. She lived from heightened moment to heightened
moment. Life was cosmic drama with a cosmic glow. She moved from
union to union, suffering agonizing disruptions of union. As often
happens with individuals who possess a strong appetite for union, she
tended to live alone. Her aloneness heightened moments of union, and
gave all experience greater impact. Aloneness protected sensitivity.

So much of her experience was organized around a nuclear sense of
rightness and certainty. She stayed close to what felt right for her, and
when she found what felt right, there was no room for doubt. She was
swept away by the intensity of perceptions, which were nearly as absolute

for her as a schizophrenic's hallucinations. For Dolores, perception was, as William Blake suggested, infinite. Thus, for Dolores, life was ever meaningful. Each moment was saturated with meaning. However, she did not recognize the attitudinal basis of her perceptions: she was not tuned in to the attitudes that organized the tone and slant of her perceptual world. In particular, she never doubted the rightness of her sense of rightness. For Dolores, what felt right was the truth of her being, her soul's verity. Above all, life was soul-feeling: what the soul felt *was* true, and what was true *must* be right.

For Dolores, life was orgasmic. Not just body orgasms, but feeling orgasms, soul orgasms, self orgasms, ego orgasms. Not all experiential impacts set off orgasmic fireworks. Dolores was an artist and actress, as well as therapist. She painted and acted soul feelings, so that states of being she lived and expressed were finely nuanced. Yet even when the volume was low, and gradation of feeling varied, life was an ebb and flow of orgasmic seas, with rising undercurrents.

Dolores *knew* life through the rise and fall of orgasmic feeling. Orgasm was a mode of cognition, a tuning fork, a magnet, a magnifier. It focused and heightened significant aspects of life. Through soul orgasms Dolores evaluated and tasted life more keenly. From the quality and feel of orgasm, Dolores could tell how good or right or wrong something was for her. Dolores read the taste and feel of orgasms (body-mind-soul-self-ego) for messages about her path. Orgasms provided destiny messages.

It had never dawned on Dolores to what extent she relied on the orgasmic sense to *judge* experience, or to what extent her ego was a *judging* ego. She had prided herself on being non-judgmental, on living openly. Now, suddenly she saw a hidden connection between orgasmic judging and ego judging, how a judgment flash that had orgasmic authority closed her down. Just as she thought she was most open, an orgasmic judge pulverized whatever person or moment filled or tore her.

Orgasm was a way of processing *and* obliterating experience. For a moment it took her closer to herself and the other. But then it turned, and the gap between herself and the other seemed unbridgeable, or filled with hurt and rage. The orgasmic flash began with sweetness and joy, but ended in fury. Lover and enemy were one.

The moment Dolores and I laughed together was free from judgment. If anything, we were gleefully judging destructive judgment, perhaps a little like kids getting away with something. But I think for the moment we found the capacity to play, to enjoy feeling alive together, to simply flow. The prison of judgment temporarily dissolved, or partly became an object of humor, rather than a totally gripping horrific reality. Dolores felt what it was like not to be gripped by a judgment that had the authority of ego *and* orgasm, a judgment that thrived on terror and rage. She found herself in an intersubjective playground bigger than the sum of parts.

In our new playground there would be battles. War was not ended. We could still be enemies, as well as friends. But we somehow *knew* the flow. There was room for it. There were moments of mystical aloneness, union, injuries to aloneness and to union, sorrow, joy, everydayness and just plain me-ness, fury, worry, reaching out, hiding, opening, closing. We *knew* we would be many ways together, we would suffer together, celebrate together. There could be no end to what we might discover. We were *joined* as a therapy couple, the sky's the limit. It is now up to Life, God, Chance, Luck, Destiny, Evolution, You Name It. We would no longer be tyrannized by rightness-wrongness, including personal, social, and professional pressures about what therapy *should* be (precocious foreclosure of what therapy *might* be). We had a right to discover what place in the universe a therapy couple can have.

Flowing

The states Dolores went through did not end, but her attitude towards them changed. She could now take in her sense of rightness, see how it tyrannized her, and see what the next moment might reveal. She *knew* one moment qualified, filled out, altered another. She became as interested in the ongoing editing and revision, as the original Word. How one moment would look different in light of another became as intriguing as immersion in the moment itself. Her *knowing* was less from top down, than bottom up, a knowing in her being and bones and nerves, less attached to rightness than possibility.

A field opened in which polarities fed each other, became interchangeable, dissolved and endlessly reconstituted. At the same time, so much happened in the interstices of polarities, that polarities became hindrances as well as anchors. The holy war was over. Self↔Other appeared with double arrow between them, the bi-directionality meaning flow, reversibility, together-apart, towards-against-away, the ever shifting distinction-union movement, zero-one-two-three-infinity, the variable *between*.

Dolores was a bit more able to take herself for granted, to settle into being *her*. It was a relief to see the beam in her third eye, instead of fighting doubleness in others. In time, consciousness of fault becomes less naive, more elastic, less cataclysmic. It is a relief to be able to take oneself in all one's guises, including enlightenment lust, with a grain of salt. A kind of loving humor makes seriousness bearable.

To be more at one with oneself means transitions between states become less ominous, more anticipated. The mystical moment may be more focused on self, other, between, within, beyond, emptiness, fullness, everythingness, nothingness, fragmentariness, sameness, difference, light, dark. Dolores had an unconscious belief that enlightenment meant achieving an unchanging state. This is akin to the philosophical dogma that God is unchanging (since change implies incompletion or lack or death). Those who strive to be like God may strive for totality, completion, a state that never changes or ends. Dolores thought herself inferior because she could not be unchanging. When she experienced a mystical moment she imagined it *should* last forever. Holding tightly to a state, trying to make it unending, may lead to nostalgia, but often worsens terror and rage.

The mystical charge moves across dimensions and objects. One can move with it, stand against it, encounter it in many keys. One develops a rich and varied relationship with one's mystical capacity. The latter is not something to neglect, or promiscuously indulge. It is one of the capacities that make us the beings we are, and like other capacities, we gradually learn how to live with it. We learn how it responds to ways we relate to it, as well as how we respond to it. In time we may become better partners and make the most of each other.

Dolores could breathe easier being able to move between ecstasies of union and difference, and their sorrows, without making one right, the other wrong. She was a bit freer from the reflex to blame others for movements of mood and spirit built into her nature. At the same time, she did not have to blame herself for not being one thing or something else. God now was freer to be the *living* God, which includes openness to what the next moment of God may be. We swim in God-fields covering us with unending movement.

Mystical Precocity and Mystical Maturation: Forgiving the Unforgivable

Mystical experience can be used to further or short-circuit personality growth. As often happens, as was true for Dolores, it does both for the same person. To what extent does it do one and the other? Can we tip the scales more in one direction or the other? To what extent ought we meddle with capacities we don't understand? How can we get to know our mystical capacity better, so that we and it may grow together?

We are not in a position to say, "I don't believe in mysticism," and turn attention to important, real matters. Too much is at stake to be dismissive. It took less than ten years for a mysticism of hate to end *Yiddish* culture in Europe. The swastika and goose step were parts of a mystical surge, a military mysticism that cemented huge portions of a nation. Words like *pure* and *super* played on echoes of holiness, placing the sense of boundless transcendence in the service of precise destructiveness.

Dolores's mysticism didn't hurt anyone but herself. Her precocious mystical capacity helped and harmed her. The gratification she got from her mystical capacity held her together. At the same time, it decreased motivation to develop her intellectual and practical potential. She barely made a living.

Most of her life she did not mind a threadbare existence, since her life was filled with *self-feeling*. Cosmic suffering and joy commingled to make her life full, rich, meaningful. The moment was enough. As a young woman she enjoyed a mysticism of the senses. Sensation and sexuality held her together. She *lived* a kind of *Tantric* philosophy, a *Song of Solomon* existence. She lived like the lilies of the field, with no thought of the morrow, in God's hands. As time went on, mystical feeling spread through her body, and led to dancing, painting, acting. She was a body mystic, yet her eyes shined with earnest, loving transcendence.

As a child she felt loved by her father, although he was perceived as ineffectual in worldly terms. Her mother was near psychotic and Dolores had a psychotic sibling, and her other siblings had marked difficulties. One could say she lived her father's life in a transposed key. She became a version of father as refuge against mother. Yet Dolores was also very much an original, her own person.

Her mother wanted her to be an intellectual, social, and worldly success. Dolores was gifted and had the potential to shine. But she fell apart in college. Head learning tore her to shreds. She felt she could not and did not want to become the showpiece her mother wanted. She would *not* be successful, at least as defined in common, worldly terms. It was enough to just *be*.

Her mother was dismissive and invasive and incessantly plunged Dolores into dire agonies. Her father's love saved her, but could not make it safe to use the intellectual, social and practical capacities that her mother desired. Dolores did what neither parent expected. She lived off a deep sense of mystical intensity that took her out of the family, into the river of life.

Dolores would be an eternal child, always young, always new. Yet she was rich with experience. Why did she seek help? What did she want from therapy? She had never wanted marriage, children, money, mainstream living. She was a child of the cosmos, a daughter of the dance of

Life. What did she want from *me*?

Our first year of work was characterized by moments of intense connection, punctuated by the latter's rupture. Moments of high emotional-erotic-mental-spiritual arousal, which bordered on exquisite ecstasy, were repeatedly smashed. Dolores would become deeply wounded and incensed at what she regarded as my cruelty or insensitivity. This is a pattern that characterized her close relationships. One could relate it to various aspects of ruptured union with parents. Her traumatic object relational history would be enough to explain the repetition. The Other alternately *was* loving, cruel, insensitive, implosive -explosive, vacant.

Dolores had years of therapy and my sense was that historical "explanations" were necessary but not sufficient. As we went through the *wounded union* moment repeatedly, I had the strong sense that we were not simply reliving, but trying to create something *new*. Our immersion in the wounded union moment allowed Dolores to experience the realness of both union *and* separateness, their swings, comminglings, sorrows, ecstasies. No amount of therapy makes them go away. They are permanent parts of experience. By our going through them together, Dolores could gradually take them as part of a larger intersubjective flow.

Our going through the wound together was different from what she did on her own. With her parents the trauma was repeated, more of the same. Our moments of trauma led to new possibilities of experiencing. We not only talked about traumatic impacts with mindful awareness, nor simply enlarged our mental frames of reference, although these were important. Dolores's heightened reactivity to my traumatic impacts on her had an enormous impact on *me*. Her sensitivity fine tuned me. I experienced my wounding impact on her repeatedly and thoroughly, and in subtle ways spontaneously reworked myself around her sore spot. I grew through Dolores's pain.

We are elastic and inflexible. No matter how I stretched and grew, I had traumatic impacts on Dolores. But Dolores saw and felt her impact on me. She *could* change me, although not entirely. She saw that I would have liked to have been different, if I could, and that her influence, at least, made *some* difference. She was not simply sloughed off, ignored. Through our interchanges I was becoming the sort of person she could forgive, although I, *also*, remained unbearably unforgivable.

Dolores's mother could not enter into interchanges that might change her. She went on blithely beyond influence, vaguely omniscient and oblivious. An oblivious omniscient individual tends to be helplessly enraging rather than forgivable. Dolores's psychic flow was clotted by *an unforgiving attitude stuck to an unforgivable object.* Perhaps some of her hypersensitivity was an attempt to burst past this barrier. She could calm down somewhat with me because her sensitivity affected my sensitivity in ways that changed my self and person. We discovered *mutual sensitivity* deeper than trauma.

When I became someone she could (sometimes) forgive, my unforgivable aspect became (sometimes) more lovable or tolerable. She could put up with me because of what she got from me, what we got from each other. At least with one person, for some moments, the *unforgiving attitude stuck to the unforgivable object* could begin to thaw. Her perception of her impact on me enabled her to let down and experience her stiff and unyielding aspect, her "soul rightness" described earlier. My painful admission of my wrongness (how I could wrong the Other), allowed her to feel how wrong her rightness could be.

In so much of life, defensive rightness in one person triggers defensive rightness in another, spirals of defensive reactiveness. Dolores's mother could never be wrong about anything basic. She was never at fault, at risk. She could not live from wound to wound, sensitivity to sensitivity, unless filtered through defensive rightness. She was not aware of the rightness that stole responsiveness: she simply *was* right. Dolores had not been aware how much her sense of mystical rightness aped her mother's oblivious omniscience. She would have been horrified to think that her capacity for mystical experience shared her mother's blindness.

Dolores's capacity for mystical intensity made life worthwhile. She never focused on the rightness or judgementalism of mystical vision. Mystical awareness was nourishing, enriching, fulfilling. It lit up existence. The blindness of mystical darkness was inherently ecstatic. That the mystical richness of life should have something in common with her mother's unconscious snobbery was unthinkable.

Without quite realizing it, I modeled the ability to feel deeply wrong in relationship to the Other. I gave Dolores a chance to experience someone feeling deeply wrong and sorry without masochistic surrender. This smoked out an incapacity to feel wrong buried in mystical rightness, an incapacity all too obvious in her mother's prosaic rightness. It never dawned on Dolores to develop a critical stance towards the sort of experiencing that enhanced her life, the area of life she felt certain her mother did not invade. If she was wrong about mystical experiencing, she was wrong about everything.

Mystical Awareness as Psychic Short-Circuit

Mystical states can short-circuit working through processes. There are moments of beatific union with self or Other that bypass painful realities. One can wait or strive for such states instead of working with personal difficulties.

Certain mystical moments are akin to being in the goal region without going through the maze. One enjoys the excitement and richness of the event, without worrying about preparation or cleanup.

One takes a direct, nonstop rocket to divinity, a mixture of sensation, feeling, intuition. Intellect is used mainly to drill deeper wells, or make better openings. One lives in and for these states, never far from ecstasy. One's cup runs over, filled to bursting with heavenly sensation and feeling. The divine moment leaves. One is alone, forlorn, in agony. One is terrified and enraged at the Other's indifference, insensitivity, cruelty, incapacity. One feels grieved for life's wounding ways. Feeling disappears. There is deadness, emptiness. Then the rocket fires again. One weeps tears of recognition, gratitude. One's heart is radiant.

The cycle repeats with many variations. Life becomes a raw affect flow, a rise and fall of naked affects. Everything else is extraneous. The affects are, alternately, blessings and curses, cosmic portals. Through the rise and fall of Self-God sensations-feelings, life is revved to infinite power.

I recall learning about rats starving as they kept pressing a bar that triggered electrode stimulation of a pleasure center in the brain. Mystical sensation-feeling can be addictive. Dolores's life was dangerously near the poverty level. Yet rich in cycles of feeling. The term "pleasure" scarcely does justice to the surge and diminishing of mystical intimations, mixtures of bliss, joy, ecstasy, suffering. One's life can be devoured by radiance.

Somewhere Isaac Bashevis Singer wrote, "God gave us so many emotions and such strong ones. Every human being, even if he is an idiot, is a millionaire in emotions." Singer seemed almost an ideological naturalist, yet his work teemed with demons and angels. He portrayed individuals who could not take the emotions or emotionlessness of existence. Peoples' lives were broken by the mystical capacity that gave them meaning. Lives also were broken by lack of this capacity, by bleakness. Whether ineffable joy or terror, human equipment was not up to what it must endure. Neither mysticism, nor lack of mysticism, was the answer.

Did Dolores substitute mysticism for life? Or did mysticism make life possible, add to life? I think both. Dolores would not have survived without it. She would have disintegrated or society would have crushed her. Mysticism fortified her within and without. It held her together and enabled her to come through repeated periods of disintegration. And it gave her a base or center from which to meet reality on her own terms.

Perhaps she dismissed or discounted huge portions of reality. But she tended to maintain enough of a therapy practice to survive, and had enough points of contact with other liminal souls to make life worthwhile. She would always live from the soul. The conventional mainstream was outside her domain. She was on another track, a mystical substream, a point in the diamond that made fractures glow.

I never felt my job was to make Dolores into a different person, to make her more "realistic." She would never have stayed with a "reality" oriented therapist. I was willing to accept that what most people called reality would be meaningless to her. Mystical reality was her home, her world. What was most important was that she make the most of the home and world *she* lived in.

For an individual like Dolores, growth within the mystical domain is more important than growth outside it. It would be harsh and unrealistic to oppose mystical radiance with practical criticism. One needs to grow along one's own track, not switch to someone else's. *One needs to become the sort of person through whom mystical experience can evolve, and who can evolve through mystical experience.*

Mystical Maturation

What is important is not mysticism versus other domains, but lack of growth within the mystical domain itself. With a Dolores therapy can not focus on the domains *her* brand of mysticism leaves out (mainstream social life, marriage, vocational ambition, economic security or greed). But one can focus on ways *her* use of mystical experience short-circuits itself.

As a young woman, Dolores became dependent on mystical feeling to offset dread of disintegration. She fell through a trap door in her psyche into a world of heightened sensation-feeling that made her feel more whole. The affect of moment was everything. Nothing outside it mattered. In this context, disintegration was part of the cycle of affects, part of a death-rebirth process. Dolores spontaneously found a way to counter disintegrating and going under. Her brand of mystical intensity saved her from madness and death.

Nevertheless, I think it would be wrong to view her mysticism as merely defensive. It tapped into and opened a deeply meaningful reality, perhaps an underpinning or counter-reality to the ticking off of conventional life. She lived in timeless time, a world in which the experience of moment was real, a world of the realness of experience as such, especially the sensation-feeling side of things.

The sensation-feeling world saved her life. She would be loyal to it forever. She dreaded the intellect's destructive potential, its role as killer of life. Her mother's emphasis on mental superiority contributed to the disintegration she underwent. She *knew* her mother's pride in mind was wrong. She experienced its destructiveness first hand. It did not work for her. For Dolores intellect was useful if it enhanced sensation-feeling and cleared the way for more intense states.

Now she had to face the fact that the capacity that opened and saved her (safety net and treasure), kept her from growing. The experiential capacity that enlarged her, made her small. She never had been in a position to think of the addictive, tyrannical aspects of mystical states, the slavery, as well as freedom, of mystical moments. These moments had meant too much to be placed in doubt.

It was more than simply finding her mother's self-righteousness buried in the heart of what she valued. This was hard enough. But the matter went beyond maternal infiltration of her deep self. Through our encounter, Dolores discovered for herself the double edged sense of "rightness" that organizes experience. Her mother's oblivious self-righteousness was damaging. But in the end, we all have to deal with the damage and benefits our sense of rightness brings.

Dolores got a first hand glimpse of what in literature and religion has variously been described as *hubris, original sin, pride, vanity, narcissism, folly, madness, egocentricity, selfishness.* The repeated wound to our close tie led to a moment of revisualization of who we were. The hidden *"me right-you wrong"* sensation that permeated experience was exposed in a way that took Dolores by surprise. Her mother was a damaging carrier of the psychobiological virus, but not its originator. Dolores had no one to blame for the astonishing egocentricity that pervades experience. Her mother's (or my own) horribleness, did not make Dolores pure.

Mystical feeling expanded to include two people who could be right *and* wrong, and for whom terms like right-wrong are crude or besides the point (unless one wants to spend one's life arguing). The mystical glow expanded to include two people fighting for their lives, finding and losing each other, combatants, friends, partners, loved ones, ready to be touched by what it is possible to go through together, ready to try again.

The glow of self expanded to include glowing selves in various states of realization. We were touched by each other through all the breaks between us. It was as if we were saying that there is a goodness in life that runs deeper than the ghastly things that happen. We were uplifted by the regeneration of this goodness, repeated miracles of refinding each other.

For someone like Dolores, who must progress within a mystical field, therapy enlarges the area of intersubjective glow or numinosity or charge, so that it includes perceived shifts in two subjects, variably closer-further from each other, in ways that neither subject can finally destroy or decisively warp. The mystical field expanded to include the possibility of a faulty relationship regenerating at deep levels. The torn heart became part of a larger flow.

We were developing a relationship that made room for changes Dolores went through alone. Not only could we go through them to-gether, we could go through much more, much else. The possibility of what two people could endure and survive together was incessantly redefined. Difficulties that would have led to breakdowns of relation-ships, became challenges for growth. We tasted what it was like to be inspired by going through places there seemed no way out of. The gates of hell could not stop us. We kept coming back for more.

This is like and unlike what Dolores has gone through in her life. Yes, her mother will always love her, accept her. But her mother does not know her, has not found her, hasn't the slightest idea who she is. The repair therapy offers involves seeing, feeling, being in ways a person can say, yes, this is me, this is more like it, a place I want more of. We discover that our relationship survives us, and we survive it. We are resources for our relationship, and it for us. We learn to take into ac-count how destructive we can be, and survive this learning.

Rebirth remains central, but takes on a different quality. It is not simply the shift from low to high or breaking through a wall that counts. There is also a sense of self-other generating and regenerating each other in many keys, always another corner to be turned. Peak intensity combines with openness to time, as notes in a phrase, parts of an ever changing song we never get enough of. We bob up and find each other just as we thought we would be alone forever. But now we know that finding is possible, that we never stop making each other possible.

Precocious Malevolence-Benevolence, Precocious Affect, Unborn Together, New Connections

Dolores was one of the least hurtful persons I've ever met. She could become furiously enraged when she felt violated. But I never felt injured by her. This is in contrast to individuals who chronically injure others, whose very being seems to be injurious. One can't get near such people without getting bloody.

Charles Manson is an extreme example of precocious mystical male-volence that forecloses flow of experience. More generally, devil cults twist experience out of shape, and glory in hate. One can not penetrate the veil of self-justificatory "rightness" that grips fanatics.

The malevolent mystic can not bear the Other's claim to goodness or creativeness. He prefers a counterworld of his making to the world's injustices. In a way, he is like Dolores, before she saw she could be wrong. Dolores, however, does not injure or kill anyone by shrinking (expanding) her world to mystical moments (although her mother may be baffled, disappointed, chagrined). The malevolent mystic requires elimination of target others, or parts of others. He can not rest until some other is injured or disposed of. If looks could kill, his job would be easier. But he usually must go through the trouble of developing or finding means to implement his evil vision. He may become a magnet for others who crave violent "solutions" for complex tensions.

Certain kinds of love also foreclose flow of experience. Maternal love that upholds her child's being, may violate the latter's person. A mother may forever picture her child as younger and other than he is. Her vision of the child's goodness may be maddening, insofar as she does not have an inkling of the tormented soul he really is. The child may desper-ately up the ante until someone responds to his grief. Individuals use various affect patterns to simplify experience and harden-soften person-ality enough to excite (or dismiss) attention and to function.

Affect, not only intellect, may be precociously organized. We become specialists in certain affects and their patternings as ways of giving ourselves identities, feeling real, or avoiding unspeakable horrors. Dolores discovered she could use intense affect moments to develop a way of life. As long as she knew she could dip into moments of height-ened affect, she would be all right. Other people functioned as stimuli for heightened states, and, to some extent, as mood modifiers. This worked well enough, until her sensitivity threatened to swallow her, perhaps swallow itself as well.

She became a heightened ball of sensitivity, so that small shifts in others triggered immense, often catastrophic changes. How long could she stay on the wild bronco of unadulterated self?

We rode the bronco together. I am a raw ball of sensitivity too, although my insulation is thicker. Therapy gave the bronco more room to bounce around. Our broncos resonated to one another. But I'm not at the point in life where I want to be totally subject to turbulence. I don't mind spreading it a little thin, so that an experience has more space and time, so that one moment is qualified by another. I don't *feel* like being so totally at the mercy of virulent emotionality, although I value intensity. As I grow older, my pleasures include looking forward to how the next moments will add to (alter) my sense of everything that went before, an incessant reknitting of life's garment. One keeps fine tuning the point where one's Archimedean lever move's the world.

I think Dolores needed to feel connected with someone who never stopped massaging his point of entree to the universe, where sanity-madness feed each other, need each other.

Our mystical capacities hooked into each other, like trains coupling. But which tracks we would take remained unknown. There was jostling for position before relaxing into deeper currents. We tugged at each other. Who would lead where? We led each other. The idea of a leader faded. We shifted positions like birds in flight, fish in water, animate, sensitive, molecular waves.

We lived and processed mystical awareness, and the latter lived and processed us. Her imaginative life more readily embraced the play of sensations, feelings, and thoughts. The gap between sophisticated ideals and embryonic realities was mitigated by the pleasure Dolores and I got by being unborn together. We blanked out and grew from null and agony points many times. We went through nothing and hell so often, and in so many ways, that faith in our radiant connection deepened. Mystical appreciation of being no longer short-circuited growth of personality, but became integral to it.

For Dolores and myself, personal growth was inherently mystical, and mystical awareness became allied with personal growth. This involved a realignment and reworking of the connection between the capacity for mystical experience and the capacity for personality growth. Our relationship became a place where capacities that did not necessarily work together had a chance to link up in new ways.

In Dolores's life, mystical awareness and personality growth fed each other up to a point. But they would become incendiary, warring parties, forcing Dolores to pull back, shrink. Mystical feelings often jettisoned Dolores's growth. The mystical capacity could become parasitic, feeding off Dolores's personality, rather than feeding it. At such moments, Dolores would be terrified of her personality *and* mystical capacity. Our relationship shifted the psychospiritual balance for the better, since it was allied both with mystical awareness *and* personal growth. We participated in a kind of psychoanalytic mysticism that enabled personal growth and mystical awareness to find, and refind each other, a psychoanalysis informed and incessantly recreated in this double helix.

Chapter 6

The Sword of Grace

The expansion that psychoanalytic theory has undergone in the past several decades allows people to apply it to literature and religion in ways which can no longer be described as "reductionistic." An important part of this shift in orientation involves an assimilation by contemporary psychoanalysis of existentialist concerns with the self. For certain psychoanalytic writers (e.g., Bion, 1977; Kohut, 1971, 1977; Winnicott, 1971) the self is not only a structure but a subjective center of personality. Personality as a whole is viewed as an open, expanding "system." Clinical drama at any moment hinges on the kind of person one is becoming or wishes to be. What is at stake from moment to moment is the very quality of selfhood.

The psychoanalyst's concern with "who am I?" brings the analyst into close relationship with religion and literature: It is no longer a matter of trying to explain one by the other. The creation of a story, a prayer, or a psychoanalytic communication are not mutually reducible to one another, nor are they mutually exclusive. They may influence one another in fertile ways. The psychoanalyst reaches out to other disciplines not to impose a body of knowledge, but to discover or deepen a personal sense of identity. The analyst must get help from varied sources to contribute as much as possible.

It is in the spirit of this quest that the present chapter brings together aspects of the work of Flannery O'Connor, D. W. Winnicott, and Wilfred R. Bion. If psychoanalysts can link in a sensible way with an author like Flannery O'Connor, it will have to be somewhat different from the methods of much applied psychoanalysis in the past. As O'Connor (1980) wrote to a friend and fellow author: "In fiction everything that has an explanation has to have it and the residue is Mystery with a capital M" (p.199). Again, "the meaning of a piece of fiction only begins where everything psychological and sociological has been explained" (ibid, p. 300). Winnicott and Bion are less concerned with psychological explanation than with experience-near description and Mystery (Eigen, 1981).

My principal emphasis will be on the interaction of certain aspects of O'Connor's and Bion's work. Of all psychoanalysts it is Bion who most explicitly uses religious images as models to explore emotional experience associated with therapeutic change and resistance. However, Winnicott's (1969; Eigen, 1981) "use of object" formulation amplifies a basic movement in O'Connor's work, and while my reference to Winnicott is brief, it is central. My aim is less to "understand" O'Connor psychoanalytically than to allow an interplay which quickens appreciation of an area of experience to which each author adds something. The result is psychoanalytically oriented, but one in which psychoanalysis and Mystery are partners.

Flannery O'Connor's Destroyers: The Shock of Grace

Most of Flannery O'Connor's stories move toward some central shock or jolt, which may convey a certain mystery, but which also seems to arise inevitably from the nature of her characters and life itself. Often these telling moments are catastrophic and do not always result in a reorientation of the characters in question. Many of her characters break under the strain of a potential conversion experience they refuse or are unable to sustain. In story after story something of a stripping down to a zero point of human personality occurs. In extreme terms, one either changes or dies, possibly both. The logic of the Biblical call to die to be reborn can be ruthless.

O'Connor's stories are uncompromising and austere. If profoundly humorous, they are ascetically so. Layers of personality are peeled to discover what is absolutely indispensable. Hers is a method of contractions. Her characters' compromises or stopping points are tested and the verdict usually is, not this, not this. Nothing less than the offering and acceptance of God's grace will do, and the latter is an incessant shock to defenses.

"Good Country People" condenses a number of O'Connor's central concerns and insights. In this story Hulga (she changed her name from Joy) has contempt for those she depends upon, partly because she is a Doctor of Philosophy and reads about nothingness. She is a 32-year-old woman with an artificial leg who is treated like a child by her mother, Mrs. Hopewell. In time a traveling Bible salesman, Pointer, penetrates Mrs. Hopewell's perimeter and Hulga decides to seduce him, although she has never been kissed. At the crucial moment Pointer asks to see where her wooden leg joins the rest of her. He tells her the leg makes her different from others. She feels superior to love but feels touched by his apparent innocence and complies. As she shows him how to put it on and off she feels he has touched her truth and that she is surrendering. The story ends with Pointer abandoning Hulga and taking her leg with him. Next to his gesture her talk about nothingness was empty. "'And I'll tell you another thing, Hulga,' he said before leaving. 'You ain't so smart. I been believing in nothing ever since I was born!'"

At her best O'Connor fingers her characters at *the point where pride and vulnerability converge*. She touched Hulga's implicit dependency through her pride and left her little to stand on. We do not know if Hulga will go further than realizing she isn't as smart as she thinks. Nonetheless, the shock is real, perhaps more for the reader than Hulga. It leaves a strong after current, which may or may not take one as far as O'Connor would like, but would be a genuine loss if one tried to ignore it.

A good many of her stories are divided between homely souls and destroyers, both maimed. Her destroyers unmask everyday complacency like the plague and bring out the spiritually perverse and infantile that pass for normal. They remain pitiless in face of the pitiable and contemptible. They usually smash the areas of self-deception that keep one from being most deeply alive. One might say that these destroyers act like avenging angels meant to clean up the psychospiritual landscape.

In "A Good Man Is Hard to Find," a banal family, led by a sentimental, controlling Grandmother, meets the Misfit, an escaped killer.

One by one the hapless family is dispatched in a way that makes the contrast between their flabby existence and the Misfit's uncompromising meanness a biting reality. The Grandmother argues for her life with an array of pieties that are helpless against the Misfit's incorruptible hardness. Up to this point the story is one of pure unmasking. Real evil smokes out everyday complacency. The Misfit acts as an inner standard against which hypocrisy falls short.

He and the Grandmother continue to talk until something real appears in her. The Misfit suggests something of his wronged self and hidden struggle with Jesus. His religious sense is of a violent intensity beyond anything the Grandmother has known. The Misfit fears Jesus. He feels if the latter is real everything is thrown off balance. Without Jesus his way of life is fully justified. He says: "then it's nothing for you to do but enjoy the few minutes you got left the best way you can—by killing somebody . . . or doing some other meanness to him." His agony evokes pity in the Grandmother who reaches out to touch him, as if he were her own child. At that point the Misfit recoils and shoots her, then lets down the tiniest bit. He was not entirely untouched by her. He shuts up a yakking buddy and tells him: "She would of been a good woman . . . if it had been somebody there to shoot her every minute of her life."

In O'Connor's work grace involves cutting through the folds of personality, soft and hard. In her work there is never grace without a sword. The cutting is done by the way characters turn each other inside out or fail to accomplish that. In O'Connor's terms the Misfit is a "spoiled prophet" who might have done great things. Not all her devils achieve this integrity. For example, Shiftlet, a sleazy devil in "The Life You Save May Be Your Own," acts from a sense of convenience tinged with self-pity. O'Connor's honest devils can be counted on to clear out psychic garbage.

One can engage a panoply of psychoanalytic concepts which relate to O'Connor's devils. One can see in them id-superego functions, the antilibidinal ego, the paranoid-schizoid ego, some combination of Winnicott's "ruthless baby" and Bion's –K, a self wounded and disillusioned by important objects, and so on. All of these play some role in aspects of her "spoiler's" make-up. Here, I wish to use Winnicott's "use of the object" to bring out further one aspect of O'Connor's "destroyer."

O'Connor's Destroyer and Winnicott's "Use of the Object"

Winnicott (1969, 1971; Eigen, 1981) depicts a process wherein the baby attacks what he imagines to be the other, only to discover the real other survives. The other remains beyond his fantasy control. After the infant vents wrath he is left with a startling and uplifting sense of self and difference from the other. Perhaps Winnicott's (1971) most memorable description of this process is the following:

> The subject says to the object: "I destroyed you," and the object is there to receive the communication. From now on the subject says: "Hello object." "I destroyed you." "I love you. . . ." "You have value for me because of your survival of my destruction of you." "While I am loving you I am all the time destroying you in (unconscious) fantasy" (p. 90).

In this interplay, fantasy operations and the sense of the real require and feed each other. A new sense of the real is born through the destruction of fantasy, while the real invites fantasy and further attacks—a continuous process of clearing the air. An experiential world is constructed which embraces both fantasy and reality fully, each feeding and breaking through the other. This double movement undercuts subtle tendencies toward depersonalization or psychic impoverishment. With good enough circumstances the baby discovers otherness beyond his own web-spinning and learns to use others for growth purposes. This true making use of others is one pole of grace. It is no mere calculation or manipulation, but an intrinsic reaching out and joyous appreciation of the shock of difference.

In Winnicott's terms, O'Connor's destroyers partly express a baby's wrath aimed at flaws in those others. They stay caught on one horn of the process; no proper holding response allows the transition from wrath to love. At the same time her destroyers do not sell out. They remain the "I destroy you" unqualified by "I love you," clear-sighted killer babies who at least know what they are. For them a certain kind of realness is all. Winnicott's picture of realness remains closed to them, although nothing less would do. In Winnicott's terms the destroyer is one term of a complex drama in which love has primacy. Both the "I destroy you" and "I love you" are valued inclinations of the human heart. They are spontaneous feelings toward others, not discharge mechanisms. This "I love you" doesn't make up for "I destroy you," but turns the latter to good use. In this context destructiveness makes love real, and love makes destructiveness creative.

Resistance to Faith: *Wise Blood* and *The Violent Bear Is Away*

O'Connor's two novels center on the struggle against faith. In *Wise Blood* (1952) Hazel Motes fights his religious urge by preaching The Church Without Christ. He takes a seemingly humanistic stand against God's cruel call for salvation and the intimidating choices it involves. He tries to make the idea of salvation irrelevant but his fanaticism betrays him. Above all it becomes clear that he is fighting all falseness with bitter tenacity; Motes holds on to a grim integrity.

He rejects those who try to "help" him insofar as what they offer involves some sort of lie. In each case he resists temptations which would have made life easier, at the cost of his perceived integrity. In effect, he throws off everything he might hold on to and does not stop at murder in this regard. He embodies the destroyer within himself who will not be taken in by anything. If he finally "succumbs" to religion, it cannot be a false one.

In time his cleansing nihilism leads to a reversal. His search turns inward and he tries to annihilate everything false or "unclean" about himself. It becomes horribly clear that he is heading for some kind of mad sainthood. He blinds himself, wraps barbed wire around his body; he is a strange, Protestant, mystical Oedipus-Tiresias with echoes of older Catholic saintly mortification. The woman who watches his dead body "saw him moving farther and farther away, farther and farther into the darkness until he was the pin point of light," perhaps as much light as she could know.

Similarly, in *The Violent Bear Is Away* (1961), Tarwater struggles against his great uncle's wish for him to become a prophet. He has an "inner friend" (a "fiend," the devil) who voices common sense truths and tempts Tarwater to break away from the old man's "madness." The tempter's voice gets help from outside parties and Tarwater undergoes the conflicts through which he gradually defines himself.

Both Hazel and Tarwater are caught in violent conflicts over what kind of person to be, what kind he really is. At critical points both become violent, and each slays some weak element. In Hazel's case it was an old alcoholic who preached a mock version of Hazel's Christless church (The Holy Church of Christ Without Christ). Tarwater kills his nephew, an idiot boy, in the act of baptizing him. Hazel kills something more obviously whorish, while Tarwater seems to kill innocence. Both destroy some blindly clinging, dependent figure, as if this person would hold them back. Their ability to be violent in the service of their integrity reflects the intensity of what they are caught in. Both commit murder to prove they are free from the idea of sin. Their very intensity plays a role in their redemption. They are too God bitten and haunted to be able, ultimately, to be at one with themselves without faith.

In O'Connor's fiction faith is a violent business. It may have always been so, but in a harsh, forgetful age it can hardly be less. There are too many defenses and warped values for faith to move through. Extreme measures are necessary for faith to gain a hearing at all. Throughout O'Connor's works one feels the subdued screams of misshapen souls. Whether grace is accepted or rejected it cannot escape the intensity of evil circumstances, especially the "banality of evil." If grace is possible, it must move through our real selves in this moment of reality.

Impoverished Containers

To a certain extent, grace must be resisted inasmuch as personal change is often painful. However, O'Connor's characters portray additional problems related to a lack of an adequate container for religious experience, a lack both personal and social. Her most religious characters are in some way broken by the experiences that save them. They do not have a support system to help channel what has touched them. They are left to their own devices and suffer the torments associated with the unconscious pride of the isolate.

Her religious heroes are backwoods Protestants, "wild" saints and prophets, untempered by Catholic reason and sacraments. O'Connor favors them over secular emptiness. At least they are dead serious and are related to Mystery. One way or another their whole beings are focused on redemption. Like our modern culture, they have little to go on but their own feel for the way they must carve out a self in the wilderness. Their fundamental beliefs are defined by Protestant orthodoxy but they lack communal guidelines to help them on their way. O'Connor (1980) writes of Tarwater, "My prophet will be inarticulate and burnt by his own visions. He'll have to explode somewhere" (p. 373).

When touched by the numinous, O'Connor's lesser characters are usually dispatched far more easily. Again, the subject's ability to be a repository for experience was not up to the experience he was touched by. In "The River," a child, hungry for identity, drowns trying to recapture the moment of his baptism. He came from an ordinary family with the material preoccupations of daily living and had no preparation for an encounter with spiritual reality. One day his caretaker brought him to a preacher who immersed him in the river and told him, "You count now." Yet where the boy lived everything was a joke. From the preacher's face he knew immediately nothing the preacher did was a joke, and the boy wanted to be like the preacher. Later he goes to the water alone to find his true home.

Other O'Connor characters wed a mixture of earthly loss and suppressed fury with a religious epiphany which proved too much for them. In "The Displaced Person" Mrs. Shortley, long-time farm help, took her family and left when threatened by a new, more disciplined arrival. This self-willed, religious woman could not bear any real threat to her narrow, controlling life. She apparently felt her presence was indispensable. Upon driving off she has her greatest moment and dies of a stroke. Only then did her face seem to register any astonishment, as "her eyes like blue-painted glass, seemed to contemplate for the first time the tremendous frontiers of her true country."

In effect, O'Connor's stories hold us fixed at the moment of potential conversion. We are ground out of shape by the challenge of personal change but misshapen without it. She writes in a letter, ". . . I don't know if anybody can be converted without seeing themselves in a kind of blasting annihilating light, a blast that will last a lifetime" (1980, p. 427). Her stories rivet us to this blast and bring home experiences we cannot bear.

In rare instances ("The Artificial Nigger") grace with benefit is offered and accepted in the midst of tumult. In others, characters are transfigured in their ordinariness with no clear sense of what will happen when the vision passes. Mrs. Tulpin ("Everything That Rises Must Converge") in her hogpen suddenly sees the souls in Purgatory and discovers "by their shocked and altered faces that even their virtues were being burned away."

Bion (1970) likens the emergence of emotional truth in an analytic session to mystical vision or the flash of genius. The new realization shatters as well as uplifts. The possibility of interior violence is part of each analytic hour. Elemental tendencies such as love, hate, and the urge to know function as resistances and fuel development in conflictual ways. Personality is prone to a certain inertia or complacency. The very intensity of one's psychic reality may be experienced as a violent threat and disturbance. As with O'Connor's characters, it is problematic whether the containing function (the analyst's or the patient's) is adequate for the emotions and realizations one grapples with.

Faith and Psychoanalysis

In recent years, something akin to faith has come to play an important role in psychoanalytic understanding of the foundations of human personality. Erikson's (1950) "basic trust," Winnicott's (1953, 1969, 1971) "transitional space" and "use of the object," Kohut's (1971, 1977) stress on positive aspects of idealization, Elkin's (1972) "primordial Self and Other," Meltzer's (1973) "superego ideal"—all tap some aspects of what might be called the phenomenon of faith.

For Bion (1970; Eigen, 1981, 1983b) faith is the very heart of the psychoanalytic attitude, a radical openness through which one aims at the ultimate emotional reality of moment, Bion's O. Strictly speaking, O is unknowable. We develop hunches, hypotheses or convictions concerning O but not certainty. Nevertheless, the analyst attempts to attend to the movement of emotional reality and for this a certain faith is necessary—faith that reaching out for emotional truth is worthwhile or even required as a principle of wholesome maturation.

Faith is the "baseless" capacity through which one aims at O. An attitude aimed at knowledge, memory, or sensuous experience misses the mark. Similarly, one's id-ego-superego desires and maneuvers become painfully obtrusive insofar as they differ from one's aim to be open to the play of emotional truth. *The explosive or catastrophic potential of every therapeutic encounter is seen in the clash between faith and all other attitudes.* Like other human capacities, one's relationship to faith may evolve with use. Within this attitude or framework, data drawn from other capacities may form meaningful gestalts that can facilitate growth. All capacities find their place within a primacy of faith. In this context, William Blake describes heaven as all out war between every human capacity in which all have their say without compromise, yet incessantly enrich and are enriched by others. Here faith functions as a boundless or infinite container.

To be sure, O'Connor means orthodox Christian faith, although Shloss (1980) feels that an internal reading of her work does not require only a Christian interpretation. O'Connor, a Southern Catholic, eschews psychoanalysis as an organizing framework, yet it is difficult to imagine her stories could have been written in an age not permeated by the discoveries of Freud, an Austrian Jew. One speaks of her characters in terms of resistances and defenses scarcely noticing it. She automatically uses psychoanalysis as part of her unmasking sensibility.

Similarly, Bion turns to religious analogues as a way of approaching psychoanalytical experience. For Bion the former do not function as a fixed framework but part of a method of discovery. The religious contribution gains fresh currency by contact with the turmoil of the analytic hour. In analytic sessions one may study and participate in the finest details of the moment to moment acceptance and refusal of grace or healing (Eigen, 1983a).

For Bion, as O'Connor, faith is personal and hard won. It is not simply the animal faith we naturally live by. To a certain extent, it runs counter to the pull of psychic gravity and opens a mental and spiritual center, which engages experience more deeply. One suffers while reading Bion and O'Connor. Their works are like hermits wrapped in wire and the sincere reader can't avoid being wounded by them. At the same time they evoke the sensation of looking through the wrong end of a telescope. The imposed distance makes one think about one's developing wound. It is hoped that the tension between these terms proves useful, although one cannot rest long in this hope.

Winnicott opts for a primacy of love. He emphasizes the positive aspects of soft boundaries and mutual permeability. In optimal conditions the self's struggle with its divisions (e.g., love-rage, reality-fantasy) continuously creates a fresh sense of self and other (see, Eigen, 1981, 1983b). For Bion, the status of love is ambiguous. He speaks of a conflict between love, hate, and the wish to know during analytic sessions for patient and analyst alike. In this context love can function seductively and addictively and may conflict with the drive for self-knowledge. Yet he also suggests that the quality of personality is partly determined by its love or hate of knowledge and the concomitant wish or ability to learn from experience. Still more deeply, love of knowledge is transcended by faith. For Bion faith involves a radical opening up and letting go. Nothing is held on to, not even love of knowledge. One's very being is changed by reaching out to an emotional truth, which is more than usual knowledge. For O'Connor, love also has this transforming or shattering impact. At her level love and faith presuppose each other; however, love without faith takes an addictive and manipulative turn.

In all three authors the tension between multidimensional realities is central. In Winnicott's use of the object, the primacy of love turns the moment of rage into something creative. Both love and hate are necessary to supply drama. In his writings on the transitional area implicit divisions make for the suspense of play. For Bion, faith creates the attitude that makes conflict between psychic dimensions most fruitful. In both Winnicott and Bion the structure of mystery exhibits a tension-in-unity which is dynamic. For O'Connor, too, tension is a necessary part of mystery and life.

Fragility and conflict are among the elemental terms of experience. Both require and feed each other and are part of one another. As noted earlier, a perennial conflict revolves around what sort of self I am, what sort should I become. These questions are not simply abstractions, but are rooted in the very quality of each moment of self-feeling, possibly in the very birth of self-feeling. Our sense of strength and deficiency can be in conflict as early as we choose—in complex ways even in infancy—to move toward more or less existence.

Chapter 7

Perchance to Dream

Saint Augustine opens the Bible and wherever his eyes fall are words God means for him this moment, this crossroad. These are destiny words. They give Saint Augustine courage and direction. It is time for him to go all the way, to give his life to God. He looks for a sign. Wherever the Bible opens, wherever eyes fall—chance is destiny.

The Hebrew *purim* means "lots." The Book of Esther tells how lots were cast to see which Jews lived or died. Behind the lots was the evil will of a man called Haman. The good and cunning Mordecai sent his adopted daughter, Esther, to seduce the king, Achashverus, to reverse the decree. Beautiful and wise Esther did the trick, not on her own, but with help of a dream the king had about the help Mordecai once gave him. The dream pricked the conscience of the king, but it didn't hurt that Esther sweetened the prick. The book is about the work of reversal, since Haman hung on his own gallows and many of his followers (perhaps many innocents) were killed. *Chai* means life, which encompasses lots and reversals.

Alan Watts used to shoot arrows in the air above his head. It was exhilarating for him to see if he would live or die. As chance had it, no arrow pierced him. He had to drink himself to death.

And what of those who play Russian roulette? Who lives, who dies? There are so many roulettes in life—disease, accidents, violence. I think of people I've known from childhood who are no longer here. I'm amazed I'm still here. It feels like borrowed time. I still have my little chance at living. By this time it feels like I've had many, many chances.

Going to School

I'm driving one of my boys to school. We pause at an intersection while a car crosses in front of us and slows down. A teenager sticks his head out the window and pukes. My boy and I were chatting aimlessly, pleasantly. I try to make light of the puking but I'm aware my son has a hard time with vomit. The day changes. He feels queasy.

"Oh, no!" I think. "Shit! Just when things were going nicely!"

The thought crosses my mind that this chance act is a cosmic message. The cosmos knows my son has a nervous stomach, has struggled with intestinal difficulties for many years. We feared he might develop Crone's disease or colitis or something worse. So far nothing of the sort happened. The fears were magnified dreads of parental minds. He has gotten much better.

The cosmos rubs it in. It finds/creates a weakness and milks it for all its worth, a kind of black humor cosmos. It keeps testing, creating challenges, forcing growth for those who *can* grow. But what of those who can't take it? Inwardly I'm moaning, "Why the hell did this have to happen now?"

I watch my son out of the corner of my eye. He doesn't complain but I see his face turning yellowish-greenish. He takes a couple of Tums. He hasn't eaten breakfast. I stupidly suggest he have some toast he took along, he oughtn't to got to school on an empty stomach or he won't feel well later. He looks at me as if I were a Martian and reminds me (as if I needed reminding), "I don't feel well *now*." The wry humor in his voice reassures me and I let go inwardly. He has tuned into the cosmic wink. It is all beyond me. He is moving along his own trajectory with its blessings and curses. I smile back with wry appreciation. Aspects of my life and personality dance in inner vision—no great shakes. His mess isn't any worse than mine. Who can measure? As it turns out, he has a good day. And so do I.

The Pain Machine

My mother is in her mid-eighties and her mental functions are not what they used to be. She has short term memory problems and easily panics when things do not go right. This means she forgets a lot and panics a lot. She lives alone in the house I grew up in and I wonder how long she can do this. She does not want outside help and does not want to move. All her friends are gone. The neighborhood has changed. The world she lived in is gone. Yet she stays on in the old house that is so small and fragile now, but which was huge and solid when I was a child.

I get a lot of panic calls. Things are always going wrong. The furnace stops working, circuit breakers shut off, a next door neighbor encroaches on her property. All these things happen and need attention. Last month smoke was coming from the circuit breaker box, and if the electrician delayed a few hours, the house would have burned down.

But she also calls when nothing is wrong or when what is wrong is trivial. She does not just call me. She calls repair men, the electrician, the heating company, helpful neighbors. She generates a support network, although her calls can be maddening. A few weeks ago, panicky about heat and electricity, she called the heating company twenty times in one evening. They finally sent a repair man to adjust her thermostat. She could not adjust it herself. Her eyes can't see the numbers. It was set too high and she was too terrified to turn it down a bit.

Some of her calls are dreamlike, nightmarish. She talks slowly, haltingly, like she walks. She has trouble finding words. Since my mind is much faster, I jump to conclusions, fill in blanks. A recent phone conversation went something like this:

"You know, everyone has one. You have one."

"What mom? What do I have?"

"You know—a machine."

"You mean a furnace?"

"No—a pain-machine."

"A pain machine?"

"A man comes and sets it. . . at night. You have one. He sets it for me. But he didn't come tonight."

"A man comes every night? A man comes and sets a machine? A man comes and sets a pain machine? Something to make you feel better?"

"You know what I mean. . . . You have one."

She mentions *time*. I imagine she's talking about a pain machine that's a time machine. I start getting into it and locate my own pain machine in the center of my chest. Then I come to and think, "This is it. She's lost it." I tell my wife and think of places to bring her, and settle on a really good hospital, although it is a very long drive. My wife suggests I call again to check things out and see how she's doing.

Almost as soon as I call she blurts out, "The timer. That's the name. Timer—for the lights." In an instant it becomes clear. She kept calling the timer a machine. She said time a few times but I didn't know she meant timer. The automatic light timer was thrown off when the electricity was shut off. A man was to reset the timer, but did not show up. She was disturbed that lights were going on and off at wrong times. When I asked about the word "pain," she said it was a pain, she couldn't think of the word "timer" and communicate what she meant.

I felt enormously relieved and so did she. "I was worried, mom. I thought you lost it." "I was worried, too," she said. We both feared she'd gone over the edge. After this experience, she became stronger and clearer for a week or two.

I filled in my mother's blanks with psychotic vision. A pain machine—

that's pretty good. As good as an influencing machine. I really saw it. I think of how I had to slow down when my children were very little. It could take hours to walk a block. They would play with a swinging gate for twenty minutes, wander up and down stoops, walk on walls, be attracted by this or that object or color or movement. If I dropped into their time world it was like being high. The play of chance opened worlds of possibilities.

With my poor mother, it was the opposite. Chance destroyed. Her world was populated with broken machines, invading neighbors, bad weather, threat of violence. Every chance event threatened loss of control, reduced her to helpless panic. Her powers of organization were slipping and what attracted her were symbols of her mental and physical inability to work. Where chance once meant opportunity, it now meant disability and the coming end. Chance once stimulated life and the building of structure. Now it poured vinegar into wounds of breakdown and deterioration. How sweet moments of intactness can be—when things come together for awhile, a breath of air, neither stupor nor panic. All the sweeter, as they become fewer and fewer.

Mousemare

A supervisee chats about a patient who chats a lot about boyfriends and sex. She loves sex and talks about which boyfriend makes her feel better how. Her mother does not care for her men and lifestyle. She fears her daughter will not make much of her life. She's fucking her life away. She, too, fucked her life away, but, at least, has a daughter to show for it. Her father was warmer and nicer but died. She worries, like her mother, about what will become of her. But she is having fun.

Fun, that is, up to a point. She feels the men she dates are beneath her. They are not her equals. Good in bed, not stimulating otherwise. She feels too inadequate to meet men she can talk with. She's afraid of men she can talk with. She is comfortable with sexy men who don't say much.

She tells her therapist how happy she is that her new boyfriend talks with her and that she likes talking with him. He's a bit stuffy in bed, not as good as her usual lovers. He washes himself off too quickly and is hesitant about mucousy things. But he makes up for it by mothering her. He tucks her in, cuddles, cooks for her, buys her presents. She's never felt so well taken care of.

In passing, she mentions a nightmare she had while sleeping with him. In the nightmare mice were all over the place, even in their bed. Did she get bitten? Will she get bitten? Are they growing in size and number? She was terrified.

She made light of her passing panic. She wanted to keep talking about boyfriends and sex. This one was good this way, that one that way. If only she could find one that combined the best of all worlds. She didn't want to break up with the mothering and talking one. He wasn't exactly bad in bed. It's just that he wasn't as into it as she really liked, but. . . and so on, and on.

The nightmare gets lost, dismissed, passed by. Her therapist didn't say a word about it. She got involved with the verbal flow, the boyfriend, the family stories, the daily ups and downs. The patient tries to make little of her nightmare, her panic. She tries to make terror into a little, fleeting mousy thing. But terror grows in intensity (size and number), until it has to be noticed. It demands an awakening of sorts.

I was sitting and waiting and letting the chat wash over but felt a rush when the terror of the night passed by. Something in me said, "Hold it. Wait a minute. Run that one again." I opened my mouth and out came the words, "The mousemare. But the mousemare—you said nothing about it!"

My supervisee gave me a funny look, not without interest. "Here she's telling you how comforting her boyfriend is, how soothing," I go on. "She's never been so well cared for. And she wakes up screaming. Terror wakes her. His motherly arms enfold her, and she wakes in panic."

I suppose we could have chatted about mice as sexual symbol, fear of the very thing she loves. Or perhaps they have to do with her mother's promiscuity, which must have frightened, as well as enticed her, as a child. Or perhaps she feels so tiny in her boyfriend's arms, tiny and afraid of being biting or bitten. Perhaps mice refer to the intensity of the baby self, too much for parents or anyone to handle well. We could say she can't bear the safety of her boyfriend's care, or that she finds it engulfing, suffocating. There are many things we could think or say. But the emotional fact is terror. Whatever we say, it has terror as its nucleus.

And it is precisely this terror she excludes from her chatty sessions and from her lovemaking. She is good at this exclusion, because even her therapist doesn't notice. She runs the terror past her session, whisks it away as soon as it is spoken. It is spoken but not heard.

It is not heard but is transmitted by my supervisee's notes. When my supervisee mentions the mousemare in passing, suddenly I hear nothing else. If the patient sees only sex and comfort, I see only terror. We are both reductionists. The dream is spokesman for excluded terror. My supervisee will learn to be spokesman for the dream.

Chance sexual meetings thrill this patient, but her mousemare tries to give terror a chance. The waves of the dream need to travel a distance before they have an impact. Isn't that, partly, what supervisors are for? Who knows what dwelling with this terror may open? Perhaps the dream is asking to give the unknown a chance.

A Horror Story

My patient, Max, is extraordinary. He has an amazing ability to perceive structural relations in financial systems and develop creative solutions for problems that might otherwise pass unnoticed and be destructive later. He is, also, a mechanical whiz. He can fix anything around a house or a computer. He is a master do-it-your-selfer, but runs into a wall when it comes to fixing himself.

His wife forced him into therapy because he was high strung, rarely home, and rageful. She feared their son would grow up without a father. If left to his own devices, he'd work all the time. To his credit, he found a lovely wife who wanted more than a furious workaholic.

I find Max engaging, endearing, charming, but I like eccentrics, especially brilliant ones. Nevertheless, his self-made-man rap tends to be off putting, especially when it leads to denigrating others, like his wife and co-workers, as weaker. His expectations are severe. He has to be the best and expects others to be the best too (best = strong, independent, supercompetent). It galls him that his wife, who watches more TV, sleeps more, needs down time, accesses a wider range of feelings than he and can dream.

Max is not a therapy type, but he comes to see me when a crisis hits because he now realizes he can be scary and that he scares himself. He makes sounds and gestures in his sleep that scare his wife, but remembers no dream. Then one session, in a recent trip through therapy, he comes in proudly, dangling an enormous dream, the first dream in his adult life.

Max brags about a horror story dream, in which he tells Stephen King that the latter's stories aren't scary. Max analyzes the author's stories and proves they are too hackneyed to be truly frightening. The author, with amused dismay, challenges Max to do better. Max rises to the challenges and creates a story on the spot, that King agrees is really frightening.

The story is about a criminal who finds a way to put doctors and nurses in a new-born baby ward out of play, then steals the babies and sells them to drug and porno rings. As the police close in, he sells the remaining babies as a group to the most evil ring of all.

So proud was Max of besting Stephen King that he couldn't wait to tell the dream. He told a colleague at work who was horrified. Max was so proud of his ability to create something scary, that he didn't realize it might actually affect someone negatively. He expected people to rejoice in his triumph, rather than recoil in horror.

"The dream is quite real," I said. "It expresses very real feelings in your life. Doesn't it express your feelings about being adopted?"

Max was an adopted child. The dream magnified feelings of being ripped away, stolen, sold into bondage. He was given a home, but at great expense. He was abused and neglected by his adopted mother, and his father was rarely home. When his father was home, he spent his time fixing the house. Max watched him and learned. Most of all, he learned the lesson of doing things for himself, since no one helped him. He was on his own and made the most of it.

Max flashed a look that said everything. For the moment, he was gifted with inner vision. It was hard to believe feelings from so long ago created a dream now. But he stared at the horror and hurt of it, if only for instants. He couldn't believe the dream was not only about victory, but about injury—his own. But he saw it with his own eyes and, for the first time, felt some connection to the scary sounds that tore out of him in the night, sounds he never heard himself.

Jouissance

In psychoanalysis, chance, to some extent, means repetition, the banana peel principle of life. When I least expect it and feel in the clear, I'll slip on a mishap my personality attracts, if not creates. A bad boss, a disastrous love object, my own shortsighted reactive patterns and sudden bursts of cruelty, a calamity that mirrors my damaged self—the sense that—oh-oh—here it comes again! Pow! Boom! Zap! Ouch!

How did I get myself into this jam again?

What seem to be chance events connect with deep patterns laid down in infancy and early childhood. At the same time, I may seize on chance events to break a pattern. I may do something destructive to escape a suffocating existence, to get a thrill. It is often impossible to distinguish between chance as repetition or breaking through repetition. It is more difficult than ordinarily imagined to tell the difference between old and new.

Desires are repetitious. Whether the play of Eros is capricious or linked to a soul mate, the experience and anatomy of desires have a, b, c's. We can list desires associated with fame, romance, power, and finding out about them for ourselves can be necessary fun. Some of us eventually develop maps of desires and learn a lot about what to expect of them.

There are patients too dead to have desires. Sometimes the appearance of desire means growth in aliveness. There are, also, patients who are frightened by desires. They feel if they could live them out, they would be cured. But there are others who live out all manner of desires, and still are searching. They feel as enchained as liberated by demands of desire. In this regard, it is worth noting that great literature of our past defines characters by their desires, particularly characteristic limits of desires. There are sectors of literature today in which characters are defined less by desire, than by extent of personality collapse or deterioration or lack of development.

Lacan (1977) writes of desire as a defense, a prohibition, a binding: "For desire is a defense, a prohibition against going beyond a certain limit in *jouissance*" (p. 322).

To modify this notion for my own use, if we posit a primary or originary *jouissance* (bliss/joy/ecstasy/juiciness), systems of desires function as paths or filters for the former. Let me follow my fantasy vision further. Let us call God *jouisssance*, then all God's creating of the cosmos, the heavens, the earth, living beings - all creating is *Jouissance* creating. Everything that is, is a path, a filter, a binding, a depot of *jouissance*. In one of its faces, chance is *Jouissance's* freedom.

In Biblical stories, unbounded *Jouissance* is annihilating. Can one see God and live? Dare one get too close to the Unbounded? Aharon's sons are burnt to a crisp, trying to bypass protective limits. Chance, too, is a filter, a sign, an opening. If one tries to bypass chance, and take an express to the Source or Goal, life ends.

Desire is a protective limit, as is the Law. For Lacan (1977) they go (grow) together. "The true function of the Father is to unite (and not set in opposition) a desire and the Law" (p. 321). If there were only originary *Jouissance*, there would be no place for creatures like us. We work with oppositions and unities of desire and Law, the limiting poles or structures that make us possible. Our identities are brakes and limits enabling living, and openings for the originary creative joy that makes living worth it.

W. R. Bion somewhere wrote, "Life is full of surprises. Most of them bad." But one senses *jouissance* seeping through the not so hidden background of his rueful remark.

Chapter 8

Originary *Jouissance*

In the beginning is *Jouissance*.

Call God *Jouissance*, and speak of God as eternal beginning, incessant beginning. Speak of now, not then. The then of moment, is the then of moment now.

In the beginning is *Jouissance*, and *Jouissance* in delirium sings, dances, creates the Word (poetry). Aliveness is ecstasy.

I'm nineteen and wretched, lonely. Pain is excruciating. I'm looking out my apartment window. Maybe my roommates are in classes or doing homework or messing around. It doesn't matter where they are. Aliveness is agony. Can I bear another moment? The suffering increases. I take a record off a stack and throw it on the turntable. Vivaldi—"Four Seasons." Everything changes in an instant. Joy! Such joy! I'm besides myself and throw open the window, like Scrooge the morning after. Everything shines, glistens. I'm so happy. Delirious. Ecstatic. Heart bursting. Heart of hearts alive, dancing. Who wants more? Vivaldi is a friend forever. His music is *jouissance*, sweetness that includes sorrow. It is not something I get from roommates, not like this.

The joyous, ecstatic, juicy Yes. I read it in Carlyle, in Joyce. Yes, Oh Yes. Not only an ideal yes. The Yes of Molly and Leopold Bloom, a sexy yes, a real yes, Molly jerking Bloom off into a hanky. Not a very fetching picture of yes, but yes nonetheless. A yes welling up from below, not simply an image, but a current of feeling. Nothing is more real.

Are the Vivaldi and Joyce Yes's the same? Parts of a Great Yes they lead to, come from? Two of many currents, moments, avenues? Like Yeats's soul clapping hands?

Desire Limits *Jouissance*

"For desire is a defense, a prohibition against going beyond a certain limit in *jouissance*" (Lacan, 1977, p. 322). Let me misread Lacan for my purpose. For the moment, let us again call God *Jouissance,* and imagine originary, boundless *Jouissance.* Let us say, "In the beginning there is originary, boundless, *Jouisssance.*"

If I, also, am God and ever beginning, then I, too, am originary, boundless *Jouissance.* But I am, also, not God, just plain me, a vessel of *jouissance,* a limit. You and I provide a playground for *jouissance* by placing limits on it. Our very desires place limits on *jouissance.* Our desires channel *jouissance,* filter it, make it this or that form. Our desires are steeped in and oriented toward *jouissance,* but express a lack, a gap, or we would not be so driven.

We hunger for originary *jouissance,* and originary *jouissance* hungers for us. But if originary *jouissance* is boundless, it is not merely lack that drives us. It is surplus, abundance, exuberance, the capacity for more and more life. We want more and more of a good thing. As in Dante's *Paradise,* one can always open more. There is no end to opening, to heavenly delights.

In delight's extremity, desire gets in the way. Desire brings us down, provides brakes. We pin ourselves to desires, rather than bathe in the stream of heavenly delights.

To pit delight against desire is silly, since they fuse in all sorts of ways. Yet it is helpful to think of desire not simply as a pointer toward infinity, but as a defense against it. Desires crystallize or organize *jouissance* in characteristic ways. They give *jouissance* "a local habitation and a name." Our equipment can't take too much of *jouissance* as such, but relates to *jouissance* through particular desires.

In literature, characters tend to be defined by their desires, and by particular limits placed on their desires. An inner push against internal/external obstacles or barriers sets the drama. Our sense of identity forms around our desires, particular configurations *jouissance* takes. But *jouissance* can explode or dissolve identity, lift us beyond ourselves, beyond particulars, reshape identity, bring us to new starting points.

Pleasure Limits *Jouissance*

Lacan, also, tells us that pleasure limits *jouissance.* "For it is pleasure that sets the limit on *jouissance*" (Lacan, p. 319). Pleasure "binds incoherent life together," binds *jouissance.* Like desire, pleasure defends against *jouissance,* acts as prohibition. Lacan links pleasure as prohibition with further development of binding, the elemental mental work Freud called primary process (which binds, refracts, regulates psychic life according to principle, a pleasure principle). From pleasure to pleasure principle, from raw sensation to never-ending showering of displacements-condensations feeding fireworks of culture.

Freud (1914) suggests that incoherent auto-erotic streamings are united by birth of a pleasure ego. Lacan pulls on Freudian threads to suggest that pleasure itself involves incipient shaping processes, stimulating further shaping processes. Lacan locates psychic brakes at the level of pleasure as such. Pleasure slows things down, binds, soon regulates. Pleasure binds the ego, as well as the reverse. It is as if pleasure involutes-convolutes to yield a law of pleasure, pleasurable shapes, shapes of pleasure, a shaping principle evolving. The ego, then, does not impose order by fiat, but carries inherent braking-shaping processes forward. Pleasure itself begins the work that ego threads through its needles.

Pleasure, like desire, defends against *jouissance*, places limits on the boundless. Formless pleasure forms the formless, reaching new dimensions through primary process work. Without pleasure, there would be only originary, boundless *Jouissance*, and nothing more to say. Without pleasure, there would not be *us*.

But if pleasure is the bread of the psyche, bliss or ecstasy or delirious juiciness (boundless incoherent *Jouissance*) is the wine. Plato feared poetic intoxication. He suspected poets, like sophists, might say anything to turn a phrase or win a verbal advantage. Yet what is more intoxicating than Socrates' Vision of the Good? What more beatific, joyous? The noble spokesman for mind, the great gadfly and midwife, lives by faith and vision. The light and goodness of *Jouissance* shines more brightly by limits traced in shadows and misconceptions.

Law is inscribed in pleasure, partly, because pleasure is already a kind of law. Freudian pleasure follows certain channels, takes certain forms (Freud, 1919). Pleasure binds and feeds, as well as disrupts identity. Pleasure is a kind of paste or glue the ego seizes and partly organizes itself around. We can say yes or no to this or that pleasure, channel it characteristic ways (according to our character). But pleasure is a ubiquitous part of the fabric of experience (what would experience be like without it?), and an intimate part of the way we form and sustain ourselves.

Pleasure, like desire, is a filter or opening for *Jouissance*, a necessary dampening, toning down. To mistake pleasure for *Jouissance* is to seriously downgrade our nature, but without pleasure we could not access *Jouissance*, at least not in a way that would grant any respite. Pleasure gives us a rest from *Jouissance*, at the same time that it lets us taste the latter. What is really pleasurable about pleasure is the *Jouissance* that shines through it.

Purity of Non-Being

"'I' am in the place from which a voice is heard clamoring 'the universe is a defect in the purity of Non-Being'. . . . By protecting itself this place makes Being itself languish. This place is called *Jouissance*, and it is the absence of this that makes the universe vain" (Lacan, p. 317).

Lacan is asking what is the I and what is the Other. Whatever I am, I am a lack, like the Other. I am a defect in the purity of Non-Being, like the rest of the universe. More tellingly, I am in the place from which I hear a voice, the place called *Jouissance*. While I am in the place called *Jouissance*, everything else that is not this place seems defective, less, lacking. Is *Jouissance*, then, the purity of Non-Being? Am I most I when I am in the place called *Jouissance*? What can it mean to call *Jouissance* a place or call a place *Jouissance*? One of the Hebrew nicknames (there are so many) for God is "The Place" (*Hakom*). When one says *Hakom* (The Place) one does, indeed, live *Jouissance*. Dare I say I am in *Jouissance* or I am *Jouissance*?

Is this precisely what I am forbidden to say? I am not *Jouissance* but in the place of hearing a voice say that I and the universe are not *Jouissance*. But without *Jouissance*, all is vain. Is *Jouissance*, then, on loan? Am I, too, on loan? If the loan is rich beyond reckoning, is it enough to rest on riches, or are we obliged to turn a profit?

I am a forbidden I because my secret is the fullness of *Jouissance*, precisely what I can't be. But it is this, and only this, that makes life worthwhile. Therefore, longing. Not only my longing. *Jouissance* protecting itself makes Being languish. The place from which I hear, the place called *Jouissance*, is also a hiding place.

Perhaps *Jouissance* hides from me, because I can only take so much of it, like Moses and God. Too much God, no more me. Is this why *jouissance* can be so tantalizing? It's dosed out according to what we can bear, or, really, just beyond what we can bear. One is always reaching, trying to take a little more. We are teased by what capacities can't quite do. At any time there is plenty, but also not enough and plenty more.

If *Jouissance* is the purity of Non-Being, then *Jouisssance* must be the lack of lacks, superlack. *Jouissance* is the background lack, a lack so purely lacking, that the lack the universe is can be visible. A lack so purely lacking that the universe can appear as ripples of lacks. How odd to call the fullness of *Jouissance* the lack of lacks. But *Jouissance* is not homogenous. Its inhomogeneities are the sparks we live by. The purity of Non-Being has defects, gaps, ruptures, variations, dislocations. The purity of Non-Being is alive, therefore spontaneous. There are many kinds of lacks, many lack-dimensions. The purity of Non-Being surprises itself by fluctuations in the field of *jouissance.*

Although we are not *jouissance*, we live in its fluctuations. Although we are not the purity of Non-Being, we do not feel ourselves without it.

Lack of Zero

Not even zero is adequate to signify the purity of non-being. Lacan (p. 318) envisions a lack so profound that zero fails to do it justice. Lacan's lack can not be described by zero, or zeroing zero. No multiplication of zeros will do. We go beyond zero to lack itself, including lack of nulling. One can lack zero but can not zero lack. Lack can not be nulled.

You and I and the universe share this lack. Without this lack, we would not be. Lack permeates and sustains Being. This lack is not simply cutting the umbilical cord or being torn from the breast, special subsets of lack. Fetus and embryo, also, are lacking beings. Is there a place of no lack in the universe?

Pure *Jouissance*, absolute fullness, is also pure lack, the purity of Non-Being. The defect in *jouissance* that the universe is, shares the lack of lacks, the peekaboo play of *jouissance, jouissance* "between the lines" (Lacan, p. 319). We are *jouissance* defective beings, other than *jouissance*, and *jouissance* is other to us. We are in the place *jouissance* might have been, and *jouissance* is the place we can't be. God as pure *jouissance*, is pure lack, superlack. God lacks us as we lack God. We seek each other, not only to fill up, but to live the lacks we are.

The ancient saying that to see (or touch) God is to die seems complicated today. It is even more true that we can not live without seeing God. God let Moses see his rear but no complete view. Moses, who spoke to God face to face, only got a bit of God, God's "tooshy," so to speak. This is not the same as shadows in a cave. He got to see a real part of God, God's ass, as it were. We know from experience how fun asses can be, a baby's ass, a woman's, a man's. How great it must have been for Moses to see God's.

Any bit of God we get is a lot, but it can not be the whole of *Jouissance* (there is no such thing), *jouissance* as such. It can only be a bit of *jouissance*, even if it is all we can feel at a time. Whatever *jouissance* we suffer or enjoy, pulsates, shifts. Lack is built into our experience of fullness. Maximum *Jouissance*, at any moment, is maximum fullness-lack. If it were only one or the other, it would not be so sweet.

Lurianic Kaballah has it that God contracted to make a place for the universe. The universe is in the place where God might have been. We are in God's place. If God is pure *jouissance*, we are in *jouissance's* place.

Does that mean we are substitutes for *jouissance*, that *jouissance* is inescapable, both?

Tradition tells us God is everywhere. We live in a God saturated universe. Can God be in some places more than others? Is God more alive in Jerusalem than Paris? Why not, if *jouissance* is not homogenous, if J*ouissance* is alive.

God's lack makes the fullness we feel possible. But how can God, total fullness, hold back? Doesn't God give God fully? Yes, but God as total lack, also gives lack fully, as much as we can bear. God protects us from God by giving us limits. But we are limit testing beings. We can not endure the suffering God can, but we have our share or more. We try to get closer to God by going beyond what it is possible to suffer. If God, our beloved, suffers absolutely and is, also, pure *Jouissance*, we can not settle for our lacks and agonies and joys, we can not settle for anything less than God can.

God is our lack, as we are God's. We try each other sorely. We, also, squeeze each other's juices. We are each other's orgasms, we come together. Coming intensifies rather than nullifies lack, although it may assuage lack for a time. The beatific moment of orgasmic plenitude gains power from the fathomless lack that supports it. That we can envision God as pure *Jouissance*/suffering/lack/fullness means God is more or other than what our capacities can shape, for if we shape it, it would not be God, but an idol. We have a need to shape a God that is more than we can shape, more than an idol. We have a need to create a God that is something we lack, a signifier of lack as such, a lack that can't be voided by zero.

Barred Other

Lacan speaks of a barred subject ($) and barred Other (S(Ø)). The bar has many meanings. It might mean canceled, nulled, voided. But it is a nulling or voiding that is essential. Where can one find the subject, or the Other subject? Subject and Other can not be localized. They can not be given a local habitation and a name, although one may try. They exceed or dodge names given to them. They remain, in inescapable ways, airy nothings.

Lacan's obsession with psychoanalysis and language gives this ancient theme special turns. We are barred from ourselves by virtue of the structure of the unconscious and language. If a repressed unconscious is essential to who we are, then the unconscious is, partly, a barred Other. Language, too, bars us from direct contact with ourselves and objects. If we are given to ourselves through meaning, then who we are depends on what we mean to ourselves and each other. Language mediates contact. Objects gain value by what they mean for us. Objects are signifiers, like words. We are barred from reaching the object bereft of what it means for us. Whatever self might mean, or God: they are values within chains of signifiers.

Lacan brings the repressed unconscious and language together by proposing that "the unconscious of the subject is the discourse of the other" (p. 55). Other has multiple meanings. Other is another subject. The desire of the other helps constitute our desire. We are inserted into worlds of meaning that orient and disorient our lives. The unconscious, also, is not simply a repository of interpersonal others, but is itself a structural other, another language. The unconscious is, partly, primary process language working through displacement-condensation, symbolization, and the like, or as Lacan expresses it, through metonymy-metaphor.

We are constituted through the barred Other (S($\emptyset$)). We are not transparent to ourselves. Our heart is bathed in unfathomable opacity. To say we are intersubjective is to say, partly, we are informed by the unconscious desire of the Other, the other as unconscious subject, the other as unconscious language, the other as primary process work. We are supported/shaken by shell games of unconscious meaning as revelation/ resistance to ourselves, unconscious creation of ourselves. Lacan speaks for the *un*—or *not* conscious—the *un*conscious work consciousness can not fully appropriate. This is not simply consciousness of lack or lack as consciousness. To think unconscious processing ought or might be overcome is megalomaniacal, if not naive. Still, our relationship with lack can deepen and evolve on many levels, including our relationship to the unconscious-conscious signifying capacity that helps make us what we are.

The barred Other (S($\emptyset$)) is a strong signifier of indelible and ineradicable lack that structures human subjectivity. When commentators try to fill in lack or convert it to something social, Lacan dramatically asserts that lack can not be filled or nulled, not by a Manna object, not by zero. S($\emptyset$) signifies lack of zero also (p. 318). Lacan goes as far as saying that the Other does not exist (p. 323). Can we get to an Other through our fantasies, images, desires? Is the Other always a signifier? The Other may not exist, but lack never stops existing.

Lacan tells us we are not simply constituted through the Other, but through a lack in the Other. S($\emptyset$) signifies "a lack in the Other" (p. 316). This lack is not something contingent on object relations, the faults of another, the other not being there. This lack structures object relations and may be dealt with in different ways in psychosis, neurosis, perversion. This is not to say that abandoning-invasive objects are not real or fantasies: they may be both. But no real or fantasy object can fill or null the lack that structures it and that it signifies.

For many, the lack that structures us is unbearable. Abandonment-invasion are, partly, attempts to escape the unbearable, cruel ways to structure the lack that structures us. On the other hand, there are circumstances in which lack is wished for, as when we wish that something bad not be there. We see posters with wished for prohibitions that use the bar: no smoking, no drugs, no war. In these cases a wish that x not be there, a wished for lack, is an attempt to null or undo or void a destructive presence.

Lacan's bar is more radical and subversive. It announces a necessary lack that is part of the creation of meaning. To trifle with this lack courts disaster. To begin to apprehend and work with this lack is saying yes to the life of meaning. Lacan, also, feels that the lack through which we are given to ourselves is precious. $S(\emptyset)$ as signifier of a lack in the Other, functions as "the treasure of the signifier" (p. 316). We may or may not be able to reach each other through our meanings, but what we mean to each other is more treasure than chests contain.

In an analogous way, Bion (1965) stresses the importance of being able to tolerate no-thing (Eigen, 1996). The need to fill gaps or lack or no-thing can turn no-thing into a thing, often menacingly. Bion notes one needs to tolerate meaninglessness in order for meaning to be meaningful. Lacan speaks of a lack inherent in the possibility of meaning. They overlap in recognition of x that isn't there, in order for whatever is there to evolve.

Lacan's barred Other $(S(\emptyset))$ expresses inherent lack that makes the treasure of meaning possible. It is a privileged signifier, since without it, meaning would vanish altogether. If the Other were not a signifier, meaning would have no meaning. Meaning can only arise in a context in which the Other means. If the Other were not part of the signifying chain, there would be no signifying chain.

Lacan's definition of signifier is that which "represents the subject for another signifier" (p. 316). It is less "I think, so am," than "I signify, I mean, and go on meaning." The I is part of signifying chains, constituted by beginingless/endless layers of meaning. What all signifiers have in common is they imply a subject who signifies, the treasure. But there is no meaning in a vacuum. There would be no signifying subject with no Other to signify, or with no signifying Other. $S(\emptyset)$ is "the signifier for which all the other signifiers represent the subject" (p. 316). $S(\emptyset)$ tells us we are subjects, an immense lack that is a treasure. We are signifying beings who access ourselves through meaning. Whatever we mean points to one who means, and the one who means is part of a never-ending flow of meaning.

Castration

For Lacan, the castration complex structures the subject (p. 318). It is signifier *par excellence* of barred subject/barred Other, signifier of gap or lack. The idea of castration is lack as threat. One thing that is lacking is the literal. The literal penis becomes a center of symbolic drama, literal no more, if ever it was. Penis transforms into symbolic phallus, signifier rather than literal thing. What is lacking is not the literal penis, but the penis as literal. The letter kills, the spirit gives life. To reduce phallus to penis is a kind of reverse castration or psychic truncation.

The more one meditates on the castration complex, the more profound and elusive lack becomes. The erectile organ grows into a symbol of "the place of *jouissance*, not in itself, or even in the form of an image, but as a part lacking in the desired image" (p. 320). The phallus becomes a *jouissance* symbol, not simply because of the pleasure the penis affords, but because even its pleasure can not fill the gap, is no substitute for the gap. The phallus becomes a kind of symbol for maximum pleasure-maximum lack.

Maximum gratification points to and opens fields of infinite *jouissance* beyond the maximum. No pleasure exhausts the infinitude of *jouissance*. What is points to the more that isn't, the other that is not yet. Castration is inherent in the phallic symbol, since everything an organ gives hints at infinitudes of *jouisssance*. The phallus is meaningful in its lack and promise, not only for what the penis can or can't do.

For Lacan, prohibition and guilt are not only induced by social pressures. They, also, structure social pressures. They are psychic brakes or filters that mediate and regulate dosage of *jouissance*. Guilt is original, not merely derived. A guiltless psyche would drown in *jouissance*. Guilt/prohibition tones *jouissance* down, enables the latter to be uplifting. Guilt/prohibition that is part of the phallus as signifier of *jouissance*, makes one appreciate all the more the *jouisssance* one experiences. For Lacan, the castration complex is a structural prism through which *jouissance* is refracted in our lives.

The psychotic tries to undo the prism of castration by being one with the forbidden object, as if there were oneness prior to prohibition. For the pervert, fantasies of becoming an "instrument of the Other's *jouissance*" substitute for lack or Ø (p. 320). The neurotic fills lack with demand masking fear of desire and substitutes an ideal of mastery of perfect or dead objects for alive relationships structured by Ø, one who lacks. The neurotic wants to be more alive but goes after life in self-defeating ways, trying to control what he wishes-fears. The pervert tastes life through his image of the Other's dominance-submission, proxy of his own. The psychotic seeks *jouissance* as such, unmediated by symbols and defaults into nameless dread.

One thing lacking in the above scenarios is "the true function of the Father, which is fundamentally to unite (and not to set in opposition) a desire and the Law" (p. 321). The father principle structures *jouissance*, and makes the latter a possibility of real living, rather than vain self-consumption. The neurotic's wished for ideal father is a fantasy that ultimately deadens life. One may wish for an ideal substitute for a bad reality, but that cuts one off from discovering what living offers. One may try to undo the symbolic father entirely (psychosis) or submit to, enslave, or tantalize an imaginary father proxy (perversion). But underneath is opposition of desire and Law, rebellion and mayhem, circuitous slavery, obedience, tyranny. The function of the Father is to unite (rather than dissolve) opposites. The symbolic Father is a conduit of *Jouissance*, an invitation to fulfillment of what one can give to life, what life one can give (as in loving God with "all your heart, soul, might"). The prophets speak of circumcision of the heart, castration that gives life.

Passage

Where do I and Other originate? We originate in *Jouissance*. Originary *jouissance* passes through the father funnel. Prohibition-Law grow out of an "almost natural barrier." But the Father is not only prohibition and Law, but a uniting principle, signifier of uniting (affirming), not collapsing, opposites (desire-Law). The Father is a Yes-sayer, not to simplified pleasures, but to complex tensions, the commingling of seemingly warring elements that make up living. No is necessary, but not sufficient. Yes alone is empty. The Father says it may be possible to make something out of the diverse elements of one's make-up, without denigrating the contribution of any sibling in one's soul. Not less than No, but more than Yes. This, indeed, is a new Father, not the father that causes one life to prosper at another's expense. Father as signifier that everything is possible, including evolution of the prohibition-desire helix.

Jouissance is not stationary, no unmoved mover. *Jouissance* is pulsating, evolving with its conduits and signifiers (us and our products), singing new songs. It is in our sinews and skin, not just our symbols. It is in our laughter, our movement between sorrow and joy. *Jouissance*, too, is a signifier, of what life can offer. It signifies, among other things, its own realness, the taste of life.

Chapter 9

Serving *Jouissance*

Castration governs desire, says Lacan (1977, p. 323). Lacan's sorcery thickens the meaning of the pivotal role castration had for Freud (1937) to the end (pp. 250-253). For Lacan, castration is a structural underpinning of psychic life, a privileged condition that makes the kind of psychic life we know possible. We would not be the sort of psychic beings we are, if castration were not a defining structural principle.

Castration is repressed, hidden, yet clung to. One clings to what one denies and denies what one clings to. Psychic formations grow around castration dread in ceaseless variation. Multiple levels and qualities of castration fantasies are used to defend against one another.

The neurotic clings to an enslaving imaginary castration to avoid a deeper, freeing castration. The neurotic hides, denies, clings to, refuses to sacrifice his imaginary castration. One's fantasy of being castrated is used as a defense to hide just how castrated one really is. At the same time, imaginary castration wards off interactions that increase the genuine play of *jouissance* between people.

Clinging to imaginary castration may heighten a master or slave position. Either may be used to bolster ego defensiveness. Lacan points out that the so-called strong ego, once a valued goal of many analysts, gains an illusion of strength, partly, by making believe it is not castrated. By denying deep castration, it ends fighting even superficial castration threats.

Denial of castration makes the ego's assertion of strength potentially destructive. Imaginary castration threats are used to justify the ego's defensive-offensive poses. Here is a list of some positions the strength that denies castration leads to:

1. *My ego is the most important thing*. (I justify the centrality of my ego as a fight against castration.)

2. *I'm not going to submit to castration by you.* (The possibility of your gaining *jouissance* through me would irritate, distress, even annihilate me if I am not credited.)

3. *I'm going to lead my own life.* (Only an imaginary ego tries to fabricate a life without the *jouissance* no one owns, given to all. Otherness protects the life of *jouissance* from perversely megalomanic ownership, i.e., destruction. We are enlivened by *jouissance* that supports us, neither created nor owned.)

4. *I'm not going to submit to your desire, your version of me.* (My fight against submission/castration justifies my not taking your desire and version of me into account. Indignation and its ploys substitute for respect.)

5. *I'm going to submit only to my own ego, and you should submit to it too.* (If anyone is to be castrated, let it be you. It is one of the great sleights of mind to imagine that my submitting to my own ego is not a self-castrating act).

In the above assertions the imaginary ego presents itself in a quasi-heroic militaristic stance. An aggressive, paranoid attack is unleashed against whatever does not support the ego. One reduces to absurdity the drive to find out who one really is, making short shrift of complexities and difficulties that beset quivering identities.

The simplicity of ego's reductive position is remarkable. In extreme form, my fear that you are going to castrate me gives me the right to have my way, even kill you. The imaginary ego presents itself as non-castrated and uses defenses to maintain its fictional non-castration against imaginary castration. Its unconscious slogan is: "I'm not castrated, never was or will be." And its corollary: "I use my denied castration to justify victimizing others." One uses shifting sands of imaginary castration to justify a position of ego mastery. Such chronic psychic oversimplification leads to inability to compromise, if compromising one's position means castration or the latter's denial.

A climax of analysis involves discovery of authentic, structural castration, which makes opening to and serving the *jouissance* of the Other possible. To serve the *jouissance* of the Other is not the same as serving the Other's desire. *Jouissance* is more or other than desire, since desire acts as a defense against *jouissance*, limits *jouissance*, prohibits the full play of *jouissance* (Lacan, 1977, p. 322). In a way, desire is a kind of filter system that configures the *jouissance* that supports it. Desire can tyrannize *jouissance,* forcing it into this or that mold or script. *Jouissance* is more primary than desire. To taste unbounded *jouissance* sets one free from desire.

There is a deep structural relation between castration and *jouissance* that subtends desire. Authentic castration serves *jouissance.* Serve here does not mean submission or anything servile. Serving *jouissance* involves getting past rigid assertions of ego fictions. *Jouissance* is freedom, if one connects with the *Ein Soph* of castration and its generic subsets, its psychoanalytic sephirot.

Imaginary castration is not the same as the castration that serves. Imaginary castration uses the servile state in service of being on top. "Poor me, I'm a victim [castrated]" gives me permission to be a bastard. A young male patient recently told me that a submissive woman he engaged became increasingly nasty and controlling. To his surprise, he got a better deal from a woman who gave him a tougher time from the outset, but appreciated him. The submissive woman blamed him for her submissiveness, and kept attacking him from behind. The more she insisted she was a victim, the more he felt victimized.

It may well be that his "submissive woman" was trying to organize unbearable traumas/injustices inflicted by caretakers and society. The practical effect was to make him wonder where the stones were coming from and run away. She initially switched on his fantasy of being master to her slave, but could not endure slavery and attacked. The drama was imaginary, the pain real. She became a relentless persecutor, blaming him for not loving her enough. He became guilty for lacking the love that would cure her. In the end, the relationship reduced itself to whether or not he would love her enough to make her pain go away. Would he be a good enough slave for her to master life's evil?

The net result of their time together was to kill *jouissance.* He sought therapy because they were glued together in pain. Her self-serving use of masochistic slavery in order to get something, tied him in knots. She wanted love, healing, justice, revenge, mastery—but got pain, and more pain. Instead of a pleasure ego, a pain ego. There are instances in which the drive to kill *jouissance* gains momentum and one secures a perverse sense of mastery by creating pain.

One points to one's castration in the imaginary key with the innuendo—"You did it. Fix me." No matter that there may be deeper wounds beneath the fiction one creates and the imaginary revenge one exacts. Real wounds are coated by imaginary scenarios that keep the former at bey, yet taste them far away. Imaginary castration is milked for all its worth by an imaginary ego bent on spoiling what it can't enjoy.

The castration that serves *jouissance* is of another order, akin to Israel as Bride of God. Israel serves God like castration serves *jouissance*. All the terms of such an analogy serve each other. For instance, we (brides) serve each other's *jouissance*, while *jouissance* is, also, bride that serves and is served. Genuine castration is like a hole in the omnipotent ego that lets *jouissance* shine through.

Ego omnipotence sees castration everywhere. Danger is omnipresent. The other exists as support or threat to ego omnipotence. Omnipotence precludes mutuality. To act as if one's wish to be Absolute Master had real prerogatives substitutes dread of failure for the sacrifice/castration that supports mutuality (serving each other's *jouissance*).

It is possible for the parties involved to elect an omnipotent ego and distribute roles accordingly, a kind of parody of mutuality, which is not uncommon. This gets into the problem of democratically electing a tyrant, which makes democracy impossible. Psychic democracy is a fragile and difficult achievement, very much in the process of evolving. Oscillation between psychic democracy-tyranny is often a moment-to-moment affair, since both tendencies are part of one's make-up.

Opening to the mutuality of *jouissance* is a decisive experience. Once tasting the beauty and depth of such an opening, it is difficult to return to tyranny without regrets. One can try to extract the Other's *jouissance* by flattery and intimidation and there is no question that such procedures are enjoyable. But once the precious, life-giving free-flow of *jouissance* is tasted, nothing is quite as good.

To get more of the best stuff, one learns to modulate one's tyrannical-servile sides. This may mean a battle that lasts a lifetime. The story of Abraham circumcising himself as an old man, in order to get closer to God, represents something of the self-castration needed to become more open. Indeed, the prophets speak of circumcising the heart, not flesh, turning a heart of stone to flesh, becoming a compassionate, feeling being.

Anything less than the spontaneous interplay of free-flowing *jouissance* pales. But what agonies one may need to go through to prepare an opening in one's heart for it, and keep opening. As fast as heart opens, imaginary ego rushes in with fictitious claims and self-serving scripts. The ego incessantly bends the *jouissance* of the Other to its prevailing catalogue of desires. Indeed, a servile tyrannical ego may be expert at attuning itself to the desire of the Other, in order to capture *jouissance*.

Jouissance bursts desire. That is, experiencing free-flowing *jouissance* puts one in touch with joy-bliss-pleasure greater than desire and the latter's control systems. One wants more and more of *jouissance* as such, and desire gets in the way. Once *jouissance* gets stronger, it creates a perspective in which desiring activity begins to look differently. So much of what ego imagined was so important shrinks, as the *jouissance* that informs aliveness grows. Uniting with *jouissance* in the world around one becomes more fun and interesting than dominating objects of desire.

Imaginary castration is not the castration that serves. Imaginary castration bolsters the illusion of ego mastery. For example, one may deny weakness and cultivate a persona of strength. Or one may milk one's sense of weakness for all its worth, using it deviously to gain momentary advantage. Even if one is a tyrant or slave in reality, the *fantasy* of being a tyrant-slave supplies the libidinal momentum, without which role playing collapses. It is what imagination contributes to power-powerlessness that makes the drama feel juicy. If, for some reason, imagination lost its hypnotic power, the power-driven ego would wilt.

Imaginary castration-mastery defends against sacrificial opening. The imaginary ego dreads discovery of the castration that frees. If it gives up the fiction of power, what will it have? If it can not cling to the illusion of mastery and control, what will become of it? What will become of its ambition, if it discovers it is dependent on uncontrollable *jouissance*?

To serve the *jouissance* of the Other involves castration of control. Once tasting the unbegrudging generosity of free-flowing *jouissance*, it is difficult to go back to control dramas. Control and anxiety will always be part of one's equipment, but the primacy of *jouissance* provides an experiential touchstone outside dominance and anxiety paradigms. The centrality of *jouissance* frees one to protect and serve the other's dignity and rights, for without the *jouissance* of the Other, there would be no *jouissance* at all.

If one can't serve *jouissance*, if one can't reach the *jouissance* of the Other in at least some mustard seed form, then one has to live a life of imaginary castration mastery. In the latter case, Lacan (1977) tells us, one feels, at bottom, "most vain in existing, a Want-to-be or Too-much-of-it" (p. 323). At bottom the "neurotic" feels his existence is vain because he keeps on boosting his imaginary ego. One could say the same of the "borderline", "narcissist" or "psychotic" by delineating specific variants of imaginary ego castration mastery dramas. Lacan's fingering the vanity underlying imaginary ego mastery (linked with denial of castration or milking the latter) contributes additional turns of meaning to the "false self" (Winnicott, 1974), with an almost biblical ring.

Serving *jouissance* is the one thing that is not vain. To put it in a somewhat Buddhist vein, we are here to bring everyone to fulfillment. Our job is to bring *jouissance* into people's lives, to inspire people to a *jouissance* life.

Is this possible in face of the hold the imaginary ego has on humanity? Why should one sacrifice imaginary ego addiction if there is nothing to hold on to? At least one can hold ego fictions to be true identities. So often society reinforces counterfeit identities as the real thing. It is difficult to drop the official, phony, uncastrated stance and say, "We don't know who we are."

The neurotic is attached to an imaginary other, a nonexistent other who demands castration, so must be fought or served. Why should he sacrifice imaginary difference for the real thing? The leap from fighting imaginary threats to an authentic sacrificial life in service of *jouisssance* seems impossible. How does one move from the castration anxiety that prohibits, to going through the castration that opens life? The gulf between maintaining imaginary ego addiction and falling into the hands of the living God seems infinite. But we are infinity dancers. We dance between infinities and from one infinity to another, hopping over and on infinity rocks on infinite streams.

The sacrificial castration that opens one's heart brings one into a saving relation with who one isn't and who the other isn't. I am not the imaginary hero of my omnipotent ego dreams, nor is the Other what I imagined. We are much worse and better than anything we thought we were or wanted.

You and I as living gods, bearers of *jouissance* who serve the *jouissance* of the Other, do not exist as something we can posit. What does not exist is the you I say you are, the me you want me to be. My version of you does not cover the territory. What you say about you does not either. To reach what counts for ourselves and each other, our knowledge of who we are undergoes castration. It is precisely the you I don't know that makes the you I know bearable, fetching. What counts more than knowing is the *Ein Soph* of you, the unknowable, indefinable You. Always, the inexhaustible Mystery. Living in the *Ein Soph* of each another is activity in the goal region.

Yet we posit the Other we don't know as existing. The unknowable Other supports our knowing-imagining activity. We even enjoy the unknowable Other. As the old saw goes, if we are in a dinosaur's dream of existence, existence exists, even as a dream (whatever existence or a dream of existence or a dinosaur may be). Existence goes on existing as we are talking about it, although it eludes our grasp.

The unknowable Other is precisely what Lacan's (1977, p. 323) neurotic can't enjoy. It is precisely what can't be controlled and known that is unbearable. "Cure" involves reaching the place where one can say, "Yes, I can serve your *jouissance*, you whom I can never know, the *jouissance* I can never control."

The neurotic wants to serve his own version of the other with a precise and exacting set of fantasies. There is little tolerance of deviation. In a sense, the neurotic has no ability to serve at all, since for him, serving is always in the service of control. Whether servile or bossy, master or slave, whichever side of the coin, the control drama goes on. Whether master or slave, one knows what one is getting into, what is expected. To serve *jouissance* is to break free, for no two moments ask the same thing. Where *jouissance* is concerned, there is only learning on the job, the surprise of *jouissance* where one least expects it.

Chapter 10

One Reality

What is your original face, before you were born? I've always loved this koan, since first reading it 40 years ago. My original face—before I was born. Just thinking this makes me breathe easier. Even now, at 60, I feel my soul smile and my body open as I think these words.

How many things can one read at 20, and still love and learn from at 60? Zen and Torah—I've not tired of either. I must quickly add, *my* Zen, *my* Torah, for I study neither formally, nor do I have a formal teacher. I go my way. But Buddhism and Judaism are among my umbilical connections to the universe, lifelines to the mother-ship, as I swim in space.

Suzuki and Buber

In 1957, I saw D. T. Suzuki speak in a big church on the seven circles of love and we had tea afterwards. I was quite an idealizing youth. I worshiped wisdom and its messengers. I doubt I was able to open my mouth around Suzuki but I sucked in his presence, through my eyes, my pores. I kept looking at him and what I saw was a man being himself, not trying to make an impression, gracious perhaps, but solid as rock.

He was very old and pretty deaf and the effect of his presence may have had a lot to do with age. But an offhand remark he made stuck with me. Someone must have asked a question about activity-passivity and he responded with a delightful outburst, "Passivity, passivity. What's wrong with passivity?" He then listed Western passive pleasures he enjoyed, such as sitting in a movie, flying in planes. I instantly relaxed—the pressure to be active seemed suddenly to have lifted. It was as if I felt guilty about being passive without knowing it. I secretly liked being passive and now it was OK. So often offhand remarks have a greater impact than systematic discourse.

The same year I read Eric Fromm's *The Art of Loving*, which I liked. Fromm had just spent several months with Suzuki in Mexico that year, but when Suzuki was later asked a question about Fromm, he didn't remember him, causing some snickers among us college kids. I wonder whether there was something too activist in Fromm, something that Suzuki's remark cut through. His outburst included yet went beyond Western hyperactivity and depreciation of passivity (Aristotle's God— pure activity, the highest rationality: God forbid God should be passive, God forbid God should have a day of rest, a Sabbath—the Sabbath point of soul).

I saw Martin Buber speak in a big synagogue around the same time. I don't remember much about what he said (nor do I remember much about Suzuki's circles of love). But I was fascinated by the *way* Buber spoke. Too mannered, perhaps, but entrancing—the way he lowered his head into his arms after saying something, waiting for the next revelation. He took time between utterances, time to pause, to listen. For Buber, speaking was a way of listening. *Shema Yisroael*: "Hear, Israel." Buber heard, and when he heard, we heard. By speaking, Buber was teaching listening.

My memory has Buber with a flowing white beard, Suzuki clean shaven. Both old men, Buber thick boned with the thunder and lightning of Sinai crackling off him, Suzuki thinner and still, unafraid to let death show in his eyes. Light reflected off Buber and gathered into Suzuki. Suzuki had a lighter, ticklier touch. For Buber, listening was electrifying. There was rest, quiet, pause between, but expect to be burnt by the tongue's fire.

Buber's death between utterances was anticipatory. One emptied self in order to be ready for the next Thou surge, from moment of meeting to moment of meeting, waves of impacts. Suzuki's emptiness was not like Buber's waiting: it was emptiness itself. What a relief to be empty, not a transition to the next God surge.

Emptiness and the I-Thou moment of impact. We thrive on both. We need more than one breast, more than one eye.

Idealization of Buddhism

There is hope that Buddhism will succeed where Western religions have failed. Many westerners look to the East for what is missing in their lives. Experience teaches us that it is dangerous to think that any one system of belief will supply everything. There is always something missing, something wrong.

Healthy skepticism protects against blind faith. Healthy faith protects against nihilistic skepticism. We are made of multiple systems capable of providing some checks and balances. It is important not to expect too little or too much of a great teaching. I don't know, for example, that freedom from suffering is necessary, possible, or desirable. In the United States, for example, many think that practicing Buddhism will end suffering, rather than change one's relationship to the latter.

Bliss, ecstasy, joy, nirvana, the beatific state are real. But how does one relate to the primacy of ecstasy? How is ecstasy used? Is faith free of violence? Buddhism is supposed to be non-violent, but is anything non-violent in fact? Like every practice, Buddhism has casualties and involves violence to self and others in many ways. Buddhist patients have the same sins and foibles as everyone else.

Owen

Owen is a dedicated meditator who fears he will do something destructive to those in his care. He is depressed and anxious and having trouble functioning. Yet he is filled with self-importance.

As he eyes me, I can feel him placing me beneath him. I'm not worthy to be the therapist of an experienced Buddhist teacher. He does not think he should have to see a therapist after years of meditation, especially one like me. He is used to surroundings more elegant than my run-down office. He has a better self-image and sense of worth than I do. He is *someone*—and I am not even a systematic meditator.

He is taking medication cocktails, but they have failed to relieve his anxiety, depression, and fear of destruction. I wonder whether he can deepen his meditation practice, rely more on meditation than medication. But how?

He complains he feels nothing, he is dead. Perhaps he is not dead enough. Perhaps he has died the wrong way—he so clings to his teacherly self.

Owen confesses that while he helps students he also has erotic liaisons with them. He is especially helpful to young women whose lives are in disarray. He is attracted to those in need and provokes erotic payment. He feels only a little guilty, since he greatly helps others who give a bit of pleasure in return. He seems to imply that what they give does not match what they get.

"Do you hear your tone?" I ask. "You seem to denigrate what they give you, as I feel denigrated by your glance."

"Yes—I do feel they owe me something. It's the least they can do. I can't help it. It comes over me. I feel it building for weeks, months, sometimes longer. I find a way to manipulate the one I want into a position where it has to happen. They follow suit, fall into it. Then I'm enraged when they don't want to do it anymore, when they want to break free. I feel they're not grateful for all I've done for them. It plays itself out. I find another one."

"You watch with a cold eye."

"Yes. And there's nothing to do about it. I can't fight it and don't really try. I don't want to stop it. It's something that happens. It's part of my karma. It's not so bad considering the good I do. It's two people doing good for each other."

"But it doesn't solve your depression."

"It used to make me feel better than it does now. Now it's more something that happens, that runs itself out. It used to make me feel more alive."

Owen's wheels are spinning. He is caught in a progressive self-deadening process. While he is popular, sought after, in the limelight, Eros deadens more than enriches him. He goes through the motions. Yet his whole life is Buddhism. He loves the Dharma—up to a point. He can give himself to transformation through the teachings only so far—no more.

The problem is not simply a matter of ego or self, but something more inclusive, more fundamental: wounds that haven't healed, have misshaped his personality, and warped the structure of his being. Owen supplied well rehearsed versions of his personal history. Doting, controlling mother, weak, nice father. He feels his problem is not that his parents hurt him, but that they indulged him. His mother idolized him, expected him to shine. (For a relevant discussion of the "idolized self" see Khan, 1979, Chapter 1.) Shine he did. He felt more catered to than injured by her domineering nature.

Yet I sense a deeply wounded, if triumphant man here. Owen can't recognize the violence done to his soul. He is, partly, a fusion of divine child and domineering/nourishing mother.

I imagine myself as Owen and look through layers of personality formation. What is it like for Owen as a new-born baby, a six-month-old, an eight-month-old, and so on? What choices does the baby have, given the conditions he lives in?

I picture Owen breathing in his mother's controlling idolization, and the subsequent growth of self-idolatry. It was not that Owen feared not being idolized. It was simply all he knew. Life had never forced him to feel lowly. He had no idea what he missed by not feeling sufficiently wounded, violated. The wounded, broken women he helps carry brokenness for him. He lives brokenness by proxy, vicariously. Is it possible to be out of contact with something missing, something never properly owned, perhaps something he was not allowed to have? Was a shattered baby intolerable to Owen's mother?

Owen became too strong, too fast. He became one who nourished others and was worshiped and Eros was part of the brew. The self-other fusion of helper-helped seemed a piece with the idolization-nourishment Owen was born into. Apparently Owen's mother was herself nourished by Owen's submission to this idolization, and Owen remained addicted to variations of this dynamic all his life—a silent warp that made him successful, but eventually deadened him.

Owen complains about deadness, depression, anxiety, fear of destructiveness—but he does not seem wounded or shattered or broken. He does not seem torn by his panicky depression, and expects to remain its master. It is as if the bad things happening to him are foreign aberrations or don't count. They are happening to him, but are not him. He does not identify with the suffering he is enduring. Has he prematurely emptied himself of self? If so, he has done so very selectively, as can be seen from his erotic possessiveness. As a Buddhist, oughtn't he see the bad things happening to him as a result of past actions, as a challenge, as something belonging to his life task? Are there ways in which Owen isn't Buddhist enough?

As a psychologist, I would argue that Owen did not possess—he was not given—the equipment necessary to process misery, disability, limits, ordinariness, warp. Hyperdetached and critical, he was a parody of separateness. His cold eye spots flaws in me, false moves, and as a result he can not allow much emotional flow between us. Owen lacks a full range of emotions—they are undeveloped, unlived. He became a specialist in reenacting the emotional dynamic he learned from his mother, and subtly amplified it as a meditation teacher. Unable to see his pain as intrinsic to the shape of his psyche, he'd rather get rid of or manage it. He does not have a desperate enough feel for the deformation he has undergone, and treats what haunts him now like dead skin he wishes to shed.

I picture how pleasurable meditation must have been for Owen as a young man. Inflated maternal support blossomed in the Void. He loved retreats and was generous to others. Any selfishness could easily be justified by his youth. He never really had to struggle with the warp, and if his teachers saw it, they did not press him. He kept sitting—letting life unfold. Since he was instructed not to hold on to what came up, he sidestepped wrestling with the internalized maternal idolization that, partly, fueled his meditation practice. He was a great student, and great teacher.

How did the warp slip through everyone's fingers? Owen must have been an ideal student, but did he ever work with a real spiritual master in a day in-day out way? I think of Schneur Zalman's depiction of the war between good and evil inclinations that is part of the wisdom path, and know Buddhism has equivalents. Owen somehow skipped this struggle. In Owen's case, is deadness growing where struggle might have been? Is deadness a substitute for wrestling with himself?

If only Owen would stay long enough to wrestle with me, but he no longer has to stay anywhere if he does not get his way. I suspect Owen suffers from I-Thou deprivation. He needs less emptiness. Fighting it out with an ordinary psychotherapist who has a taste for wisdom would be a start. Owen managed to incorporate the Buddhist world in clever extensions of the mother-son field, permutations of idolizing nourishment coupled with critical detachment. But he never wept through the night because of his faults.

It would be harder to bypass himself in a therapeutic relationship. If one stays in therapy, sooner or later one comes up against what is wrong with the therapy relationship. What is wrong with the therapy relationship is not something one can easily manipulate one's way out of, short of leaving, or agreeing to lie to oneself. It is something to weep over and try to change. Oddly, trying to change the unchangeable, and weeping over inability, promotes a kind of growth. The tone and texture and resonance of personality deepen.

Owen might or might not need erotic connections with dependents all his life. But struggling with his warps, his limits, his personal impossible might lead to fuller, less manipulative and exploitative relationships, possibly it might even lead to more pleasure. Of course, Owen may need to be devious. He is addicted to silent slyness. But his acceptance of his style is too easy, premature. The reconciliation that comes after doing battle with oneself, does not have the same offensive-defensive tone that lifelong avoidance does.

Battering his head against a wall in therapy could make Owen more appreciative of what he really takes from others. Owen denigrates the other because he does not feel the latter gives freely—a Catch 22, since Owen slyly coerces the other into giving. A basic issue in therapy is determining whether give and take is possible outside of coercion. It would not be surprising to learn that Owen's denigrating tongue and cold eye are manifestations of pervasive self-hatred. It is easy to imagine that the hyperidolization his mother subjected him to (deforming his growth), offset her own self-hatred as well.

Owen may well have done enough good in this life to slip into a human form again in his next incarnation. Perhaps the struggle with self will be joined a bit more in his next life. But there are opportunities in this life as well.

Jesse

Jesse sought help for what other doctors had diagnosed as chronic fatigue syndrome. He had tried a number of medical treatments but still felt listless and nauseous much of the time. Self-employed, he did very well crunching numbers for Wall Street firms.

Now is his late thirties, Jesse was a serious meditator, and had been a Buddhist for nearly fifteen years. Meditation catalyzed his creativity and heightened his already acute awareness of shifting sensations, moods, feelings. Enlivening thoughts and visions would come to him. His teachers told him to let contents of awareness freely come and go, but some times he was guided to slow down and direct his attention to aspects of what he was experiencing so as to better observe, control and explore certain states. To some extent, meditation acted as a container for his sensitivity but could also be a stimulant that exploded containers, now soothing, now heightening.

As I got to know Jesse, I discerned a curious, repetitive pattern that characterized his meditation sessions. While meditating, he developed convictions about women he should see or break up with. It would dawn on him that a woman he hadn't properly considered, was really right for him. He would call her and they would get together. As time went on, he came to know, with equal conviction, that she wasn't right after all. He could do better. This sequence might involve the same woman on and off for years, or different women.

Something similar happened professionally. While meditating, he would get ideas about what sort of work would be better and how he might go about improving things for himself. He was able to make a lot of money with minimal exertion by the time I met him. He scarcely had to move three yards or put in more than a few afternoons a week (or every couple of weeks) to make more than enough for a month. However, his material success did not translate into successful relationships—unless one measures success by numbers. His insensitivity to the women in his life amazed me. He was so in touch, so sensitive, with what was right for him moment to moment, that the havoc he left in his wake escaped him.

He used meditation to develop a kind of openness with women. While meditating, he would observe his feelings, so that he could be undefensive, vulnerable, and honest. Women appreciated this, but would get enraged at how controlling he was. He remained open and un-defensive in the face of their rage, a high-class steam-roller who man-aged to get his way.

I suspected that he ate himself up with his feelings and his compul-sion to stay with what felt right, especially since what felt right kept shifting. He simplified work, but his emotional life was torn in two directions, towards intensity and diffusion. Perhaps his delusional openness was wearing him out. Unable to do much more than lie in bed got him out of an emotional meat grinder, at least temporarily. Illness gave his over-run psyche a reprieve.

Therapy with Jesse was not easy. He held on to the idea that therapy focuses on the past and on tracing particular patterns or problems. He expected to get a working map of his personal history and psychological life and learn how present difficulties related to past upbringing. He wanted to control what therapy should focus on and what might be achieved.

My own version of therapy tends to be more fuzzy and open. W. R. Bion (1970) suggested approaching sessions without memory, under-standing, expectation, or desire. For me, psychotherapy is a psycho-spiritual journey. I don't have a preset idea of where it might lead. It might lead into spiritual experience, childhood trauma, inklings of future possibilities, recounting past lives. It could become, for a time, the focused cognitive-behavioral tool desired by Jesse and managed care.

Jesse wanted to keep meditation separate from psychotherapy. Therapy was to be treated as a tool to address certain problems—fatigue, nausea. It was not something he would give himself to. It did not dawn on him to think of therapy as something to discover, to wonder about, to create. Therapy was a kind of psychic engineering for him. Its busi-ness was ameliorating symptoms, not soul-making. Jesse set therapy and meditation in opposition, the former inferior to the latter. He did not experience both as outgrowths from the same psychic body.

Jesse's attitude towards therapy threw me into doubt. Isn't it reason-able to have a specific focus and to adopt a method capable of achieving success? After all, this is what insurance companies seem to feel therapy should do. Am I wrong in thinking that therapy involves one's whole being and that it is impossible and even undesirable to know where it might lead ahead of time? Am I a dinosaur for feeling that psychic life has value in its own right, and that the struggle to be open to it for its own sake is part of the "cure"?

I felt enormous pressure, as though Jesse were strangling me. How self-assured and controlling this sensitive, vulnerable man was. Or was I the controlling one? Did I try to control him by my view of therapeutic openness? His meditative openness, my therapeutic openness—how did they get into such a power struggle, a battle for control? Who was controlling whom? Was he relentlessly squeezing me more and more tightly while tightening the grip on himself as well—or was I putting the squeeze on him? How controlling ideologies of openness can be!

In fact I fed Jesse some of the things he asked for. I helped him contact early wounds and connect past trauma with present defenses. He filled in more of his story. I helped him do this, partly, to demonstrate the limits of such understanding, although the process was helpful. It gave Jesse a sense of background support that he was lacking. I supported him in his search, and the support was as important as the search. This work made him feel a little better, but the fatigue and nausea continued.

It began to dawn on me that the muted battle for control was perhaps the real work of our therapy. The struggle was a basic emotional fact, something I felt with him session to session, week to week. It was hard to pin down just where it came from. His voice was soft, even, somewhat monotonic, and his movements were slow, measured. It seemed to me that his muscles (back of neck, shoulders, lower back, sphincters, even face) were too tightly clenched. He did everything slowly, deliberately, as if he did not want to do anything faster than he could observe.

I felt overly constrained in Jesse's presence, even claustrophobic. It was as if he were trying to adapt life to his version of mindful awareness, rather than let the latter be part of life. He tried to make life conform to his vision of it and was slowly suffocating himself. Whatever feelings he experienced in my presence—anger, sadness—were quickly dampened, reported, studied, deconstructed, understood, let go. I rarely got a sense of immediate, free-flowing contact. Everything was filtered through the activity of watching. Meditation—the way Jesse used it—was making him sick.

I unsuccessfully tried to communicate my sense of being controlled by Jesse as well as the immense pressure he put on himself. I pulled back and reflected on the sense of deadlock and battle I was experiencing. My shoulders, back, and body tightened. I imagined what it was like being Jesse.

It would be easy to make something up to explain the pressure, contraction, and control, but it was more important to feel it, and continue feeling it. Weeks and months passed, and I became familiar with the tight feeling. I turned it over, tasted it, relaxed around it. We continued to talk about whatever we talked about—girlfriends, work, parents, meditation, therapy, moment to moment states, breakdown, never getting better, what it was like being together, this, that. I remained coiled around Jesse's tightness, in me, and eventually became less defensive-offensive about it, less up tight about the tightness. Not simply that I took it for granted, but psychosomatically I made room for it. I did not have to recoil, contract, or point at it in futile dismay.

What happened *felt* miraculous, although I'm sure there's logic to it. As the months went on, Jesse became more attractive to me. At times, I loved his expressions, the quiet twinkle in his eye, the glow of his face. I felt the tightness—his tightness in my chest and belly, the tightening skin and muscles of my face and arms and legs—but I tingled with joy sometimes just seeing him. For a few moments, the tightness melted.

When he came in, I no longer had to hold myself back somewhat fearfully, nor did I worry about his need for control. I smiled—really smiled. I liked seeing him. Nevertheless, as I sat with him, the struggle continued and pressure mounted. My inner smile would come and go. Then when I least expected it, when the self-tightening process seemed like it would last forever, Jesse's soul would tickle me, and joy would take me by surprise.

Within a year, Jesse's nauseous fatigue had lifted. I doubt that any particular thing we said or did had much to do with it. My guess is that his tightness found a place in someone else. It was not just that I let him in—I did and I didn't. Rather, the work my psyche did with the tightness kept me—and him—out. Whatever the reason, something in Jesse blocked our spontaneous contact. My attention gravitated to the barrier, to the x that blocked contact.

It was precisely the barrier or wall that lodged in me. Jesse's tightness obtruded, burrowed in, made room for itself. Had I resisted, *it* would have had to keep fighting for space. That I spread around it and got the feel of it opened the possibility for something more to happen.

My hunch is that Jesse's controlling tightness must have arisen in response to the traumatizing characteristics of those who cared for him. He controlled himself to better fit in and control those who threatened and nourished him. His yo-yo pattern with women suggests that his attempts to control traumatizing aspects of mother were only partly successful. And his unfortunate success in controlling his workplace (such a reduction of work life!) suggests too easy a victory over father. Jesse, too, may have had a predisposition for self-tightening as a spontaneous form of self-protectiveness and mastery.

Meditation was a way for Jesse to control his emotions. However, the more control he exercised, as he got older, the less room there was for himself. He was both master and victim of his own controlling process. To make room for himself, he assigned too great a value to moment to moment changes of feeling. He was compelled to follow what felt right, even though what felt right kept changing. The master of control was tossed and torn by changing emotional winds.

Jesse sat at meditation centers for years, but his need for control coupled with emotional lability and diffusion prevented him from ever really engaging another person. Meditation teachers threw him back on himself. He tried to manage himself and eventually fell ill. His meditation teachers challenged and encouraged him, but did not supply the kind of personal engagement that he so needed. Jesse needed simple, human contact, not enlightenment.

One Reality

I've spoken at a number of conferences on spirituality and psychotherapy the last several years, and at each one a Buddhist has gotten up and said that practicing Buddhist meditation can shorten psychotherapy by years. They might be responding to some of my case presentations, in which psychotherapy goes on for decades. I find it fruitless to pit religion and psychotherapy against each other. I find it especially cruel for either religion or psychotherapy to advertise itself as an agent for that which it can't deliver. Hopes unfulfilled by psychotherapy are not necessarily going to be fulfilled by religion, and vice versa.

The Buddhist path requires a lifetime of practice—perhaps many lifetimes. It is no shortcut. The cases presented in this chapter serve as a warning not to idealize Buddhism, or any other path to liberation. No religion or therapeutic method holds the best cards in all games.

My use of Buddhism and Judaism is idiosyncratic and does not pass muster as being strictly true to either. I invent them as I go along and they invent me. I draw from texts and teachers and colleagues and friends—whatever hits me. If I do not draw from the Holy Spirit on a daily basis, I become a semi-collapsed version of myself. We are sustained directly by God, not only through others. We are sustained by others, not only by God.

Buddhism helps me empty myself out, Jewish prayer fills me up. There is poignant longing in Jewish prayer and song, a sweet, wailing connection to God. Tears and joy are one in it. Buddhism clears and cleans me. In meditation, chains of identities go up in smoke. What a relief to be free of self! It is like detoxifying the air we breathe.

But we learn from Owen, that self re-forms. It is more than failure to be hard on himself. True, Owen does not wail repentantly about the warp that stains his efforts. He does not throw himself down, rend his garments, don sackcloth (images of soul's desire to cleanse itself). He refuses to anguish over his psychic deformations. Owen does not believe in punishing himself.

Yet over and over, gains in meditation are poisoned by the sickening feeling that tinges erotic exploitation. He has his moments of sexual exaltation, yet senses that he is acting debased. Owen is punished by success.

If one does not punish oneself for what needs punishing, sometimes punishment comes some other way. Owen and Jesse see the world as a playground filled with infinite possibilities. Life presents them with endless arrays of objects suitable for the exercise of creativity. Meditation opens space for repatterning of what is possible. But it is the very surplus of possibilities than enables Owen and Jesse to sidestep themselves. They do not have to create a boundary and say, "I'll hang in and wrestle with this."

Meditation is a way to get off the hook for them. They believe meditation will help them grow—indeed, it does. But something wrong in their relationship to meditation impedes them. Owen remains poisonously self-indulgent and can scarcely stand the taste of himself. To deaden that taste, he has become dead. Jesse could not bear the weight of his whirring whims and could scarcely get out of bed.

Individuals are both too hard on themselves and not hard enough. Often the balance needs restructuring and qualities of hardness-softness need to evolve. Missing in both Owen and Jesse is an ability to be transformed by others' responses to them. They do not—can not—take to heart what others say to them. They can always find people who say nice things to them, and the bad things do not strike deeply enough.

Each has virtually created a world he dominates and does not have to hear or be affected by what eludes domination. Neither has linked with another in a way capable of generating the journey into self-correction. They do not grab hold of themselves and say, "This is it! The buck stops here!" They think the next moment will be different, easier.

Perhaps they are waiting to grow the equipment to grapple with themselves. Meanwhile, self-deadening collapse accelerates.

Their lovers level plenty of criticisms and complaints. Owen and Jesse are good at paying lip-service but, on the whole, manage to escape. They easily dismiss the lover's criticisms: the lover is reacting to rejection, is too needy, is angry because Owen or Jesse do no not act as they want, the lover is not the right one, the lover is a passing moment, and so on. Owen and Jesse get off free, but pay with illness.

An inability to listen and be transformed by what one hears is characteristic of illness. What sorts of developmental deficiencies make being transformed by the other difficult or impossible? What conditions are needed to enable growth of transformational responsiveness? To what extent can psychotherapy and/or meditation and prayer enable growth of this precious capacity?

For many individuals meditation and prayer are forms of psychotherapy and psychotherapy is a form of meditation and prayer. The boundaries between them are not clear cut. There may be a point where the branches diverge, but for most people, there is enormous overlap. Too rigid a conception of what one ought to get from which "discipline" can make it impossible to open oneself to the work of the One Reality that flows through all. We are all partners here.

Chapter 11

Where the Wind Blows

"A thing can never be unless it both is and is not" (W. R. Bion, *Transformations*, p. 103).

". . . for my vision almost wholly fades, and still there drops within my heart the sweetness that was born of it" (Dante, *Paradiso*, Canto XXXIII, lines 61-63).

It is a remarkable fact of life that suffering and ecstasy nest in one another. Hell, purgatory, and paradise are linear distillations of a quite mixed reality, the parts of which slide into one another. The joy-agony nucleus is, for many, the most precious and intimate fact of experience. Yet we try to wish this fact away, talk ourselves out of it, act as if it isn't so.

Even in heaven one wonders how much of a good thing one can take. Aren't there heavenly torments? One dips in and out of greater-lesser ecstasies and yearns for more and more. A most fetching fact in Dante's *Paradise* is that the soul keeps growing. The more a capacity gets used, the more it can be used. Exercise is important even in heaven. The more divinity Dante's being tolerates, the more it can tolerate. One builds tolerance for love, as well as toxins.

The word "tolerance" seems colorless, when one considers the opening of soul Dante portrays. One opens and opens. If there is no end to opening, no limit to sweetness, whence bitter-sweetness? Is there always poignancy of remainder, of less-more? Does bitterness come from body, soul, ego, mind, psyche, self, illimitable reaching of desire? Can there be loss and grief in welcoming and gain? I am one with God but not God and the not is the rub? Surely Dante's heaven goes beyond the rub of not? Yet even the beatific does not do away with bitterness in a life. The soul is always homesick, especially in heaven.

Still, a taste of the divine can provide a measure of reconciliation, even if one remains tormented. Dante's beatific vision or Job's awesome mystery of divine might (*mysterium tremendum*) can shut one up. But one resurfaces and goes on, deepened by silence. Dante's exile, poverty, humiliations—through all he maintained a sense of adventure and could not stop God-writing. The glow of divine wrath and love illuminates his writings. One wonders, when he lay dying of malaria, if his fevered brain burst with its most luminous visions of all, his fevered God bursting with him in ecstasy.

Job had it easier, yet his good fortune, after surviving the worst, ought not be denigrated. I have had patients who, after nearly destroying themselves, return from the Great Destruction with inner peace. They rebuild their lives with a happiness they never knew before. Where there had been walls and impossibilities, they now see opportunities for living, rainbows after storms. They take pleasure in ordinary living and seeing what they can do with the problems each day brings.

I remember, as a young man, going to sleep many lonely nights, aching and desolate. The aloneness was bottomless. How surprised I was when, eyes closed, head on pillow, my heart opened and the words, "I love you," came pouring out. The first time this happened was more surprising than my first wet dream, some fifteen years earlier. The possibility of having physical orgasms was spectacular enough, and certainly revolutionized my life. But heart orgasms, soul orgasms—even more revolutionary!

Who was speaking? Who was spoken to? Parent and child saying I love you to one another? My heart reaching toward an as yet unknown (unknowable?) sweetheart? Was God the speaker and the spoken to? A remarkable thing was that no one was there, no one at all. Just "I love you" welling up from the depths. No parent, no child, no sweetheart, no God—just "I love you." Or perhaps this "I love you" contained all possibilities, not reducible to any. For the moment the whole universe, my lonely universe, was nothing but "I love you," an intrinsic "I love you," for its own sake (mine and yours), with nothing outside it but its own pulsations. I fell asleep with a weepy, joyful, blissful smile in my heart, on my face.

I was surprised to learn, as time went on, not everyone felt "I love you" in the night. Without formulating it, I assumed something everyone felt finally came to me. Work with patients taught me I couldn't be farther from the truth. For many who sought help, love was, at best, a tormenting fiction dangled over lives by evil spirits. I worked with burnt out craters, black holes, shrieking voids, vegetative emptiness, lethal weaponry, warps and poisons. There were others for whom love was alive and real, although destructive forces worked against it. But for many, the fantasy of love was a mockery of existence. Self-loathing was the most basic fact of life.

Lucy straddled both worlds. For Lucy, love was real, but so was the black hole that swallowed it. We spoke of conflict between life and death, love and self-hate, and the many forms conflicting forces take, but conflict language did not go far enough. When the depressive movement gathered strength, it left no room for conflict. It swallowed everything. Life dissolved in it. The whole universe was made up of wave after wave of depressive self-loathing and torturous, blistering, formless rage.

At those moments all Lucy could think of was suicide. What kept her alive? The memory of love, of potential goodness? The thought of killing herself before her children died—the idea of leaving them without her? Conscience? Some surviving, beaten down fidelity to the promise life once made to her?

Lucy's previous therapist jumped out a window to his death. Her husband's therapist killed himself in a car crash on a mountain road. Why should she live, if those who supported life couldn't?

Death had been close to her since childhood. Her father tortured her with grisly depictions of the holocaust. He had no direct involvement with it, but Nazi brutality obsessed him. He made Lucy feel guilty for being alive or having any happiness in face of the misery of so many. Her mother, too, lived a sparse, self-depriving existence, asking nothing for herself, except Lucy's obedience. They made Lucy scared of herself and her life urges. She couldn't breathe.

For many years Lucy was in and out of a depressive pit, mostly in. Her depression would spike, and she felt agonizing spasms of self-hate, akin to acute physical pain, only more devastating. We went through cesspool after cesspool. No point seemed low enough. No matter how ghastly she felt, she had a gift for feeling worse than before. She was convinced there was no way out.

As the time we spent together became years, Lucy had better moments more often. She recoiled from them, paid for them, did not have ability to support them. But they came back, and she gradually built more capacity for them. There were sometimes rapid swings in and out of the mire that drove her and her husband crazy. But the overall movement was in the direction of getting better, of more life.

A session a few months ago shows how far she has come:

Lucy: "I wasn't supposed to be happy. My parents were grim. My father was always talking about children being gassed, and how disease and dirt were everywhere. Nothing was as real as dangers and disasters everywhere. Anything that wasn't a catastrophe was trivial."

"But I was supposed to be happy to make them happy. I was supposed to make a show of happiness to make them feel good. Not *real* happiness. Real happiness was too exciting, disturbing. Any happy moments I had with them got ruined. They couldn't take *my* happiness. I had to keep it a secret. They could only take happiness fabricated for *them*.

But I had my happy moments, my *own* happy moments. One stands out from the rest. It feels like the only time I was ever really happy. I was sitting in a tree singing to my dog, when I looked and oh, his eyes were smiling! His eyes were smiling, and mine too. I'm lucky I had a moment."

M.E.: "Yes. Ready for more?"

Lucy: "I'm scared. I was happy painting too. But it didn't make noise. She had no idea how happy I was."

"I went back and forth between being a good girl and bad girl. When I was good, I got ice cream. When I was bad, I got rage. And my own rage? Where was it? After awhile of being good I'd say, 'This sucks. I'm giving up my life. Who needs them?' When I got older and left them I couldn't take care of myself. I'd sink. I'd drown in wretchedness, try more, cave in again."

"Now I do things. I take care of what needs to be done without spending hour after hour in bed, hiding in the house. I'm not just a good girl or rebel. I can be and do. I go about being happy, noisy, quiet."

It was terribly important that for many years I did not try to take Lucy's misery away. Of course, I couldn't take it away if I wanted to, but it was good I didn't try. It was equally crucial that I acknowledged and supported surges of aliveness when they came and went. Therapeutic "neutrality"—I prefer calling it therapeutic "openness"—can be experienced by the patient as a freeing gift. It may provide the individual, often for the first time, a sustained relationship which is neither overly abandoning nor intrusive.

I would not exactly call my state of being "neutral." I often felt badly when Lucy did, and joyous when a momentary breeze of life uplifted her. I became a kind of background sea of feelings that supported, touched, connected with hers. We were parts of a stream of life together. Yet there were times—many times—I could not *be* with her. Not because I didn't want to, or didn't try. There are moments when it is as important not to be with someone, as to be with her. There are moments when it is important to be parts of the stream of death, alone together, or simply alone.

Lucy's agony could be so great that there was no room for anything else, not even herself. There was only pain, more than pain, something approaching absolute torment, pure hell. At such moments Lucy knew herself only through her urge to kill herself. Her one remaining desire was to end the agony.

We learned a lot from lesser agonies. When she was not so totally consumed by pain, she could rage against her parents for ruining her. She raged at her husband for his rages and controlling nature. But most of all, she raged against herself. It was as if she had become a child tortured by Nazis—a concentration camp victim—and the horror went on and on. She could not bring herself to be a survivor. She had fallen into the misery her father forced her to look at. He did his job so well, she could not turn away. She had become what he feared she would not see.

As years ticked by, Lucy learned much about what went into making her father and mother the way they were. But understanding did not mitigate the pain, the rage, or depression. The fury was still there, if, at times, tinged with grief. Perhaps it would not hurt so much if she did not love them so deeply.

Lucy suffered so much, so long, that her personality, her very being, underwent a mutation. It was not simply that her personality built itself around an agonized core, became addicted to suffering, or was masochistic and depressed, although all these may be so. Freud (1937) wrote of an "alteration of the ego" (pp. 238-240), the result of early employment of defenses in face of conflict and trauma, an alteration so lasting and devastating that it works against recovery. I believe it sometimes helpful to view this alteration as a mutation that cuts through all levels of personality, not just ego. The personality is reshaped through intensity of suffering, so much so that realms of experiencing become possible that would have remained closed, if not for the effects of prolonged misery.

Without therapy, I'm not sure Lucy would have survived, or survived well. The pain would have been too much and have no meaning or use. I don't think therapy absorbed or took the edge off Lucy's pain, so much as provided a context where it could be expressed—where it could be *known*. More than known—where it could *be*. It may sound odd to say that Lucy's pain, which consumed her life, had no place to be, but I believe this was so.

Her parents could not tolerate her pain. They insisted she be happy. Her father, who insisted she know the pain of others, could not permit her to know her own. Her mother died each time she felt her daughter was unhappy. Her pain enraged her husband. He wanted a joyous wife.

There was no *place* for Lucy's pain, although she felt it was everything everywhere.

At times, when the intensity of pain mounted beyond a certain point, Lucy would vanish, or begin to vanish. This is, partly, the result of natural defenses against pain—numbing, blurring, blotting out, falling into oblivion, stuporous self-obliteration. However, if the pain that triggers vanishing comes often enough, as it did for Lucy, one begins to anticipate it, and vanish before it comes. Vanishing of mind, body, self, psyche, or being becomes not only part of life, but a way of life.

One's situation becomes somewhat like Berkeley's tree falling in the forest. The pressures to produce sound must exist, but what sound can there be without a sensory apparatus to transform these pressures into hearing? Similarly, whatever might produce pain in Lucy kept going, but she would not be there to experience it. She would "meet" pain by simulating, hallucinating, or bringing into being a counterstate of no-pain, which was no-where.

The study of Lucy's pain gives one a glimpse of how complex psychic states can be. Pain mounts to an unbearable point. Lucy goes under, vanishes, dies out. Consciousness varies, so that Lucy fades in and out of agonizing states. At the same time, something in Lucy turns off, numbs, dies, is not there. There is permanent vanishing, oscillating agonies, and temporary vanishings. All of this happens at once, as well as successively. There is, also, confusion over complexity of what one is experiencing, since one does not have a frame of reference, a picture of self, broad enough to encompass the full range of variable and enduring tortures one suffers. No wonder therapy is often experienced as enemy, if it encourages study of pain. Yet what relief such study can bring.

Therapy could not undo the no-place chronic vanishing in face of agony opened. It could, however, recognize the reality of the mutation that occurred, and perhaps allow the latter's contribution to evolve. Lucy became a different sort of being by becoming a vanisher. She became a being for whom no-place was real. But who in her life could she share no-place with? Was it possible to share the unshareable?

Therapy gave pain a place—in a way, a *no-place*. Insofar as Lucy's pain saturated everything, there was nowhere it could go. To an extent, therapy enabled nowhere to be—a nowhere greater than the sum of pain. It is difficult to describe this experience, but important to signal that it exists. Many individuals require some inkling of it in order to survive and thrive.

All human relationships have much in common, whatever their differences. Therapy is no exception. Yet therapy's uniqueness lies in individuals coming together to wrestle with *psychic reality* in ways that further growth. There is nothing quite like it, even though it can happen outside therapy too. That there should be a portion of the day or week set aside for growth talk with another person is thrilling.

Yet how chilling it can be going nowhere with agonies, even if nowhere may be the only place to go. When agony obliterates everything, nothing/nowhere is left. Being nowhere with Lucy changed over the years. In the beginning, nowhere was clotted, dark, heavy, airless, thick, inert. At the time of writing, nowhere often is freeing, lighter, pleasurable. We have private nowheres neither of us can reach, but also share a variety of nowheres. What is important is that nowhere—many kinds of nowheres—can *be*. Therapy became a semi-shared no-place, for Lucy's strangulated no-place to breathe.

There are individuals who need a therapist who has gotten the knack of being nowhere and adept at going through agony ↔ nowhere sequences. A therapist who has been transformed by enduring agony ↔ nowhere may be less defensive about a patient doing so. I suspect there are therapists who specialize in different sorts of nowheres and different sorts of agonies. Such therapists, pressed by intensity of agony ↔ nowhere, likely have first hand experience of mutations personality can undergo.

Sometimes it takes a mutant therapist to recognize and validate a mutant patient. A mutant therapist, if lucky, has learned a thing or two about working with the regions one finds oneself in. One learns to work with mutant states, rather than simply fear and fight them. It's a little like learning to walk in space or swim—one gets used to the medium one lives in.

It would take many years before Lucy had any inkling there were communities of mutants spread across worlds, across times. There are invisible bonds or paths leading from one unreachable no-place to another. For many years, therapy provided the only no-where for Lucy's non-existence, a place/no-place where pain could reach vanishing points, and vanishing points could reach pain. Nevertheless, nowhere has a history, a story very much in progress. It is possible for individuals to feel part of larger, evolving nowhere.

Transformations in O

Milton's "void and formless infinite," Eckhart's Godhead (Darkness and Formlessness potentially yielding distinctions), Dante's 33rd canto of the *Paradise*, negative definitions in mathematics (e.g., not infinity): these are some images Bion provides to evoke a sense of unknowable reality (O) that psychoanalysis is part of, grows with, and expresses

(Bion, 1965 , pp 154-155; p. 162). Psychoanalysis is rooted in nowhere, as well as its historical contexts and antecedents.

Terms like "nowhere" or "no-place" are, of course, inadequate depictions of unknowable reality (O). The Kaballa speaks of *Ain Soph*, or infinite of infinites, which can not be represented, yet gives rise to energy forms and filter systems that constitute the psychospiritual universe. Bion uses the term, "not infinity," to suggest that even infinity (or infinite of infinites) comes up short. Neither negative nor positive terms are substitutable for lived transformations in O. Terms like "unknowable reality" or "O" are signifiers meant to keep us faithful to the more they are not.

Nevertheless, there are individuals who appear to substitute negative and positive terms for lived transformations in O. Such people can not get from words to life or life to words in ways that work for them. A simple example is the intellectualizer who substitutes knowing for becoming. But the problem is deeper and more subtle.

Lucy wasn't an intellectualizer, yet her ideas about herself and others, connected to a real sense of being wounded, kept her isolated. Feeling her wounded self was her full time job. Everything else seemed phony. People who acted confidently seemed unreal to her. Much of the adult world was out of reach or irrelevant. Lucy would see the black hole at its center, and mock the charade. At the same time, if she could not find the other's wounded center, she felt excluded, alone, angrily bereft.

An ideology of being wounded formed around real wounds. Lucy all too readily accused others in her mind for being insensitive and out of touch with the wounded core. She could only relate from wound to wound, not strength to strength. If she deemed the other's empathic tenderness insufficient, she withdrew. She was withdrawn much of the time, since she rarely found a presence hospitable enough for her to come out of hiding.

Her ideas about life acted as a protective coating. She *knew* what life was like, so did not have to experience its myriad nuances. She was the judge and jury who found life guilty for hurting her and sentenced life to exile. She was right of course. She had the pride of the expert. She felt few people knew as much about injury as she. She could only be with people who shared this superior knowledge—a secret society of exiles who knew more about wounds than others. In her anger about the wounds she saw everywhere, Lucy sentenced life to death and sought deadness in others. Alive people looked like they were faking it.

Many people, including therapists, tried to get Lucy out of her depressive mire. Life's banquet was laid before her, but she scarcely touched it. It was as if she were in protest, on strike: if life did not change its ways, she refused what it might offer. When we met, she was in a situation where those closest to her were enraged with her. She refused or could not avail herself of what they offered. She was starving in the midst of plenty, and those around her furiously fought against being deprived by her deprivation. The barbed wire around her wounded self cut both ways.

Lucy taught me that refusing to eat was merely a specific and limited form of anorexia. She looked down at people for living. What made others able to pretend they weren't as defective as she? If everyone (including herself) were absolutely honest, all would commit suicide on the spot. If life was not possible (inedible or indigestible), what kept her (and others) alive?

Lucy could not say that we are more than the sum of our pain, but neither could she say we were only our pain. She was zero, yet hovered over zero. She was nothing, an agonizing cipher, a wretched being nulling herself, barely holding on to life. It took years of our being together before she felt her zero part of a larger therapy zero.

Lucy and I liked each other. We had basic good feelings for each other. Good feelings were important, but not enough to mitigate the fierce waves of agony that blotted Lucy out. There were periods that the best I could do—all I could do—was feel the full noxious paralysis that put us out of play. Our therapy life together became a dead, noxious paralysis.

I attempted the discipline of being without memory, understanding, desire or expectation and started each session as openly as possible. What would this session bring? Who was this person today? Who or what was I this moment? With Lucy I could feel the pressure to go blank in a poisonous way. Something was poisoning her, killing her, making her stuporous. I had urges to fight it and give in to it at the same time. In a way, I did both. For periods, I went under with her, knocked out by lethal forces. Years of going through horrific states taught me I would resurface and come back in time. How does one convey such learning to another? How does one help another develop resilience?

From time to time, Lucy found someone with her where no one had been before. We were in blank, noxious deadness without any contact, having lost a sense of each other's existence. Now and then we jostled or bumped each other in our lightless world. Sometimes we came up to breathe, moments of reprieve, then back to malignant nowhere.

I thought of the void and formless infinite, Meister Eckhart's god-head, and the like. I understood we were jumping directly into God. But God got obliterated. There was nothing but the underbelly of being—worse, formless poisonous obliteration going on and on. The O we had reached was a sort of anti-O, a null-O, an O of poisonous blankness. It is important to stress that this poisonous blankness was very real, the only real reality while we were in it. When it gripped us, the idea of hope seemed like child's play.

I don't know when or how I became aware that things were changing. Years were passing. At first Lucy's reports of being better were short-lived and had little meaning. After feeling a bit better, she would feel much worse, bad as ever. I dared not place much value on momentary reports of better or worse feelings. I recall my dawning relief and amazement upon sensing that some of her better states were like birds flying to Noah's ark after the flood. The pounding waters and winds diminished. I wouldn't say there were rainbows—but there might be in time.

I have no idea what happened, because I wasn't there when it did. I was gone. After years of states approximating many kinds of suicides, I found myself revived by changes in Lucy's life. She sounded better, lighter, fuller. The chronic death we lived together was receding. Did she bring me back to life or did I bring her to life? Where did the malignant O go?

The malignant O was by no means gone forever. The dead O did not die. But it did not take up as much room in her personality and life as it once did. Did we outlast O? Give O a chance to evolve? Did Lucy transform in O? Thoughts about what happened seem insignificant next to the fact that something happened. The malignant O lifted or gave somewhat, and Lucy had more room for living.

Lucy's long, encounter with a malignant O changed her. She was caught between killing herself, living a miserable life, or growing into something better. The Lucy who came through O, was not the same as the one buried in it. She appreciated the difference. Coming through prolonged malignant deadness is felt as nothing short of miraculous. An individual who comes through immense suffering can not be the same as one who aborted or did not need such a task.

Why Life?

Perhaps the capacity to doubt kept Lucy alive. In spite of the certainty of injury that proved life was rotten, Lucy had some experience of alternate realities. Out of the corner of her eye she watched her husband reach out for her, and appreciated the persistence of his refusal to give up—even if he were reduced to reaching out through fury. She liked people who spoke from the heart and not simply to create impressions. She loved art. She valued moments of quiet peace, reminiscent of her tree top *satori*, although these times were too fragile and intermittent to decisively offset self-destructive spins. Thus the absolute totality of her worthlessness and life's worthlessness was not absolutely total. Although she was absolutely certain, she could not be merely absolutely certain.

She also fought suicide because of her children. Her relationships with them were agonizing, but she was bound to them. She feared killing herself would injure them, push them over the edge. They were over the edge enough as it was. Staying alive exposed her to the dreaded possibility that one of them would commit suicide before she did, but it was a risk she took.

Yet pools of goodness and her tie to her children might not have been enough without help, and help might not have been possible without the former two. Lucy was sinking in a self-destructive process gaining in momentum. It took years to make a decisive difference. In therapy Lucy repeatedly experienced total annihilation of self, other, and therapy, without the annihilation being final. In daily life, individuals do not take well to being killed off, as one does not take well to being killed by others. We nurse grudges, strike back, coerce each other with hidden agendas. Therapy gave Lucy a place to be destroyed and destroy, to nurse and gratify destructive needs, without hurting anyone or anything but herself, her therapist and therapy. It gave her a place outside everyday life to practice annihilation skills, to get used to the fact of destruction.

Lucy was suffering, in part, from destruction deprivation. She never had an arena where she could destroy herself and others to her heart's content. She had to be a good girl, and the more she tried to be good, the more dread of destruction mounted. Therapy is by definition a real make believe place. "Let us destroy each other," is part of the therapist's invitation. "Let us be totally annihilated and survive." Insofar as therapy goes on, destruction is not final.

Sometimes therapy does not go on. Therapist or patient can succeed in putting an end to it, completing actual destruction. Lucy and I did not let that happen. We "clicked" as a therapy couple and weathered the storm of ourselves. We survived dying together, although the process (or non-process at times) was hair-raising. So many sessions turned me into a corpse, numbed and poisoned my psyche, made my inner being hideous. But by the next session I was fresh, ready to die or become monstrous again. Was Lucy watching me out of the corner of her eye, dreading and appreciating her effect on me? Was I a kind of model for the nuclear sequence: *being destroyed – surviving destruction*?

It took a long time, but Lucy began undergoing the sequence herself. The being destroyed – surviving destruction cycle began working in her. I don't believe Lucy simply introjected-incorporated-internalized my ability to die and survive. I think being with someone who exercised this capacity over a long period of time jump-started her own. My bouts of grueling agony/numbing out/dying and starting fresh eventually stimulated her own sleeping or under used capacity to reset herself after destructive spins.

To have faith in one's capacity to come through the worst is a priceless achievement. It enables a reshaping or refounding of personality around a kernel of resilience. It enables one to bounce back more deftly without denying the weight of living in the valley of the shadow. Our being together enabled Lucy to develop a taste for starting fresh. As she grew more confident in the freshness following depressive orgies, the circuit between destructive spins and starting fresh became more attenuated, less virulent. She could go through the cycle in a briefer, premonitory way.

Most importantly, zero states were no longer simply or mainly menacing. One repairs to zero as a kind of home base or safe harbor, an emptying of personality and its anxious concerns. Zero becomes part of the swing from depression to freshness, an O-zone where one is unknowable and free.

One of the reasons Lucy's zero had been so malignant, for so long, was that it never smiled at her before, or she could not see the smile. She saw only the wounded zero, the enraged zero. The smiling zero failed to have a biography. It remained a moment in childhood in a treetop, a reference point rather than daily bread. Now the zero winked at her. She could see the twinkle in its eye and smiled back.

Chapter 12

Pecking Away

Anthony Molino: As a starting point, I was wondering if you could comment and elaborate on a statement you once made: "Freud is right to think of psychoanalysis as wounding the Western ego, although it does not create the wound so much as grow out of it." What is this wound and how do you conceptualize the Western ego?

Michael Eigen: In terms of the wound, of psychoanalysis wounding Western narcissism, Freud had in mind the three great revolutions which kept decentering the human being, so that the human being was no longer the center of existence, nor the ego the center of human existence. In a way Freud's psychoanalysis presents a series of wounds, a series of trauma, a series of woundings, from birth trauma to abandonment anxiety, annihilation anxiety, castration anxiety . . . There's a catalog of anxieties, a catalog of catastrophic states that the infant and child go through, that the human being goes through. It's sort of an anthology of catastrophes. In Freud's informal presentations he depicts these as humiliations, humiliations that the ego goes through, humiliations to self-esteem . . . blows, blows to the ego . . . and he means "blows" literally, not just metaphorically: like a stab to the heart or a blow to the face, the way a poet might mean it. So that his picture of the human being is of the human being going from one wound to the other, and of how the personality congeals, grows, displaces itself around wounds.

When I was in the Nevada desert, a guide told me a cactus would grow straight forever, would grow forever straight if it didn't get wounded, and that the branches of the cactus grow out at the place where it's traumatized, at the place where it's wounded. Freud depicts the personality in the same way, displacing itself, or deforming itself, around the point of impact, of wounding impact. Hit the psyche, and it displaces the self like ripples or waves, it deforms itself around the points of wounding. And Freud describes those woundings in so many different ways, in terms of different developmental phases. But the wounding Freud talks about has always to do with displacements: with how the self-importance, or the self-centeredness, of the human being, the amazing arrogance of the ego, keeps getting wounded by re-centering itself in a larger existence. Psychoanalysis is part of this revolutionary decentering process, another in a long history of ways of placing or replacing the self in a larger context, while breaking the relation to being a big fish in a small pond.

A.M: If we somehow conceive of re-centering or decentering the self, there still persists the *idea* of a "center." Do you have an operative idea of a center when you talk about decentering or recentering?

M.E: The first nub, of course, is the seed. There's just the seed of a self . . . . But I nevertheless do feel a sense of the value of the idea, in spite of deconstructionism. In certain exercises, for example, I feel more centered. But what that center is, or how to describe it, I wouldn't know. It's not an idea I have an investment in. I wouldn't fight a holy war for one picture of it over another.

A.M: I'd like to address what I see as a confusion that surrounds a set of concepts invariably central to psychoanalytic theorizing. How do you understand the terms *ego, self* and *subject,* all three of which appear prominently throughout your writings?

M.E: I have never thought these things through, basically. I've thought about them at different points of my life, or through different theoretical systems: for example, what the subject is for Lacan, what the self or ego is for Jung or for self psychology or for ego psychology, or for the British school or Sullivan. What the self or ego is, or what the subject is, shifts in meaning. It is partly a matter of context: what seems to be subject in one context can be object in another. It could be like a Chinese box, or a shell game . . . . For Freud the ego is a kind of "I" subject, but it's also a system of functions, it's also the love object of the id. So in a sense it's subject in one context, the system of autonomous functions in another context, a personal "I" in another context, and an object in yet another. So that even in Freud's work, the meaning of ego keeps shifting according to how it's used. I wouldn't want to go to bat for pinning down a single meaning, because it's really dependent on context.

A.M: Your own use of the term *self* is very elastic and multi-faceted. You don't hesitate, for example, to resort to the plural notion of "selves"; you speak of a "body self" and a "mental self"; frequently, of the "growth" of self, and the "gift" of self. Sometimes the word *self* is preceded by the article "the," sometimes not. Can you clarify and expound on your own usage and understanding of such terms, both theoretically and clinically?

M.E: Maybe I've used the word *self* at different times, at different points in my life, for different growth purposes. So maybe the term has meant different things to me at different crises, at different junctures. Sometimes I think I've held onto the word "self" as an organizing principle, to make me feel more whole. At other times I use the word to give a context or horizon, a vantage point outside of the smaller ego. Sometimes I've used the word "self" because it refers to a feeling of own-ness: a kind of feeling of my own, something very personal. But I don't know that I would be intellectually equipped—or that anyone is especially intellectually equipped—to pin down the many meanings of the word. My use of the word *self*, at this time in my life isn't quite the same as it was when I was 20. I think our capacities generally involve some mixture of how we experience ourselves: on the one hand, there's a personal, warm and immediate experience; on the other hand, there's an awareness of being given to ourselves as pretty anonymous, as pretty impersonal. What we do, then, with what's personal at one moment and what freaks us out as anonymous, or as standing against us from within ourselves in another moment, can vary. I don't know whether I can add anything to the subject in terms of intellectual clarity. It's a matter, I think, of informal use and what mileage one gets from a term like *self at* a given point in one's life.

A.M: Would you feel comfortable providing some anecdotal sense of the kind of crises you mentioned, that may have distinguished a shift in your own personal understanding of what "self" might have meant at any given time?

M.E: I can think back at when I was in my 20s, on a bus, being in extreme agony. I just suddenly lost consciousness and dipped into this sense of agony, and stayed with an agony that seemed to be located in my chest. It was a terrible psychological pain, not a physical pain so much as a horrendous emotional pain, that I imagined and felt in my chest area. I went further and further into it, and I doubled over on the bus, and then all of a sudden, quite surprised not having any mental frame of reference for what was happening the pain opened up and became radiant light. Where before there was just agony and horrendous pain, without my knowing what had happened, suddenly there was bliss . . . . It turned into a terrific light that left me wishing it would never end. Of course, the pain didn't go away, but the bliss has never left me either.

A.M: In your "Afterward" to *The Electrified Tightrope*, you write: "There is much pressure not to hear oneself (or selves)." Clearly, the idea of the self's potential multiplicity is present in your thinking and experience. First put forth, arguably, by one of your early teachers,

Marie Coleman Nelson, it's an idea that's been taken up recently by the likes of Stephen Mitchell, Jane Flax, even Christopher Bollas. How is the concept present in your thinking and, more importantly, how does the idea of multiple selves bear on your practice of psychoanalysis?

M.E: I guess I came into contact with the idea first through literature rather than through psychology. In psychology, my first contact with it was through an early book by Erich Fromm, *The Forgotten Language*, and through Jung's writings, when I was still a teenager. How it finally translated for me personally was when I came to be amazed by, or thrown by, or utterly flabbergasted by, the changes of state that one can go through in a single day: the amazing changes of state of which the psalmist writes, how we go to bed crying and wake up laughing . . . . How that happens is astonishing, is amazing. Freud wrote about how the very fact that we dream is a signal that it might be possible to cure psychosis. Because if we can dream, if we are plastic enough, elastic enough, to go through such amazing changes of consciousness from normal waking to dreaming states and back again, then why shouldn't it be possible to cure psychosis? The idea of multiple selves, that we are all these things, the actual concrete, immediate experience of change of state, is problematic: what does one do with that? Is one different people when going through these different states? William Blake talks about states, all states, every state being eternal: how all states, once experienced, are forever . . . . Or we have to try to picture a unified personality identifying with different states, going through different states. Jung depicted an archipelago of selves. But I don't think either vision is necessarily comprehensive. I think the crucial thing, now, is the debate about multiple personalities or dissociated personalities. I think it's really quite useful, quite wonderful, because it brings the problem out. Perhaps it makes the problem of multiplicity sound strange or unusual, but I don't think it is very strange or unusual at all . . . . What do we do with the amazing plasticity and range of states that we actually go through in a day? From feeling more in one's body, more out of one's body, more mystical, more realistic . . . more in love . . . . Isaac Bashevis Singer somewhere writes about how all human beings, how even an idiot, is a millionaire in emotions . . . . It's a fantastic gift, a gift and liability we're given, to have this extravagant experiential capacity. And it's not at all clear that we know what to do with it as yet. One of the amazing things about going through all these states, for me, is the fact that I'm going through them at all, that I can feel so differently in so many different contexts. It's not a different self that's going through them; it's sort of, how can I be all that? But it's still me being "it"; it's not a different self, or a multiple self necessarily. It's me. It's me being other to myself too. But how is that? How can I be other to myself? How is that possible? It's mind-boggling. The kind of beings we are is really mind boggling. That we are somehow other to ourselves; that it's "not me"; hey, it's not me!

A.M: Then what's the difference between Michael Eigen saying this to me now, and what you've explored and experienced clinically with so-called multiple personalities or in dissociative states?

M.E: I think one of the big differences, is that I'm more used to it. Someone else, a patient, may not be able to make the links, may not be able to stomach the multiplicity, or take it in and digest it in some psychic way . . . . A patient might not be able to say: "Hey, that's me . . . . Oh! hey that's not me!" There's not always a place big enough, in a patient's psyche, a house big enough, to make space for these different rooms . . . . Someone comes upon another room in the house, and imagines being completely in entirely different territory. They might not realize: "Hey, I've just moved from here to there . . . that the link between. . . . "

A.M: What provides that link?

M.E: That's what we're working on, at the cutting edge of psychoanalytic praxis. Winnicott's whole career was a testament to the fact that depersonalization, not feeling real to oneself, is the central clinical problem. I believe the link, then, lies in those conditions that make it possible to feel real to oneself.

A.M: Depersonalization, or what you refer to in your present writings as psychic deadness. . . .

M.E: The sense of a life not having meaning is a phenomenon that's struck me. Nowadays, more and more people come in and actually say that they don't feel alive. It's experienced by many of them as a very painful situation. Now that's a good prognostic sign, because if they were not experiencing this as painful, the situation would be even worse . . . . Somehow, these people know what it's like to be alive, if the absence of vitality so troubles them. It's becoming more and more common to get people in practice who feel dead and who want to come back. . . .

A.M: What are the factors behind this pervasive sense of psychic deadness?

M.E: The most obvious, I would imagine, is the general degree of over-stimulation. A patient comes to mind who had a massive dose of over-stimulation all at once. He pins down his dying to a time when he was about eighteen, to an evening when he, his mother and his father were sitting having dinner. The father went into an unusually pitched rage at him and walked out of the restaurant screaming. The boy felt himself collapse at that moment, and die out, and he's been dead ever since. It was a massive shock that he felt, and it made me think that in some way or other so many people are numbed out or shocked or put in a state of shock by a kind of massive implosion, or massive impact . . . almost like a scream, or someone screaming at them . . . it's almost as if there were a silent scream that is deafening people, who can no longer hear themselves, and are thrown out of balance. . . .

A.M: You mentioned wanting to substitute the idea of "multiple states of being" for "multiple selves." That very distinction is, to a large extent, at the crux of the postmodern debate on the self. James Glass, for instance, in a book entitled *Shattered Selves*, is highly critical of the seductiveness of the postmodern exaltation of multiplicity. Conversely, Jane Flax talks about "fluid subjectivities" as a defining characteristic of this postmodern epoch, and seems to be suggesting something along the lines of what you're talking about: a condition where these fluid states do not necessarily involve fragmentation. What is your understanding of postmodernism and its distinguishing features? How has psychoanalysis and your own practice been influenced by a supposed postmodern turn?

M.E: I've liked parts of what I've read of Derrida; I've heard him talk a few times. Still, I can't always figure him out, because a lot of the results of his work seem to reflect what we as therapists were doing clinically. I'm sure I haven't grasped the depths of his writings, but I haven't learned anything new yet. What I like is the analysis. I like the poetry of the analysis in the people I've read. I've been entranced by some of the poetry of the prose, which is breathtaking. But clinically postmodernism hasn't added all that much for me. What it's confirmed, though, is that one can transcend almost any clinical situation, and look for another way to handle it: so that whatever lock, whatever impasse is created by the patient and therapist together, one knows in one's being, as well as theoretically, that one can always be doing and being something else. One gets to know that it's always possible to pick another loose end to organize oneself around, to costume oneself in; it's always possible to pour oneself into another mold, and come at a situation from another way so that one always recognizes and utilizes the plasticity of the materials at hand. One doesn't have to be resigned to being boxed in. There is, I suppose, a certain transcendental element in how free one is or can be with any particular patient . . . so that one can imagine becoming someone else, can become another self, or another part of the self, or enter into another state that might yield a different effect on the clinical situation.

A.M: There's a section in *The Psychotic Core* entitled "The Point of No Return." There you write: "Many patients complain of an endless sense of aloneness. They do not find a social milieu in which they can feel they really belong. The usual categories of connection such as family, race, nation, work, various subgroups and friends do not work for them . . . . (F)or an increasing number, nothing can truly palliate the nagging sense of being different and not quite connecting. In some basic sense, one is not understood and does not understand oneself. One has nowhere to go. One is on one's own." Looking at this, I couldn't help but think of it in cultural and historical terms. Is this aloneness somehow different, say, from the angst of the heyday of existentialism?

M.E: I don't know whether it is or isn't. I think it's like a blind man having each hand on a different part of the elephant, or like the same echo at a different point of time, the same wave at a different point in space. When I wrote that, the person in particular, and the people in general, that I had in mind were totally disconnected. They had no place, were off the map, completely had no hope. They had no hope of ever making a connection they would regard as being on the map. And yet it really was miraculous that some of the people I was thinking about at the time did manage to become part of the tapestry of life, without compromising in some essential way the alone self that had been hopeless, that had earlier been hopeless to connect up. Now, how that did happen is rather baffling: persistence, staying with it, staying with the aloneness, making room for the aloneness.

I think that in that passage I was being a therapist to the alone self. I was trying to establish a context for it, for that alone self to be, to be validated and valorized. I remember certain people I've met in my life, like Winnicott, Allen Ginsburg, or the rebbe Menachem Schneerson. When I was with them, I felt it was okay to be the sort of person I am. With them it was okay for me to be somehow off the map, beyond the map; it was okay for there to be in life such a person as I was. In that passage, then, I was trying to encode, for whomever it would reach, something like a message in a bottle. Floating on the sea it might then reach some people, who would hear the message that it's okay for them to be the sort of alone person they are. And by some miracle, by making room for such a message, some of these people, through the course of years, have tentacled out, have tapestried out. They've found themselves situated in a larger tapestry that makes room for the sorts of being they were and are, whereas earlier there didn't seem to be any place for them. Now, how did that happen? How was room made for them, a space for life to begin? . . . . It's miraculous, making room for the multiple selves . . . . Again, I'm not so sure I like the term "multiple selves" . . . . I suppose it's comforting, in a way. And I don't know that "multiple states" is much better. But the idea of making room for this alterability, or multiplicity, or self/non-self, self/otherness that one is, is one of the functions of therapy.

A.M: Is this what you mean perhaps when you write about a "friend-ship of self"?

M.E: Make friends, yes. And it's okay to be your own enemy, to be adversarial and antagonistic too. It's okay to be your own worst enemy. It's inevitable. I think the idea of normality can be horrendous, because one carries around this picture that normal people aren't insomniacs, or normal people aren't so hyper-nervous, or they don't obsess, etcetera . . . . So you have this picture of what normal people are, but then . . . where are all these people? If you find them, they're probably driving someone else crazy. What's normal is that there is a background radiation of the universe with different, molecular densities that different worlds issue from, and we are part of that universe.

A.M: Within a historical moment that either privileges or generates an excess of psychic disconnection and dislocation, and makes of geographic dislocation a basic experience, can psychoanalysis somehow confront the economic and social structures that generate this surplus of social fragmentation?

M.E: I'm more Buddhist there. I don't know that it's my job to, or that I can. To think about doing that, on a small level analysts should be less frightened of speaking out publicly about public issues. For example, it is becoming more commonplace to see how so much of political discourse hinges on winning lies, so that a one-up/one-down structure, or an adversarial structure, is becoming increasingly prevalent. Take, for example, the Clarence Thomas/Anita Hill hearings, where from one vantage point you could see so many different political maneuvers to gain the upper hand. It was less important to determine the truth than it was to see which lie would win, or which spin would win; or how best to appear as the more aggressive, the clearest, the one who could knock the other person more efficiently. The premium was not so much on truth as on who could present the clearest, most aggressive and effective image. The choice being offered was rather sickening . . . . Within the same arena, one of the things I like about Clinton is that whatever is wrong with him, or whatever the problems with him, he at least makes vacillation, or oscillation or indecision, part of the public milieu. Part, and only a small part, of the reasons he's come into so much trouble is not because of what he's done or not done, but how he's appeared. He hasn't been able to cosmeticize his vacillation or oscillation, or his unsurety, in the public domain, and he hasn't been able to present an effective one-sided, me-against-you, adversarial, axe-man approach. He hasn't been able to develop a winning enough lie to stand by, with which to knock others down. Personally, and without any delusions about my effectiveness, I like to feel that if I make a public appearance, I'm a spokesman for ambiguity, or a spokesman for oscillation.

A.M: In the epilogue to *The Psychotic Core* you specifically address the deforming effects of television and what you call "the collective brainwashing inherent in the maneuvers of contemporary political campaigning." For you who have written so extensively about psychosis, to what extent do these phenomena play a part in its genesis?

ME: I don't know if the media plays a role in promoting psychosis, though it certainly can. I think psychosis and the media are different branches of a deeper, more pervasive tendency toward madness in the human in general. I think madness pervades so many human dimensions, that it is not so uncommon at all. What's uncommon is unmadness. It would be rather unusual to find something happening that isn't quite crazy. But the fact that human beings have invested so much in one-upmanship and territoriality and economic riches . . . me-against-you, me-above-you . . . this has a madness to it. It's kind of crazy in a way . . . but I suppose not doing it would be mad too. I think that our tendency to live a dream, to live according to a fantasy . . . a fantasy of what one would like to be like, and of what life is like, that tendency is rather widespread, and madness is not a rare thing at all.

A.M: The polarized debate of the "singular" versus the "multiple" self seems to fit within a dialectical structure that is elemental to your thinking. You've written: "For practical purposes, I posited a *distinction/union structure* that characterizes the self at all of its developmental levels." I was wondering if you can elaborate on this idea, even in terms of its acknowledged antecedents in the work of Federn, Mahler, Winnicott, Grotstein. . . .

M.E: Since I now have to use words, and not just grunts, let me say that it's along the lines of what Winnicott has in mind, when he portrays the psyche as being essentially paradoxical on all levels of development. To use words like distinction/union, to become united with this double capacity, runs through the human psyche at all levels: cognitive, emotional, relational, and social. And we don't really know how to conceptualize this capacity except to point to it, and say something seems to be there . . . "I am," but I am in a context, in an intersubjective context . . . . I'm you, you're me . . . but I'm not you and you're not me . . . . It's a matter of what one can come up with, what one creates with that dichotomy . . . . In this sense, I think psychoanalysis today is a kind of poetry. Nowadays, I think of psychoanalysis as an aesthetic, as a form of poetry . . . . You have all these psychoanalytic singers and poets trying to express their aesthetic experience: of a session, of the emotional content of a session, or of the impact a patient generates in session . . . . It's all portrayed as a cultural microcosm. We have all these wonderful and moving psychoanalytic singers opening up worlds of experience, and it's a matter of whether someone moves you along at a certain point, promotes your own growth towards openness.

A.M: When you talk about this "distinction/union structure that characterizes the self at all its developmental levels," I get the impression that you're not talking simply or only about the Freudian developmental schema, of oral, anal, phallic, genital stages. I get a sense that you have implied a different, or at least a complementary, idea of what it means for the human being to develop. Could you illustrate that idea?

M.E: Well, it originally grew out of my early work with regression, with so-called "primitive" patients. I was very influenced early on by the British school, where there were a number of people working who seemed to see a positive, regenerative value in what used to be called regression. . . . I remember noting at the time how different theories seemed to suggest that one could regress as far back as to a symbiotic state, or to an autistic state; but if that were true, then regression would be extremely dangerous, and the farther back one went, the more isolated or the more fused or the more self-less, in a negative sense, one might become. So, instead of regression being regenerative, it would have to be destructive, and the best thing to do would be to build up defenses against regression. Nevertheless, my clinical finding was that so-called regression or opening up of the self or letting down the boundaries, could be extremely fruitful. . . .This seemed more wholesome, in common sense, and healthful to presuppose. . . . My myth, my story was: "In the beginning there was both separation and union, or distinction and union . . . ," so that one doesn't have to be frightened of going all the way . . . that, as far as one can go, whatever world one enters into, you'll be both self and other in various forms of relationship and non-relationship, and that one doesn't have to make a decision, doesn't have to decide whether to be simply alone or simply with others. It's more fun, and less frightening, to be and allow for all of these possibilities: to just glide along, or be able to flow from one state to another. Or to be in mixed states at different times, without prejudging: "Oh my God, I shouldn't be this now," or, "I can only be this now!"

A.M: I was wondering whether your emphasis on psychic structure and polarities of experience was somehow influenced by the work of Lévi-Strauss. I haven't seen him mentioned in your writings, but I'm reminded of a book of his called *Totemism*. . . .

M.E: Well, I never got as immersed in Lévi-Strauss as I did, say, in Bion or Winnicott or Lacan. It's just a matter of luck, a throw of the dice, what authors I got immersed in at an earlier age, and he wasn't one of them. But when I did read him later, I found his work fascinating. The connection, for instance, in my mind and lots of other people's minds, between structure and process, is truly baffling. Years ago, I think it was Gene Gendlin, in a book called *Experiencing and the Creation of Meaning*, who saw an enormous difference between process and structure. I don't understand how he derived the idea, of structure as something more solid and fixed, and process as something more fluid and moving.... (thinking *out loud*) Gestalt psychology, I think, suggests that bones, for example, are the results of slower, more fixed processes . . . but it's not like bones are process-free . . . they're made up of slower, relatively stabler patternings. . . . The bones of the system on which the flesh and nerves all hang, that's all process too . . . I don't understand the difference between structure and process. I've never felt the need to posit a difference. Just talking about structure is a very creative thing because one picks how one's going to slice it, you know. . . . One is always selecting the processes that one's going to talk about, and in what form. . . .

A.M: In elaborating this idea of the structure/process, you hint at what could be called an originary matrix of being, at what you call the "living experience of union and distinction out of which the self arises." Your own contribution in this sense is unique, in that there seems to be a "maternal" dimension of the infant's originary experience that somehow goes beyond object relations and even predates the relational embodiments and personhoods of mother and child. Again, we're stuck with words: but you seem to suggest a living experience of this union/distinction structure that actually predates the self, as well as the personhood of mother and/or child. . . .

M.E: I think that's right. . . . Something that both mother and infant get situated within, though I'm not sure what to say about it. The age-old folklore that we're children of God before we're children of our parents probably hasn't been tapped as well as it might in psychoanalytic thinking, where we're always children of our parents first. . . . It actually may take quite some time for an infant to de-infinitize . . . where the infant may go through different states, now more finite, now more up against the solid, real facts of things, and at other times be more and more in an infinite field or infinite horizon. . . . To actually come into the realization that I have to be where my body is, that my body is this bounded packet, really takes quite some time and quite some sophistication. Some people feel that schizophrenics resist this development, or that certain sorts of schizophrenics resist packeting themselves that way, or have an inability to tolerate the physical limitations of embodiment. It can't be taken for granted that the sense of infinity or of the emotionally infinite doesn't somehow antedate the experience of the mother or even of the infant.

A.M: You seem to be reclaiming for psychoanalysis an actual, experiential dimension of mystery, of the infinite, of the immaterial: words that have always suffered the weight of Freud's "oceanic feeling...."

M.E: Well, I've felt the oceanic feeling. The term itself has unfortunately watered down psychoanalytic discussions of mysticism because mystics themselves, while enjoying oceanic feelings, sometimes were often brought up shore and left terrified by the onset of a numinous awakening. They were overturned, and shaken to their core. The prophets, whenever God or an angel appears, get the dickens scared out of them, they get scared stiff, and it's terror, terror. . . . So God has to say, "grab your balls and stand up like a man, let's get down to work," because there's such a terrifying impact of the uncontainable, and it's not all peaches and cream and oceanic bliss. . . . That's the way it is with mystical experiences, or encounters with the divine. They can be too much for the human equipment at a certain time. Flannery O'Connor, in her short stories, depicts this over and over, where even religious, fundamentalist Protestants are broken by the discovery that what they were preaching actually has reality, and so they become shattered by the actual experience of what they had only been rehearsing. Over and over, her characters are shaken by a divine or demonic happening that makes real what before were only words. It's like the experience of a child, who is intensely wishing or praying for something. In the absence of the desired object, that kind of wishing can make for an altered state. Even as a child, one gets a sense of being different than one imagined one could be, and that sense can grow. It can even have a biography: the sense of the infinite can have a biography.

A.M: All your writing is imbued with a deeply charged sense of religiosity, of mystery and wonder. There is throughout the evident sensibility of a mystic. You speak of Bion as a mystic; you often cite Buber's *I and Thou*, and speak of the co-union or communion, not only of self and other, but of self and God. . . . You've written on evil and often mention the devil. . . . You talk comfortably of both prayer and Buddha. In your epilogue to *The Electrified Tightrope*, you astonish a reader with ideas like: "From the depths of one's being it is as easy to get to God as libido. For Freud libido seeks an ideal imago in traditional terms, ultimately God. The unconscious does not do away with God so much as provide a privileged point of contact with the unknowable." Later, you mention your father's death, and your subsequent immersion into the roots of Jewish mysticism. You then continue: "I used aspects of Oriental and Roman Catholic teachings to organize my mystical propensities. The paradoxical, dialectical, dialogical way of listening/speaking that marks clinical practice mitigated against religious orthodoxy, but my encounter with Judaism made me a richer and better person.

"The flow between divinity and libido is so much freer now."

This kind of language, this kind of revelation, if you will, in both senses of the word, is courageous on the part of an analyst. Beyond the oceanic feeling, I'd like to invite some free-flowing reflections of yours on psychoanalysis and religion, from both your clinical experience and your own life history.

M.E: Well, at the risk of sounding utterly trite and trivial, so be it. From the first session I've ever had with anyone, I've always felt a sacred element in psychoanalytic psychotherapeutic work, and I've never quite understood the animosity so many analysts have had against the mystical. I'm astonished, for example, that as terrific a worker as André Green tried to argue it with me. I was astonished that, in his reading of Bion, Green played down or totally parenthesized, nullified, actually, Bion's use and reference to faith. He emphasized almost exclusively what Bion called K, or knowledge, or the scientific approach to knowledge, and was convinced that Bion too thought as he did. But as Bion's work evolved, he more and more transcended the primacy of K, or the lust for knowledge, or the search for and use of knowledge, within a faith context, and as a matter of fact, he proceeded to almost define the psychoanalytic attitude as an act of faith. And he uses those words. . . . Now I think Green is a terrific analyst and thinker, but this blanket statement, with regard to an enormously important part, the climactic part of Bion's work, is astonishing. I take that incident to be a paradigmatic example of how, even with the most imaginative and generative people in the field, there seems to be a strong animosity against the faith freaks. Why faith is played down, though, is puzzling. Maybe there's the threat of fanaticism, or of losing scientific ground; but I think one can be a fanatic in the other direction as well. One can deplete experience in different ways. One can be too realistic, one can be too fantastic, one can be too scientistic, one can be overly fanatical and zealous. . . . Rather than have a war between all these different dimensions of experience, it's much more fruitful to keep open the possibility that each have a voice, that each have a say in the play of voices, and to see what happens. . . . But whatever faith is, Bion associates it with opening, with the propensity to become open. To go in the other direction, towards K, would be a premature exclusion of one voice in favor of another, as opposed to a plurality and balance of voices. Jung has his funny things too. I can certainly imagine a Jungian saying I'm wrong, but in my reading of Jung, there's so much that is devastating if one takes it to heart. For example, his attitude toward dependency can be shocking at times. He puts down certain neurotics as mother's boys and addresses them with a certain contempt. There's a contempt for dependency and weakness that runs through his writings, which is kind of odd, because he seems to really have generated a lot of positive transference, and then from that position seems to have a contempt for weakness. So there's a kind of double bind that I imagine Jung put a lot of patients in: "you must worship me, but if you do I have contempt for you." It's a funny thing. Now Jung, of course, feels he pulled himself up by his own bootstraps. As a neurotic or psychotic adolescent, he felt he'd strengthened himself and deliberately conquered his weakness, transcended his weakness, by hard work and creative endeavor. And so he developed a certain mistrust of people who can't do that. He may have made his living off of people who can't do that, but he nevertheless seemed to look down at affliction and adversity. So while Jung had a certain depth that few people reached in psychological writings before him, there was an attitudinal problem I recognized. So I tended to gravitate toward the British school partly because, for the first time in psychiatric writings, and in a consistent way, there didn't seem to be a contempt for weakness or a contempt for dependency. It seemed like dependency was now getting its due or valorized as being a legitimate part of life, that ought not to be precociously short-circuited or treated abruptly . . . or dealt with by just tugging at your bootstraps and acting bigger or stronger again. The emphasis in the British school is on staying with the dependent streak until the growth process can come about. It was that different attitude toward human weakness that appealed to me, I think. In practice, the British school also did a lot of goosing into independence, pretty much as Jung did in his own way; so the dependency business does get rather scary with the tendency, even in the British school, to perpetuate it. Nevertheless, there is an attitudinal shift, away from Jung's contempt for weakness, that is evidenced at least in Winnicott's writings.

A.M: You've written about faith as you see it in the work of Bion, Winnicott and Lacan. What is faith for Michael Eigen?

M.E: Different things at different times. I guess there's spiritual faith and there's natural faith. I place a great deal of weight on natural faith. I've nothing against spiritual or mystical faith . . . but there's an awful lot of faith that springs simply from sensory experience, from how good it feels to be able to walk down a street and move one's limbs and not be in prison. . . . It brings up a feeling inside that, while it might be stretching things to call "faith," I really do have to call it that . . . . It makes one feel good to be alive, it makes one feel that life is good. . . . The body seems to have this faith. . . . Very often I've been astonished by how a dying animal seems to not know it's dying, by how it acts in the face of death, and seems to live, to be moving or trying to move or live to the last ounce. . . . It just keeps going to the end. . . . Or even when it stops moving and gets into a dying position, it doesn't seem to be angry or yelling about its imminent end. Somehow there seems to be an acquiescence, a simple ebbing of energy in the direction of death. It's a kind of body faith, a faith the body has. I suppose one could talk about an affective faith or an emotional faith: the "ouch!" and "yum!" of things. . . . "Ouch! That hurt!" . . . or "Yum! That was worth it!" So it's more than pleasure and pain, I think. When one talks about a pleasure principle or a pain principle, one's de-animated it, because it's not simply bad or good, it's heavenly, it's heavenly . . . It's wonderful! . . . it feels yummy all through. . . . You know, one would have to be totally mad not to have a secular or ironical self and see the limits of things, but I rather like siding with this feeling of "good to the last drop" in psychoanalysis. . . . Like a bug that never stops moving. . . . There's just a sense of never giving up . . . never giving up on a case . . . not giving up on anyone. . . . Who knows better? . . . .

A.M: All this begs another question. What does Michael Eigen mean by God?

ME: God only knows! I think I have to be honest to say I mean a biblical God, the God of Abraham, Isaac and Jacob. . . . But having said that I can step back and say: "Hey, well, what I mean by God could be anything, because I don't know. . . . " In a sense God is a total unknown, and yet in others the very notion ties the so-called biblical, personal God closer to me than I am to myself. . . . And then there are times one can just lift up one's hands and say, "Wow, all this out of nothingness!". . . which feels wonderful . . . to blank oneself out and be totally open to whatever currents pulse this way or that . . . whether you're into body, or emotions . . . Taoist or Buddhist, whatever, it feels good. You know, in the Kabala, God has . . . is . . . goes beyond names . . . the *Ein Sof*, the infinite of infinites, the great unknown, the "I-itself". . . . By the time God gets named! . . . .

A.M: I had a patient once who, in the midst of a fierce negative transference, blurted out loud "I am that I am," without any apparent sense of the phrase's Biblical echo. The woman was stating her difference and uniqueness in a rather commonsensical sort of way, but the sheer power of her words was unmistakable.

M.E: That's wonderful. I think Ben, in my book *Coming Through the Whirlwind*, does something like that at one point. It's what we're doing all the time: we're "am"-ing . . . and we're "am"-ing each other too . . . we're enabling each other *to am*.

A.M: In getting back to that early "am," you seem to have supplanted the centrality, for psychoanalysis, of both the real and the metaphorical breast in the early life of the infant, with what you imagine to be the infant's formative relationship to the face. The face almost becomes as important, if not more important, than the breast. In a way, the face takes on a mythic quality in your work. . . .

M.E: Well, that comes again from a Winnicottian sense of paradox, from the idea that we shouldn't ever favor only one element of a dichotomy. Why should psychoanalysis have opted for a primacy of the tactile and diminished the visual? Why oughtn't both grow about together in a mutually constitutive way, feeding what everyone calls mind, or self, or being. . . . Bion can be quite funny sometimes when he talks about *common* sense, or getting the senses to work together . . . which can't always be taken for granted, you know. . . . In an autistic state, for example, a child can be pulled one way by one sense and another way by another sense. . . . We oughtn't to need, in theory or in practice, or even in our personal lives, to compromise the multiplicity of the senses, and the different information they provide. But there's more! The different senses don't just give information. They give different worlds, or different qualities of worlds, or different textures to live in, not just information to process, but different tastes, different ways the world tastes through touch, or through the other sensory organs. Or there can be harmony, at various times, between distance senses and closeness senses, a paradoxical interplay again between near and far. It seems quite limiting to say we are primarily near-creatures or that we're primarily far-creatures, or touch-oriented, or vision-oriented. . . . In other words, and this seems obvious, as Freud already noted and Derrida points out in "Freud and the Scene of Writing," there is a primacy of multiplicity.

A.M: This is the first answer where you've privileged a theoretical reply as opposed to an experiential one. Since so much of psychoanalytic theorizing about the breast involves the writer's fantasies of what the infant experiences or "phantasizes" at the breast, what does Michael Eigen imagine the infant's experience of the face to be? What does the face do to and for an infant?

M.E: Well, there is the eye-to-eye contact, where the eyes are shining or dull or a shade in-between. . . . The eye-to-eye contact, together with the skin-to-skin contact, generates, so to speak, different sets of feelings, currents and subcurrents of feelings. From eye-to-eye and skin-to-skin, there are currents and subcurrents, some antagonistic, some harmonious. But part of the fate of eye-to-eye contact or face-to-face contact is to enclose worlds, worlds of experience. The face does shine, you know! So I can get a double faith . . . I can get a faith from the breast and faith from the face. Normally, now, that's not the case; normally, they very often tear each other apart, with fights for the upper over the lower; fights for the lower over the upper. . . . Normally, there's probably a state of war between capacities; but optimally, that may not be necessary.

A.M: A few more things about the early developmental stages. Is there an echo of Lacan's mirror stage in any of this?

M.E: I love Lacan, but I twisted him out of shape for my papers, for my writings on faith . . . because face for him, Lacanians insist, really has to do with seduction. The face for Lacan is part of a seductive enterprise, as it also might be for Sartre. On the other hand, for Winnicott the face can be the center of an experiential movement that goes beyond seduction, that connects up with Levinas' sense of the face as infinite. It strikes me both viewpoints are right, and there is much to say about each. We *do* seduce each other through our looks, as well as through much else. One can't localize seduction. Seduction is everywhere. Nor can one localize faith. . . . You can have breast faith and face faith. One could have breast faith and not have face faith; and one could have a face faith and not have breast faith. There is faith sliding into Klein's or Lacan's early paranoid, aggressive play of desires, a seductive, demanding faith, enticing-ruling, being enticed by-ruled by the desire of the Other. Levinas writes about the face as it evokes the infinite, or as part of the experience of the infinite, of infinity, of opening infinity. How could one decide between Lacan and Levinas? Why should one have to?

A.M: I have a few more questions on issues concerning postmodernism. . . .

M.E: Those are funny terms, aren't they? Postmodernism . . . modernism. . . . I sort of picture dinosaurs walking around. . . . It's funny . . . . bit names. . . .

A.M: There's another passage from *The Psychotic Core* where you evidence a clear awareness of what might be termed a postmodern sensibility: "Writers today emphasize how present-oriented, episodic, and fragmented our experience is. We no longer simply gain identity from well-defined social roles and institutions." Similarly, in *If on a Winter's Night a Traveler*, Italo Calvino writes: ". . . (L)ong novels written today are perhaps a contradiction: the dimension of time has been shattered, we cannot live or think except in fragments of time, each of which goes off along its own trajectory and immediately disappears. We can rediscover the continuity of time only in the novels of that period when time no longer seemed stopped and did not yet seem to have exploded. . . ." If what Calvino says is true in some way, if time and space have been compressed, or if our experience of time and space is different than it might have been twenty or a hundred years ago, how does that experience now unfold in the analytic situation?

M.E: I'm intimidated by questions like that because they're so broad
. . . though I love descriptions like the one you read because they're so
fun! From early on in my writings, I've been drawn to particular portrayals of time worlds for people, and of time worlds in analysis. In an early
paper called "The Recoil on Having Another Person," I write about the
importance of time experience in the constitution of self. It's about how
temporal meanings of the Other, dimensions of time in the experience
of the Other, relate to approach-avoidance patterns, to two people being
drawn to each other or repelled by each other. The exploration of the
concept of time has a long history, in philosophy, literature, and in
human experience. . . . Condensing time, or exploding time. . . . Erik
Erikson or Alfred North Whitehead portray a kind of emotional time, or
an affective time, or time in terms of pulsations . . . how long, for example, it takes for an experience to develop and be seen through.

By implication, I think of John Dewey's work, *Art as Experience,* where
he talks about how an experience has its own particular build-up time,
development time, shifts around, comes to a climax and denouement.
The question, perhaps, is how is it possible to help people allow this
process to happen, and not short-circuit seeing an experience through
. . . or how can we enable them to sustain the tensions necessary to fully
go through and not thwart an experience? . . . . Even the question is
hard to organize, because time is such an intimate part, in analytic work,
of allowing time to be, of allowing an experience to be.

A.M: Has there been, in your clinical work, an experience of time
shattered or subverted that was fully shared with a patient?

M.E: In general, the so-called borderline personality presents the
problem of not giving time a chance, of not giving the analyst or analysis
a chance. It's all tooth and nail. . . . Time gets eaten up, gets eaten away,
gobbled up by the patient in analysis. Let's relax into giving time a
chance to develop its own flow, and allow that there should be a "later"
. . . or a "then," or enough room or enough of a gap, so that some kind
of approach, of movement from here to there is possible. So that analysis
can be possible, and develop over time. So that development, over time,
can take place. In this sense, you might want to help a person view
therapy as a kind of psychic gymnasium, to help build up tolerance, at
certain times, for just seeing a moment through . . . for the patient to
know, "ah, look, something was just about to happen between us, but it
got short-circuited. Where did that moment go? It looked to me like you
were about to feel afraid or angry, and suddenly it's gone!" . . . or maybe, "You suddenly felt relaxed here . . . you relaxed here because I
wasn't bugging you about anything. All of a sudden. . . . Where did it
go?" Therapy as a strategy to outflank the thing that kills off or short-

circuits the possibility of experience, of letting a moment grow. . . .

A.M: What about space?

M.E: I love space. But I've come to have the odd view that there's a primacy of time in analytic experience. I know that most of the literature is concerned with analytic space and preserving the integrity of analytic space. But I think there comes a moment . . . a time . . . when space dissolves, but time keeps going . . . a kind of timeless time, where the person becomes, gets dropped into, gets immersed or in touch with some unfolding of affective nuance, of affective resonance. And space, for that time, seems to dissolve, while a kind of pulse time . . . a kind of psychical artery time keeps on going. It's as though one discovers time by losing space at a certain point . . . a kind of timeless time. . . .

A.M: The inverse phenomenon of the spaceless space where time dissolves?

M.E: I've experienced many patients overly obsessed with space, who have no playful space whatsoever. What they have, actually, is not so much a playground as a coliseum, where there's a battle for survival going on: a territorial battle over who's going to survive in space. These patients inhabit a corrupted space, a violent TV-like space, where the emphasis is on who's blowing away whom; where the violence makes for one explosion after another. So the session itself becomes a kind of explosive or violent space. It becomes an annihilating space, a space that eats up, where the obsession with space again blows away the possibility for time to develop.

It's a void space, in a way, or a big-bang space, or a black-hole space that seems to foreclose the possibility of letting something unfold. Just as something's unfolding, a violent enactment blows it away, so that the experience doesn't get a chance-in and of itself-to come to a conclusion. You never get a chance to find out what the experience could be because the sort of space it occupies nullifies it. It nullifies the experience, blows it away before it has a chance to complete itself. Clinically, then, the problem is one where negative space eats away at the possibility of letting an experience be. It's a very violent, Pac-Man, black-hole kind of space that explodes the possibility of giving people time to complete any particular trajectory of experience.

A.M: Would that scenario preclude or diminish an essential capacity like introjection?

M.E: I think that's certainly true. But the problem is even more pervasive, because it precludes the possibility of completing a perception. On a sensory level or a perceptual level, you can't even perceive or see what the world would look like without something blowing the experience away before it has a chance to build. So, it wouldn't be a matter of just precluding introjection or projection. It's a matter of stopping actual innate capacities from having a chance to operate.

A.M: Regarding those "innate capacities," one of the writers you address extensively in *The Psychotic Core* is Federn. You talk about his concept of "I-feeling," and his radical contention that mental ego-feeling (and not the ego-feeling related to the body) is the first to be experienced by the child. This seems to have provided a springboard for your own ideas. I was wondering if you could comment on this, and on how our sense of the psyche gets spatialized within us?

M.E: Wow! I seized on the Federn business because it was pretty unique. I mean, no psychoanalyst before him had theorized in that way. For the general psychoanalyst, the ego is first and foremost the so-called "body ego," and it was kind of stunning to see that, for Federn, the psyche is first a mental ego. How did he get to that? Probably because he read Husserl. He was a student not only of Freud but of Husserl; so that a Husserlian-kind of phenomenology of consciousness informed his work. As a result, even while he was a staunch Freudian and remained in Freud's camp throughout his career, Federn wasn't able to begin his account of the ego's origins as a body ego. Now, that's an amazing position for an analyst to take!

It also occurs to me, in working with psychotics, and if we think of how psychotics describe their own experience, that Federn's descriptions fit certain sorts of psychosis: with regard to how the body ego can fade away, while an I-feeling still remains. Of course, this I-feeling can be lost too, in more dire states of depersonalization; or the I-feeling itself can persist, but feel unreal. One could also have the I-feeling without any quality of its being warm or immediate or real . . . or a sense of painful estrangement from the I-feeling, that the "I" is going on but I can't experience it. One can have even further I-losses. . . . But Federn, in any case, has this range of experience of working-through with psychotics, where he can have the body feeling unreal, or the "I" going on after the body drops out. . . . And there's a long tradition in esoteric religious thinking that also fits Federn's descriptions. One sees this, for example, in the esoteric Gnostic tradition, where you have ideas of one existing prior to the materialization of the body.

In a way, the Freudian enterprise implicitly has to do with getting the mind into the body. Freud's whole oral, anal, phallic thing is about ways the mind is incarnating, or a way the spirit incarnates. It's about phases of incarnation, or a development of incarnation. Whereas Federn's question, in working with psychosis, is: "Well, what if I don't incarnate? What happens then?" It's not like R. D. Laing's question, which is more: "How did I get out of the body?" For Federn, the question is: "How do

I get into it?" What happens if I don't want to get into it, or if the body isn't sufficiently inviting for me to want to be a part of it? Or if the body subjects me to too much horror?

You know, in the Gnostic myths, the soul has to be enticed or seduced or fooled or tricked into going from the dry domain into the wet. . . . Contrary to so much analytic thinking, the first fall isn't from womb to birth. The great catastrophe isn't in going through the womb to getting born. The great catastrophe is going from heaven into the womb. I think that's a worthwhile distinction to remember, especially as experimental psychology is now finally catching up with Gnosticism. We now know that the womb is not such a very perfect place at all. The fetus has traumas in the womb too, and maybe so does the embryo. . . . Can you imagine what it must feel like, if there are things like feelings at so early a stage, to go through such momentous upheavals or growths, one after another? It's more titanic and cataclysmic than the unfolding of geological ages on the earth, with its cyclones and earthquakes and climatic changes and ice ages! I mean, what the embryo undergoes in a short period of time is monumental. . . . And should anyone be there experiencing it, God knows what sort of experience it must be!

A.M: About Federn's notion you write: "Primordial I-feeling drenches the entire cosmos.... Original I-feeling is infinite." Through your reading of Federn, there's a mystical quality in his work that seems just as radical as his argument for the primacy of a mental ego. I'm wondering if this was something that you were aware of or sensed an affinity to. . . .

M.E: Well, I have my own tongue-in-cheek love of that kind of thing, because in the way Federn presents his ideas, the question becomes: "How do we all, who begin life as mystics, become anti-mystical?" How do we develop anti-mystical properties as our ego contracts into our body and into the spatial world filled with the objects that we know and love and hate. The so-called "I"—whatever that is—begins as a bigger I, as a bigger, more cosmic I, and then contracts through coming up against the hard facts of life. It develops a contraction, and we then develop a smaller, more realistic "I" that maps out the spatial realities we have to deal with. The problem then becomes: what happens to the big "I"? What happens to the cosmic "I"? Does it get funneled through the smaller "I"? Does the smaller "I" draw nourishment from the bigger "I"? Are they at war with each other? Do they battle for supremacy? Is one psychotic when one meets the cosmic "I" and delusional when one gets to the smaller "I"? If a developmental statement such as Federn's has anything to it at all, what kind of relationship can be worked out between larger and smaller "I" states? How do we get along? Can we make a playground big enough to accommodate the bigger and smaller states?

A.M: Again in *The Psychotic Core*, in writing about Federn, you state: "The subject often encounters pain when he acts on his sense of bound-lessness. He meets the resistance of spatial realities and other I centers." It's the notion of I centers I'd like to explore. Is this somehow an early prefiguration of the idea of a multiple self, or what you call multiple self states?

M.E: Well, I think of the joke about the guru who convinces his disciple that he's God. Years later the guru meets the disciple, and finds him limping along, all crippled and bandaged up. So the guru asks: "What happened?" And the disciple says "Well, this guy riding his elephant was in my way, and I kept thinking and telling him 'I am God, I am God . . .' and he ran right over me." And the guru says: "Schmuck, he's God too!" An entire range of phenomenological and existential and philosophical literatures have explored different phases, or different aspects, of what it means to be a being who sees himself through the eyes of another, a being who sees by displacement, where I see you through me, or you see me through visions of a free-floating "I," or through the "eye," the organ of sight, that floats freely. . . . A free-floating "I" that in any particular moment presents any number of vantage points. That's partly what can fuel resistance from a good borderline patient . . . this "anything" that anyone says, anyone could have said something else . . . any "I" could have acted differently, at any given time.

So a good borderline patient can always say, "Well, why should I listen to what you're telling me . . . it is after all you telling me." But there can be an impact between patient and analyst, through which I, the analyst, develop a truth of the moment, a truth which grows out of the impact, that I somehow select and through which I become aware, in an aesthetic way, of the impact's growth. . . . I become aware, then, of what it might feel like for the patient to be impacting on me in this way. And I'll develop trains of words or images that grow from the aesthetic nucleus of the impact which, without functioning as a definitive truth or perspective, can still give rise to an infinite number of other possible perspectives. . . . Then the one truth, the one perspective I select and present to the patient, becomes a poem, my song of the patient at that moment: and through it, I can access the patient's feeling states. We impact each other with our momentary dream presentations.

A.M: You've written of yourself: "From the outset it seemed clear that I could never be a strictly orthodox analyst." It's uncommon to find an analyst truly free of the shackles of schools and doctrine, one able to embrace—and I mean the term "embrace" rather literally—figures as diverse and far-reaching as Freud and Jung, Lacan and Kohut, Winnicott and Bion. What is the process, what is the attitude that allows for your incessant efforts at synthesis, and how have those efforts been accepted in the greater and often rival communities of psychoanalysis?

M.E: From early on, it was never a theoretical or technical matter. It was desperation. It was a hunger, a need, a personal need that I met, in reading each of these people at a given time. In an inner sense, I was reconstituting an aspect of myself or area of myself. If I read Jung, or Freud, or Winnicott, I felt that some other part of me was coming into being, or was being mediated into life through these various midwives. So it was, in essence, a salvation quest . . . or a matter of integrity as a person, getting more of myself into being and developing more of a life for myself. I gravitated towards the people who, at different phases of my life, seemed to be midwifing what needed to be midwifed at that particular time. . . . And as I have a sense of loyalty, I remain loyal to all my various loves from those different phases of my life. I read Jung before Freud. For some reason I didn't understand Freud when I was younger. I tried and tried and tried to read him, but it was too painful and didn't make much sense. But Jung was easy to read, Erich Fromm was easy to read, and I devoured their writings in my late teens and early twenties. . . . So in a way I did it backwards. I evolved into a Freudian later. . . . I was a Jungian before a Freudian, instead of the reverse, which ought to be the case, developmentally, according to Jung. Of course, I couldn't be a Freudian either because of Freud's anthropology and reductionist picture of what particular fantasies were important. Not being a formal theorist, it wasn't much of a problem to go through these different so-called schools or theoreticians. It was actually a matter of dire need. . . . It wasn't a theoretical matter, it was a concrete personal matter involving the constitution of the self . . . of my own self.

How has it played out in the field at-large? I really don't know. I don't know what position I have, I don't really see myself in the field at-large. . . . This much is somewhat clear to me at any rate. When I was in graduate school and going through training, and I stumbled across people like Searles or Winnicott or Marion Milner, I felt inwardly very much like William Carlos Williams describes himself in medical school. . . . He said that writing poetry got him through medical school. My having fallen upon people like Searles and Winnicott very early on, long before they were popular, got me through graduate school. . . . They got me through training. It's as if discovering them made me feel it was okay for a guy like me to exist, because it was hard for me to get that kind of validation, in the formal training that existed at the time. I like to feel that I've encoded, in my writings, the message that it's okay for people to be and develop in their own way: that we mutants are very real and have a very real contribution to make, and that the world would be poorer without us. We have a right to walk around in the sunlight and to stretch and to play our music and to sing and dance. . . . And maybe it's okay for grown-up children, for analysts like us, to help keep the balance, to help keep things afloat. I have, thank God, gotten confirmation from diverse sources: from many good souls who've read my writing and have been deeply stirred or affected by it. I've gotten numerous calls or letters or invitations from people who have had the experience, in reading my writings, of hearing their own voices in a deeper way, of feeling they had a right to be in their own particular way. . . .

A.M: Of these influences, Bion and Winnicott seem to stand out as being particularly dear to you. You've studied both for decades, and Bion you knew personally. Can you say something about these two men?

M.E: Two great mutant men! Winnicott, I suppose, one wouldn't ordinarily think of as a mutant because he had this myth of normalcy about himself. But, you know, in his writings, especially in his writings about Jung, in his "splitting headache" dream related to reviewing Jung as well as in his actual review of Jung's autobiography, Winnicott talked about having been somewhat liberated, of having been able to achieve a degree of madness in his work. Whereas I don't think Bion had to go through that process of apology for his madness. I think he worked more explicitly with and from his madness pretty much from the onset. I got the impression from his biography that he probably knew quite early that he was quite mad and didn't know what to do with his madness. At a time when people weren't all that concerned with problems of madness and the role of madness in human life, Bion, especially, offered some of the most stunning portrayals ever of the mad dimensions of life.

Winnicott? I visited him in 1968, I think, when I was in London. I was having a terrible time in graduate school, especially with one clinical teacher who'd wonder how I would come up with the things I'd come up with. She would always feel they were right, but didn't know how. I got them. So she was put off by me because she didn't get my methodology, even though she seemed to agree with the results. So during this horrible time in graduate school, I go to meet Winnicott, and he greets me at the door saying: "Hello, Dr. Eigen. I'm sorry I haven't read your work." He greeted me as if I were someone. I was quite thrown because my experience of my life in New York didn't exactly convince me that I was someone or, for that matter, anyone. So, here I am, being treated like a king by this old man, who seemed very gentle and sweet, who offered me sherry and then went on trying to convey to me something about the sort of work he did. In the meantime, he felt free to move about the room, or sat at the end of his couch in a corkscrew kind of way, which seemed rather awkward. . . . He didn't seem shy, so much as awkward. . . . What would it mean to be awkward without being shy? His was a kind of awkward intensity, in which he was digging, digging for the experience that he wanted to convey and the way he wanted to convey it, the way that he could feel it could be conveyed to me. And as I looked at him all corkscrewed up in this awkward, intense way, I found he looked very much like an old woman, in his old age. . . . So here he was, screwed up in this awkward intensity, when I had this feeling and thought: "Oh my God, he's sort of like me!" . . . that somehow we shared this awkward intensity in our attempts to get at something, in trying to get at the thing itself and find a way of conveying it. I wouldn't be so delusional as to put the two of us on the same plane, but it was a freeing moment for me. . . . It was as if he was not afraid to be in this unsmooth, rough-hewn way, in order to try to get at something. . . . Ultimately, something about him conveyed permission. It's as if his message was: "If I can be Winnicott, you can be Eigen!" It was a beautiful moment. . . .

It was a different experience entirely when I went to have consultations with Bion. I walked in, and the first thing I felt, that took me quite by surprise, is I felt he looked like a bug. . . . He looked like a bug! . . . . He looked frightened . . . like a frightened bug. It's as though he were putting himself under me somehow, in order to understand. . . . He was putting himself below me, and I felt for that moment empowered. It's as though he were empowering my narcissism by operating from a position of dread. As the session went on a lot of his pronouncements seemed to me oracular, or orphic, and I felt he could be talking to anybody. I felt that I, as a person, didn't exist for him, and I felt very uncomfortable with that. I found him rather joyless, and began telling him how joyless he was. Then, as things went on, we talked about Plato, and he talked about his analyses with Rickman and Klein, of how his earlier contact with Rickman helped save him from Klein. Then out of the blue he started talking about the Kabala, asking me if I'd read it. I told him yes, I had, but not very much. And he was quick to say that he too hadn't read it much. But it dawned on me as the session went on that he was implying . . . that he was talking to me at a level that I wasn't used to being talked to. I write about it in the afterward of *The Electrified Tightrope*, actually, how he anticipated my development by almost a decade. Anyhow, by the time I left him after the session, again I had a parallel feeling, though not at all like the one I got from Winnicott, because Bion was more bug-like with me, more cryptic. . . . But again I had the feeling that if it was okay for him to be Bion, if he could do his thing with me the way he did, then perhaps I could discover a way of finding out what my thing is and to do it with a sense of freedom. Both men had this capacity, I felt, to give permission, to give permission to be different, to be in one's own way.

A.M: Were your consultations with either man anything like a traditional analytic or supervisory relationship?

M.E: I only saw Bion when he was here in New York at the IPTAR Seminars, and everyone was presenting cases to him. I figured I would try to get the most out of the situation, so I presented myself as a case. He told me to get married, and to stop psychoanalysis. He told me I had been overanalyzed, that I'd been in analysis long enough; that I should break away, and get on with the nasty business of finding my own self. In retrospect it's touching and odd and uncanny and inspiring, uplifting, that many of the ingredients of the conversations we had, while he was here in New York, about Plato, about Klein, about the Kabala, about the weirdness of one's own idiosyncratic nature . . . that many of these ingredients turn out to be generative bits and pieces of my own inner world. It's as if the riches that he spontaneously shared about his own life matched a few gold pieces in my own treasure chest. His words, then, hadn't been random; he wasn't talking only about himself. His own unconscious mind was making selections that resonated with treasures buried in my own being, treasures that our sessions helped animate. It was something like psychic acupuncture, where he was getting to certain nerves, certain pressure points that could be stimulated.

A.M: There are two other figures who seem to have left their mark on your work and life. I'm thinking of Marion Milner, with whom I understand you've corresponded for years; and of your first analyst, Henry Elkin. Your admiration for Elkin seems filled with generosity and gratitude, and yet, you write that your analysis with him did not end well

M.E: Henry had a strong destructive side, in terms of being intuitively dogmatic. But he had depth and weight, and I had a very deep attachment to him. Implicit in our contract was the sense that something would come of this attachment. And as I began seeing him when I was quite young and quite hopeful, when he left New York I found myself feeling abandoned, looking, perhaps, for a way I was going to survive without this relationship, to carry on without a dependency that had seen me through some decades. How does one resolve a transference of this nature? I don't know. It's not all that clear to me even now.

Milner? I originally loved her appendix to *On Not Being Able to Paint*. I taught it in my seminars for many years. My reading of Milner was, again, like the other people I'd read, really for my own life. It wasn't, however, her concept of undifferentiation that helped me to reconstitute myself in any way. It's when she couched her findings in terms of a paradoxical formulation, in an "I-yet-not-I" kind of structure or dynamic or process, that I felt moved along. It was the "I-yet-not-I" feeling I got from her formulations that led to the first article I wrote about her work. It was one of the first major articles published on her work, and I thought it was a positive article, a helpful article. Pinchus Noy wrote me from Israel at the time saying how helped he was by it. He told me I'd put my finger on elements of Milner's work that had bothered him, that he couldn't grasp, so that he now felt released to assimilate what he had always loved about her in a more undiluted way. That was the effect I had hoped for, generally. My article on Milner's work, however, apparently precipitated antagonism from Margaret Little who, unbeknownst to me at that time, had used the concept of undifferentiation to couch an awful lot of her own work. Apparently, she felt that I had hurt Marion with this paper. I felt badly about that, because I was trying to help midwife a process, help catalyze a process further. Marion and I had written to each other, and her surprise baffled me, since I'd already sent her my review of *On Not Being Able to Paint,* which contained some of the main ideas spelled out by my longer paper. So I explained to her that what I wrote was the result of a process for me, and that it seemed, from the letters I'd received, to have had some use, at least for other people. So I had, then, to simply find a way of standing by my own reality, by my own experience, while at the same time tolerating, or finding a way to go through the flak, and all that it precipitated.

Well, Marion and I kept writing back and forth for quite some time over the matter. Then, much later, she wrote to me saying I was right in what I'd said; that she felt the article had also been helpful to her, in that I had actually freed her from a dead language that wasn't necessary for the experience she was trying to convey. I think that our love for each other survived whatever it was that momentarily came between us. Our love and what we get from one another survived the vicissitudes of that time. I think in a way that's a good model for therapy, and for living . . . that we lived through the pain and agony of a broken union. We very much value our contact with each other.

A.M: One striking aspect of your work, already present in *The Electrified Tightrope* and, more recently, in *Coming Through the Whirlwind,* is the candor with which you convey your own history and inner realities. In your books you highlight elements of biography, early experiences of religion, family, sexuality, college. In *Whirlwind. . .* you portray the rich world of the analyst's internal struggles with two tremendously engaging patients. Were these kind of revelations difficult for you, or did they issue very naturally? It's not common for analysts to write about themselves so frankly and openly: especially, for example, about their erotic reactions to a patient, as you document in your *Whirlwind* case study of

Cynthia.

M.E: What's more difficult is how much I haven't done. I would be happier if I could do more of it. Each time another shell is shed and I come out of the closet a little more, I get so much more out of it myself, and so do my patients. Therapy, I suppose, has not simply been a profession, it's been . . . it is my life. Therapy has been less of an external, professional process than it's been an internal birthing process. I wonder if more therapists wouldn't benefit from being more open about how much they get from their patients.

I think we get an awful lot from our patients that helps us grow; our patients help organize us, and we grow an awful lot through the work we do . . . or at least I and certain other people that I know do. Therapy can be unlike other professions in that there's less of a separation between what one does and what one gets out of it. For example, I've seen writings in the literature about therapist burnout, and I'm wondering what it means for a therapist to burn out. Perhaps the person was using the wrong model for therapy, was trying to be more external with patients to make the work more of a "profession," like a lawyer would make it. I get many lawyers who come in and hate what they do, who feel unreal about the ways they have to make themselves function in the external world. A therapist has a chance to have much more of a connection with the work that he's doing. . . . Part of doing therapy is that one is always in therapy, one's always in one birth process or another, or is evolving in a deep, inner way in connection with other people. As I can see so far from the effect on others and on myself, the more openness of a certain sort the better, I would think.

A.M: You write in *The Electrified Tightrope*: ""In the long run my work as a patient is what made me an analyst." Can you talk about that experience, and about that dimension of "the work"? Of the work that is intrinsic to any authentic therapy, and to the fashioning of a life through the interweaving or marriages of our many selves?

M.E: Jung said a long time ago that a great psychologist doesn't have much of a choice: that his only choice, so to speak, is whether to spend his life inside a mental hospital as a doctor or a patient. That's kind of tongue-in-cheek, I would think, but the truth is that, for the therapist who lives and "professes" his work inwardly, being a therapist is being a patient in a way. One is always engaged in this kind of evolutionary experience, always working on oneself, and that doesn't make for much of a distinction. The distinction between patient and therapist fades away. Of course, I have to do something for the patients in order to feel justified for earning money for my work. But very often I'll take money from a person and thank them for it, and wonder what I did to earn it:

because I probably got at least as much from the experience of being with them as they may have gotten from me.

Actually, as I become a little less frightened of being open, I become more and more aware of how I grow with certain people, and how inter-acting, especially with so-called "difficult" patients, promotes my own development. For example, if there's a person I cannot help, for whom anything I do strikes out, that person is forcing me, if I'm going to help them, to find a way of being with them that I hadn't exercised before. And if I fail to find it, it will be a failed treatment. . . . In a way, it's like a baby bird pecking at the mother, pecking the mother into developing the maternal urge to feed. . . . Well, there are certain patients who have to keep pecking away at the therapeutic field until, somewhere along the line, the field develops the capacity to help this particular set of birds develop. And when one of them arrives in the office and you cannot help them, when you can feel their anger or their drive to get help pecking away at you, it's not always easy to recognize that we've yet to evolve a corresponding capacity to respond to their particular kind of pecking. But if one does stick with the process for a long enough time, whether it's ten years, five years, two hundred years or a thousand years, sooner or later, that capacity will evolve or get pecked into existence by the bird's own persistence. By not giving up, that bird, somewhere on this earth, will evoke the particular set of responses that it requires and is looking for. And when that actually happens with a patient, after weeks or months of being stuck, it's marvelous! When all of a sudden, because of an internal shift in one's own being, the case moves on: because the therapist's being has actually changed, and has entered another phase of living, in response to getting pecked at in a way never experienced before.

A.M: Thanks for letting yourself be pecked at.

M.E: You're welcome. I'm sure!

Credits

The author and the publishers gratefully acknowledge permission to reprint the following material:

Chapter 1: "Stones in a stream," originally published in *The Psychoanalytic Review*, 1995, 82: 371-390. ©National Psychological Association for Psychoanalysis. Reprinted by permission.

Chapter 2: "The fire that never goes out," originally published in *The Psychoanalytic Review*, 1992, 79: 271-287. ©National Psychological Association for Psychoanalysis. Reprinted by permission.

Chapter 3: "Infinite surfaces, explosiveness, faith: Wilfred R. Bion," originally published in P. Marcus and A. Rosenberg (Eds.), *Psychoanalytic Versions of the Human Condition and Clinical Practice*. New York: New York University Press, in press. © New York University Press. Reprinted by permission.

Chapter 4: "Musings on O," originally published in the *Journal of Melanie Klein and Object Relations*, 1997, 15(2): 213-226. © SFR Translation and Publication Fund, Inc. Reprinted by permission.

Chapter 5: "Mystical precocity and psychic short-circuits," originally published in E. G. Corrigan and P. E. Gordon (Eds.), *The Mind Object: Precocity and Pathology of Self-Sufficiency*. Northvale, NJ: Jason Aronson, 1995. © Jason Aronson. Reprinted by permission.

Chapter 6: "The sword of grace: Flannery O'Connor, Wilfred R. Bion, and D. W. Winnicott," originally published in *The Psychoanalytic Review*, 1985, 72:335-346. ©National Psychological Association for Psychoanalysis. Reprinted by permission.

Chapter 10: "One Reality," to be published in Anthony Molino (Ed.). *The Couch and the Tree: Dialogues in Psychoanalysis and Buddhism*. New York: North Point Press, 1998. © North Point Press. Reprinted by permission.

Chapter 12: Michael Eigen. Interview by Anthony Molino co-published in *The Psychotherapy Patient*, 1997, 10: 105-141; in Anthony Molino (Ed.), *Elaborate Selves: Reflections and Reveries of Christopher Bollas, Michael Eigen, Polly Young-*

References

Balint, M. (1968). *The Basic Fault*. London: Tavistock Publications.

Bion, W.R. (1961). *Experiences in Groups*. London: Tavistock.

—— (1965). *Transformations*. London: William Heinemann. (New York: J. Aronson, 1983.)

—— (1967). *Second Thoughts*. New York: Jason Aronson, 1983.

—— (1970). *Attention and Interpretation*. London: Tavistock Publications. (New York: J. Aronson, 1983.)

—— (1982). *The Long Week-End: 1987-1919*. Abingdon, Oxon: Fleetwood Press.

—— (1985). *All My Sins Remembered* and *The Other Side of Genius*. Abingdon, Oxon: Fleetwood Press.

—— (1991). *A Memoir of The Future*. London: Karnac Books.

—— (1992). *Cogitations*. Edited by Francesca Bion. London: Karnac Books.

—— (1994). *Clinical Seminars and Other Works*. Ed. Francesca Bion. London: Karnac Books.

Bollas, C. (1989). *Forces of Destiny: Psychoanalysis and Human Idiom*. London: Free Association Books.

Buber, M. (1957). *I and Thou*. Translated by R. G. Smith. New York: Charles Scribner's Sons. (1970 edition translated by W. Kaufmann. New York, Scribner.)

Calvino, I. (1981). *If on a Winter's Night a Traveler*. Translated by W. Weaver. New York: Harcourt Brace Jovanovich.

Derrida, J. (1978). Freud and the Scene of Writing. In *Writing and Difference*. Translated by Alan Bass. Chicago: University of Chicago Press.

Dewey, J. (1959). *Art as Experience*. New York: Capricorn Books.

Fromm, E. (1957). *The Forgotten Language*. New York: Grove Press.

Ehrenzweig, A. (1971). *The Hidden Order of Art*. Berkeley: Unversity of Californa Press.

Eigen, M. (1981). The area of faith in Winnicott, Lacan and Bion. *Int. J. Psycho-Anal.*, 62: 413-433.

—— (1982). *Coming Through the Whirlwind*. Wilmette, IL: Chiron Publications.

—— (1983a) On demonized aspects of the self. In M. C. Nelson and M. Eigen (Eds.), *Evil: Self and Culture*. New York: Human Sciences Press.

—— (1983b). Dual union or undifferentiation? A critique of Marion Milner's view of the sense of psychic creativeness. *Int. Rev. Psycho-Anal.*, 10: 415-428.

Eigen, M. (1983c). A note on the structure of Freud's theory of creativity. *Psychoanal. Rev.,* 70: 41-45. (Collected in *Selected Papers.* London: Free Association Books, in press.)

—— (1986). *The Psychotic Core.* Northvale, NJ: Jason Aronson.

—— (1991). Winnicott's area of freedom: The uncompromiseable. In N. Schwartz-Salant and M. Stein (Eds.), *Liminality and Transitional Phenomena.* Wilmette, IL: Chiron.

—— (1992a). The fire that never goes out. *Psychoanal. Rev.,* 79: 271-287.

—— (1992b). *Coming Through the Whirlwind.* Wilmette, IL: Chiron Publications.

—— (1993). *The Electrified Tightrope.* Northvale, NJ: Jason Aronson.

—— (1995). *Reshaping the Self.* Madison, CT: Psychosocial Press/ International Universities Press.

—— (1996). *Psychic Deadness.* Northvale, NJ: Jason Aronson.

Elkin, H. (1972). On selfhood and the development of ego structures in infancy. *Psychoanal. Rev.,* 59: 389-416.

Erikson, E. (1950). *Childhood and Society.* New York: W. W. Norton.

Field, J. (M. Milner) (1934). *A Life of One's Own.* London: Chatto and Windus.

Freud. S. (1913). *Totem and Taboo. SE,* 13:1-162.

—— (1914a). On narcissism: An introduction. *SE,* 14: 73-102.

—— (1914b). The Moses of Michelangelo. *SE,* 13: 211-238.

—— (1921). *Group Psychology and the Analysis of the Ego. SE,* 18: 65-143.

—— (1923). *The Ego and the Id. SE,* 19: 1-59.

—— (1927). *The Future of an Illusion. SE,* 21:5-56.

—— (1930). *Civilization and its Discontents. SE,* 21: 59-145.

—— (1937). Analysis terminable and interminable. *SE,* 23: 216-153

—— (1939). *Moses and Monotheism. SE,* 23: 54-137.

—— (1940). *An Outline of Psycho-Analysis. SE,* 23: 141-207.

—— (1941). Findings, ideas, problems. *Standard Edition* 23: 299-300.

—— (1985). *The Complete Letters of Sigmund Freud to Wilhelm Fliess. 1887-1904.* Translated and edited by J.F. Masson. Cambridge, MA: Harvard University Press.

Gendlin, E. T. *(1962). Experiencing and the Creation of Meaning.* New York: Free Press of Glencoe.

Glass, J. (1993). *Shattered Selves: Multiple Personality in a Postmodern World.* Ithaca, NY: Cornell University Press.

Green, A. (1975). The analyst, symbolization and absence in the analytic setting (On changes in analytic practice and analytic experience). *Int. J. Psycho-Anal.,* 56.

Heidegger, M. (1957). *Identity and Difference.* New York: Harper & Row, 1969.

James, W. (1902). *The Varieties of Religious Experience.* Republished by Random

House in The Modern Library.

Jaynes, J. (1976). *The Origin of Consciousness in the Breakdown of the Bicameral Mind*. Boston: Houghton Mifflin.

Joseph, R. (1996). *Neuropsychiatry, Neuropsychology, and Clinical Neuroscience*. Baltimore: Williams & Wilkins.

Jung, C. G. (1958). The transcendent function. *Collected Works*, 8: 67-91. Princeton, NJ: Princeton University Press, 1963.

Khan, M.M.R. (1979). *Alienation in Perversions*. New York: International Universities Press.

Kohut, H. (1971). *The Analysis of the Self*. New York: International Universities Press.

—— (1977). *The Restoration of the Self*. New York: International Universities Press.

Lacan, J. (1977) *Ecrits*. Translated by A. Sheridan. New York: Norton.

—— (1978). *The Four Fundamental Concepts of Psycho-Analysis*. Translated by A. Sheridan. Edited by Jacques-Alain Miller. New York: Norton.

Lévi-Strauss, C. (1963). *Totemism*. Translated by R. Needham. Boston: Beacon Press.

Matte-Blanco, I. (1975). *The Unconscious as Infinite Sets*. London: Duckworth.

Meltzer, D. (1973). *Sexual States of Mind*. Pertshire: Clunie Press.

Milner, M. B. (1957). *On Not Being Able to Paint*. New York: International Universities Press. (Reprinted 1979.)

—— (1987). *The Suppressed Madness Of Sane Men*. London: Tavistock.

O'Connor, F. (1952). *Wise Blood*. New York: Harcourt, Brace & Co.

—— (1961). *The Violent Bear It Away*. New York: New American Library.

—— (1971). *The Complete Stories*. New York: Farrar, Straus & Giroux.

—— (1980). *The Habit of Being*. Edited by S. Fitzgerald. New York: Vintage Books.

Phillips, A. (1988). *Winnicott*. London: Fontana Press.

Rodman, R.F. (Ed.) (1987). *The Spontaneous Gesture: Selected Letters of D. W. Winnicott*. Cambridge, MA: Harvard University Press.

Rosenberg, D., Bloom, H. (1990). *The Book of J*. New York: Grove/ Weidenfeld.

Scholem, G. (1974). *On the Kabbalah and Its Symbolism*. New York: Shocken Books.

Shloss, C. (1980). *Flannery O'Connor's Dark Comedies: The Limits of Inference*. Baton Rouge: Louisiana State University Press.

Steinsaltz, A. (1988). *The Long Shorter Way*. Northvale, NJ: Jason Aronson.

Winnicott, D. W. (1950) Some thoughts on the meaning of the word "democracy." In C. Winnicott, R. Shepherd, and M. Davis (Eds.), *Home Is Where We Start From: Essays by a Psychoanalyst*. New York: Norton, 1986.

—— (1953). Transitional objects and transitional phenomena. *Int. J. Psycho-Anal.*, 34: 89-97. (Chapter 1 in *Playing and Reality*. New York: Basic Books,

1971, pp. 1-25.)

Winnicott, D.W. (1958). *Through Paediatrics to Psycho-Analysis*. New York: Basic Books.

—— (1965). *The Maturational Process and the Facilitating Environment*. New York: International Universities Press.

—— (1969). The use of an object and relating through identifications. *Int. J. Psycho-Anal.*, 50:711-716. (Chapter 6 in *Playing and Reality*. New York: Basic Books, 1971, pp. 86-94.)

—— (1970). Living Creatively. In C. Winnicott, R. Shepherd, and M. Davis (Eds.), *Home Is Where We Start From: Essays by a Psychoanalyst*. New York: Norton, 1986.

—— (1971). *Playing and Reality*. New York: Basic Books.

—— (1974a). Fear of breakdown. *Int. Rev. Psycho-Anal.*, 1: 103-107.

—— (1974b). *The Maturational Processes and the Facilitating Environment*. New York: International Universities Press.

—— (1986). *Holding and Interpretation: Fragment of an Analysis*. New York: Grove.

—— (1989). *Psycho-Analytic Explorations*. Edited by C. Winnicott, R. Shepherd, and M. Davis. Cambridge, MA: Harvard University Press. (Reprinted 1992.)

Zalman, S. (1984). *Likutei Amarim: Tanya*. New York: Kehot Publication Society.

Index

14, 13-143; (super) lack, 138, 139,
140, 141; mirror stage, 195; and
psychoanalysis, 15; purity and
non-being, 138-139; signifier,
142; *The Four Fundamental Concepts* (1978), 14, 96
Laing, R.D., 198
Language of clinical encounter, 33;
of wholeness, 52
Levinas, E., 195
Lévi-Strauss, C., 188
Libido, 11, 149, 190, 191
Little, M., 205

Madness, 21, 86, 93
Mahler, M., 187
Malevolence, 98-99, 103
Matte-Blanco, I., 47, 83
Meaninglessness, 142
Meditation, 11, 27, 97, 143, 155,
157, 159-161, 163-165
Meltzer, D., 124
Mental, 113; activity, 75; apparatus,
72, 100; capacities, 75; fitness, 75;
health, 63; organization, 95; processes, 68; space, 68; turbulence,
91
Milner, M., 13, 27, 41, 34, 32, 47,
77, 201, 204, 205
Milton, J., 62, 78, 173
Mitchell, S., 182
Molino, A., 179
Monism, 51-54, 58; paradoxical,
37-42, 51-54
Mortification, 121
Moses, 91
Murder, 87, 88
Mystic(ism), 11, 12, 15-17, 19, 20,
22, 24, 27, 28, 33, 36, 37,43, 64,
77, 83, 102, 103, 108, 111, 112,
190, 199; awareness, 111; capacity, 102; emotion, 22; and empti-

ness, 13; infantile ego states, 11;
and Lacan, 20; maturation, 107,
112; moments, 104-106; neurochemistry, 22; precocity, 95, 107;
and psychoanalysis, 116, 190;
states, 104

Narcissism, 87, 113, 179
Nelson, M.C., 182
Neurosis, 19, 141, 144, 145, 150,
151
Nihilism, 33, 121
Nothingness, 39, 46, 70, 77, 97,
107, 118, 119, 140, 173, 193
Noy, P., 205
Numinosity, 31, 102, 114, 123, 190

O, 74-79, 81-94
Oceanic feeling, 13, 28-30, 191;
bliss, 190; fusion, 31
O'Connor, F., 117, 118, 120, 125,
190
Oneness, 22, 28, 30, 31, 41, 50, 53,
58, 79, 143
One Reality, 153, 163-165
Orgasm(ic), 39, 73, 77, 79, 105, 106
140; generativity, 14; joy, 14

Paranoia, 104, 146
Parent(al), 56, 87, 96
Penis, 143
Phillips, A., 15
Plato, 62, 68, 137, 203, 204
Poincaré, H., 62
Postmodernism, 180, 184, 195
Primal, 82; ur-group, 83
Ps↔D, 33, 34, 64
Psyche/psychic, 29, 35, 40, 41, 55,
66, 70, 73, 77, 86, 87, 92, 96-100,
102, 112, 120, 125, 126, 137, 143,
145, 146, 148, 157, 160, 162, 163,
167, 172, 179, 183, 186, 187, 197,

198, 204; apparatus, 98, 99; birth
process, 71; breakdown, 96; deadness, 183; drama, 29; economy,
40; equipment, 17; evolution, 89;
field, 73, 88; flow, 41, 91, 110;
formation, 145; grouping, 20;
growth, 72; heart attacks, 56; inability, 97; invagination, 49, 89;
nutrient, 73; power, 85; process,
64, 71, 98; reality, 72, 124, 172;
rhythm, 33; short-circuit, 95, 111;
states, 172; structure, 27, 188;
time, 99
Psychoanalysis/psychoanalytic, 11,
13-17, 22, 24, 27, 29, 34, 39, 46,
53, 59, 62, 65, 68, 72-74, 81, 84,
85, 92, 99, 104, 116, 117, 118,
124, 125, 133, 140, 173, 174, 179,
180, 182, 184, 186, 187, 190, 191,
193, 194, 201, 204; attitude, 66,
124; concepts, 120; dramas, 63;
existential, 117; experience, 27,
62, 81, 125; jouissance, 15;
method, 79; movement, 74; mystic, 27; poetry, 95; process, 13,
16; situation, 46; theory, 117,
124; work, 11, 33
Psychology, 46, 96, 117, 180, 182,
189, 199
Psychosis, 19, 45, 74, 96, 102, 141
Psychospiritual, 86, 88, 102, 116,
119, 160, 174
Psychotherapy, 78, 116, 160, 163,
165, 191

Rachel, 49
Reality, 51, 53, 57, 58
Rebecca, 49
Reich, W., 13
Religion, 11-13, 15, 30, 33, 41, 83,
84, 113, 117, 119, 121, 122, 125,
154, 163, 191, 205; analogues,

125; attitude, 29; awareness, 30;
changes, 83; dimension, 41;
epiphany, 123; experience, 28,
122; expression, 82; forms, 25;
images, 118
Representation, 65
Repression, 55
Resistance, 75, 90, 124, 125, 141
Restauration, 69
Reversibility, 63, 65
Rodman, R.F., 45, 46, 96
Rolland, R., 28, 30
Rosenberg, D., 47
Ruah Elohim, 11

Saul, 51
Schneerson, M., 185
Scholem, G., 62
Searles, H., 201
Self, 18, 19, 25, 38, 87, 90, 97, 99,
101, 106, 113, 122, 180, 182, 184,
185, 206; embryonic, 99-100;
false, 51-54, 57; feeling, 59; fetal,
18; nature, 99; states, 18; true,
51-54
Sense of rightness, 102-103
Sensory, 79; apparatus, 172;
configurations, 78; experience,
124, 192
Shakespeare, W., 52
Shloss, C., 125
Signifier, 142, 143
Singer, I.B., 111, 193
Socrates, 137
Solomon, 85
Subjectivity, 141
Sullivan, H., 180
Sunyata, 19
Superego, 124
Superpersonal, 37
Suzuki, T.D., 153, 154
Swift, J., 34

220   THE PSYCHOANALYTIC MYSTIC

Taboo father, 28
Tao(ism), 24, 32, 46
Therapeutic change, 118; method,
   163 encounter, 124; gravity, 73;
   struggle, 67; work, 66, 207;
Torah, 12
Transcendent(al), 50, 53
Trauma, 98, 99, 147
Tree of Knowledge, 12, 40, 81
Tree of Life, 12, 40, 81
Tree of Words, 12
Trickster, 50
Truth, 12, 25, 47, 51, 105

Unconscious, 14
Unsayable, 65, 82

Vagina, 41
Visual image, 65, 95; perception,
   96; precocity,
Vivaldi, A., 135
Van Gogh, V., 36
Void, 38; formless, 20, 47

Watts, A., 127
Whitehead, A.N., 196
Williams, W.C., 201
Winnicott, C., 57

Winnicott, D.W., 13, 32, 45, 46, 47,
   47, 52, 54, 55, 56, 57, 58, 59, 92,
   93, 95, 96, 97, 117, 121, 183, 192;
   agony, 92; baby, 120; false self,
   95; "Fear of breakdown" (1974),
   15, 55, 96, 149; paradox, 194;
   Holding and Interpretation (1986),
   57; "Living creatively" (1970), 54;
   Playing and Reality (1971), 15, 16,
   31, 32, 96, 120, 124; psychic democracy, 54; *Psycho-Analytic Explorations* (1989), 15, 16, 17, 92; and
   realness, 121; "Some thoughts..."
   (1950), 52; "The use of an object
   and relating through identifications" (1969), 34, 36, 124; "Transitional objects and transitional
   phenomena" (1953), 29, 124; tormented consciousness, 57; unintegration, 45, 46; use of object,
   120, 126; wholeness, 57
Wordsworth, W., 11

Yeats, B., 135

Zalman, S. 158
Zen, 34, 79, 153